MARRIAGE
WITH MY KINGDOM

By the same author

THE YOUNG ELIZABETH
DANGER TO ELIZABETH

MARRIAGE WITH MY KINGDOM

ALISON PLOWDEN
The Courtships of Elizabeth I

M

ISBN: 0 333 15792 3

First published in Great Britain 1977 by
MACMILLAN LONDON LIMITED
4 Little Essex Street London WC2R 3LF
and Basingstoke
Associated companies in New York Dublin
Melbourne Johannesburg and Delhi

Printed in Great Britain by
WILLMER BROTHERS LIMITED, BIRKENHEAD

For Ruth with love

Contents

List of Illustrations

between pages 112 and 113

Thanks are due to the following for permission to reproduce the illustrations: Her Majesty the Queen (Windsor Castle Collection), 1a; The Marquis of Bath, 1b, 7b; Trustees of the Chatsworth Settlement, 2a; The National Portrait Gallery, 2b, 7b; The Wallace Collection, 3; The National Museum, Stockholm, 4a; The Mary Evans Picture Library, 4b; Bibliotèque Ste Geneviève, Paris, 5a; The Hon Gavin Astor, 5b; The Courtauld Institute, 6; The Methuen Collection, 8a; The Duke of Buccleuch and Queensberry, 8b.

Yea, to satisfie you, I have already joyned my self in Marriage to an Husband, namely, the Kingdom of England. And behold (said she, which I marvell ye have forgotten,) the Pledge of this my Wedlock and Marriage with my Kingdom.

And therewith she drew the Ring from her Finger, and shewed it, wherewith at her Coronation she had in a set form of words solemnly given her self in Marriage to her Kingdom.

William Camden, *Annals of the Reign of Queen Elizabeth*

Prologue

On or about 28 August 1556 a young Englishman, with his hawk on his wrist, took a gondola out of Venice hoping to enjoy a day's sport among the islands. But the bad luck which had dogged Edward Courtenay, Earl of Devonshire, throughout his life pursued him even across the Venetian lagoon. A violent squall of wind and rain caught him on the tiny, shelterless island of Lio and the young man in his light summer clothes was quickly soaked to the skin. A gondola was useless in such conditions, and the Earl and his party were fortunate to be picked up by a Venetian naval craft cruising in the area.

Edward Courtenay was travelling abroad at his sovereign's command rather than his own inclination. He took no part in the social round of Venice, keeping himself resolutely to himself and admitting to his friendship only a small group of those gentlemen eager to make much of the romantic English milord. Five days after his adventure on the lagoon, which had brought on an attack of malaria, the Earl of Devonshire had a fall on the stairs of his house and decided to move to Padua. The University of Padua was famous for its medical school, and an invalid could expect to receive the most up-to-date treatment from the city's doctors.

Most people travelled the twenty-five miles from Venice by water, patronising horse-drawn barges which plied up and down the River Brenta. But Edward Courtenay, either from obstinacy or impatience, 'took the worst way and came by a certain waggons called coches' — a form of transport which, in the opinion of Peter Vannes, Queen Mary's agent in Venice, was 'very shaking and uneasy'. Vannes was himself temporarily resident in Padua to avoid the plague which reigned in Venice during the summer months. News of the Earl of Devonshire's arrival reached him late one Saturday night, and next morning he hastened to pay his respects to the distinguished visitor. Vannes found the Earl very weak and feverish after his uncomfortable journey, and although two of the best available physicians were summoned to his bedside his condition deteriorated rapidly. The last representative of the old royal house of England, whose grandmother had been a Plantagenet princess, lay alone in his lodgings, gripped by 'a continual great hot ague', nursed only by his servants, too ill to see anyone but Peter Vannes and the Italian doctors.

The end came on 18 September. Vannes reported that he believed the Earl of Devonshire had died a good Christian who could hope for God's mercy. He had listened meekly to spiritual exhortation, lifted up his eyes and knocked himself on the breast in token of repentance of his sins; but by this time 'his tongue had so stopt his mouth, and his teeth so cloven together', that he had been unable to receive the sacrament.[1]

Knowing that news of Edward Courtenay's death would come as a considerable relief to at least one European power and as a serious disappointment to another, Peter Vannes took the precaution of securing sworn statements from the Earl's servants, from the physicians who had attended him and the surgeons who had carried out the post-mortem examination that to the best of their knowledge he had died from natural causes.[2] Vannes was also saddled with the responsibility of making the funeral arrangements, which he hoped to contrive 'with as much sparing and as much honour as can be done'. In the event, there was more sparing than honour. Vannes was currently suffering from such an acute attack of penury – the chronic affliction of sixteenth-century ambassadors – that he described himself as being 'next door to going a-begging', and Mary Tudor proved unresponsive to suggestions that she should pay for the obsequies of a kinsman she had small reason to regret.[3]

Half a century later, an English tourist exploring St Anthony's Church in Padua was deeply shocked when a plain wooden coffin containing the mortal remains of Edward Courtenay, Earl of Devonshire, was pointed out to him stacked casually in the cloister and 'having neither epitaph nor any other thing to preserve it from oblivion.'[4] It was then five years since the House of Tudor had followed the House of Plantagenet off the stage, and the name of Edward Courtenay had long since been forgotten. Worthy Thomas Coryat, gazing on the sight of a noble Englishman so ignobly buried, was struck by compassion and remorse. He was not aware that he was also looking at the last resting-place of a man who, as the predestined bridegroom of Elizabeth Tudor, might so easily have altered the whole course of English history.

CHAPTER I

The King's Last Daughter

WHEN Anne Boleyn gave birth to a girl child between the hours of three and four o'clock on the afternoon of Sunday, 7 September, 1533, Catholic Europe sniggered behind its hand over the devastating snub which Providence had dealt the King of England and his concubine. Messire Eustace Chapuys, the Holy Roman Emperor's ambassador at the Court of St James's, did not attempt to conceal his malicious amusement.[1]

Te Deum for Queen Anne's safe delivery was sung in St Paul's Cathedral in the presence of the Lord Mayor and Aldermen of the City of London, and the 'high and mighty Princess of England, Elizabeth', was given a splendid christening in the Friars' Church at Greenwich.[2] Over these proceedings, however, there hung a faint but palpable air of defiance. No amount of pompous ceremony and displays of official rejoicing could conceal the embarrassing fact that the flamboyantly masculine Henry VIII had once more failed to get a legitimate son. In his quest for a male heir, Henry had repudiated his blameless first wife and offended her influential relatives; he had challenged the Pope and resigned from the Church of Rome; he had ruthlessly manipulated the accepted laws of God and man to suit his own ends – and all he had got for his pains was another daughter.

In 1533 the break with Rome was not yet irrevocable. In July, Pope Clement had solemnly condemned the King's separation from Catherine of Aragon, denounced his second marriage and framed (but not published) a bull of excommunication.[3] In November, at a meeting with the Pope arranged under the auspices of the King of France, Henry's representatives made what seemed a deliberately provocative appeal against the threatened excommunication to a future General Council of the Church.[4] But still the way to reconciliation was not finally barred. For years now Clement had temporised and delayed in the matter of the King of England's divorce. If he could have devised some face-saving formula, he would, even at this eleventh hour, have used it thankfully. As for Henry, if he had been offered a settlement on his own terms, he might, even now, have accepted it. The King's position was not unlike that of a man who has quarrelled with the committee of his club and left to set up a rival establishment, but who, at the same time, cherishes a sneaking desire to be invited to return.

The invitation never came. On 23 March 1534 the Pope was finally forced to give a ruling on the divorce. Twenty-two cardinals in secret consistory pronounced in favour of Queen Catherine – declaring her marriage to be lawful and valid, and optimistically enjoining the King to take her back as his wife.[5] Later that year Parliament at Westminster passed the Act of Supremacy, 26 Henry VIII, recognising the King, his heirs and successors, without qualification, as 'the only supreme head in earth of the church of England', with all the 'honours, dignities, pre-eminences, jurisdictions, privileges, authorities, immunities, profits and commodities ... belonging and appertaining'.[6] After this, nothing short of unconditional surrender by one party or the other could heal the breach between England and Rome.

The King's divorce, the Great Matter which had occupied Henry's thoughts and energies almost exclusively for the past seven years, had come to overshadow every aspect of English domestic and foreign policy, and had had the effect of forcing the country further and further into the arms of France. France might remain the ancestral enemy, Spain the traditional ally, the Netherlands – now a Spanish apanage – the trading partner on which England's economic prosperity depended; but unfortunately Charles V – ruler of Spain, Lord of the Netherlands, the Franche-Comté and Austria, King of Naples, Sicily and Sardinia, suzerain of the Habsburg fiefs in Germany and northern Italy, and Holy Roman Emperor – also happened to be the nephew of the discarded Queen of England. Charles, with the cares of half Europe on his shoulders, menaced by advancing Turkish hordes in the east, harassed by heresy in Germany and by French territorial ambitions in Italy, was naturally reluctant to add war with England to his problems. Common decency and the obligations of family honour compelled him to protest at the humiliation of his aunt, and to promote her cause by all the diplomatic means at his disposal. More than that he had not, so far, been prepared to do. At the same time, the Empire represented the greatest power-bloc in Europe and the Emperor could, if sufficiently provoked, make things very uncomfortable for the King of England. It had, therefore, seemed a necessary precaution to strengthen English ties with France.

In 1532 a new defensive treaty was negotiated between the two countries and in September of that year the *entente cordiale* was sealed by a meeting betwen the two kings – Henry and François – at Boulogne.[7]

Their alliance was based on mutual self-interest. Henry needed a promise of French assistance in case of an Imperial attack. He also needed friends in Rome, especially since he had dispensed with the invaluable services of Cardinal Wolsey. François needed English support in his perennial feud with the Emperor – with English help he could close the Channel and cut sea-borne communications between Spain and the Netherlands. To embarrass Charles, he was prepared to side with Henry in his battle for the divorce, and French cardinals were instructed to use their influence at the Vatican on his behalf. The King of France was not, however, prepared to offend the Pope and certainly not, as Henry appears to have believed, to join England in schism. François needed papal backing for his Italian ploys and in 1533 acquired the Pope's niece, Catherine de Medici, as a daughter-in-law. He was, in fact, attempting to perform the increasingly difficult feat of running with the King of England while hunting with the Pope.

Then, in the autumn of 1534, Clement VII died, to be succeeded by Paul III. Though an Italian, the new Pope was said to be 'a good Frenchman'. He was also said to have been pro-Henry in the matter of the divorce and soon after his election began asking for advice on 'what means he should take to win back the King of England'.[8] François, always an optimist, began to hope that here might be an opportunity to realise his long-cherished ambition to weld England, the papacy and perhaps even the German Protestant states into a grand alliance directed against the hegemony of the Empire. In terms of practical politics this had never been a particularly realistic scheme, and in 1534 it was probably less so than ever, but the Emperor was sufficiently disturbed by the general trend of events to make some friendly overtures to François and to send the Count of Nassau on a special mission to France. The English government maintained an attitude of elaborate unconcern although, in the opinion of Eustace Chapuys, Nassau's visit was 'a flea in their ear'. English immunity from fears of Imperial vengeance depended largely on the continued animosity between France and the Empire, and Henry was haunted by a suspicion that François would not hesitate to stab his ally in the back any time it suited him.

It was common gossip that the Count of Nassau had come to

discuss 'great affairs and marriages' with the King of France, but no one seemed to know any details. The details were, in fact, being carefully concealed, for Nassau had brought a top-secret proposition from Charles that François should suggest a match between Mary Tudor, Catherine of Aragon's only surviving child, and his own third son, the Duke of Angoulême. It was true that Mary had recently been bastardised and disinherited by Act of Parliament, but in the eyes of Rome, and therefore of all orthodox Catholics, she was still the legitimate English heiress. This was to be pointed out to François, together with a reminder of the various financial and political advantages to be gained by himself and his son, and a hint that if he co-operated with the Emperor, the thing could be carried through whether the King of England was willing or not. In other words, France and the Empire could jointly exert enough pressure on Henry to force him to restore his elder daughter to her proper place in the succession.[9]

Charles naturally took a close interest in his young cousin, who was currently being bullied and threatened by her father and step-mother, and made to yield precedence to her baby half-sister. The Emperor was not without human feelings and, besides, Mary was a potentially valuable weapon in his dynastic armoury. If the King of France could be induced to make an offer for her without revealing the Emperor's interest, it might kill three Imperial birds with one stone; it would divert François from further Italian adventures, drive a useful wedge into the Anglo-French alliance – Henry could scarcely miss the wounding implication that not even his closest ally recognised his do-it-yourself divorce – and might also provide an escape-hatch for Mary.

Unhappily for these amiable intentions, the only effect of Nassau's cautiously worded approach was to impress François with a sense of the Emperor's disquiet and to strengthen his hopes of being able to make a successful challenge. A few weeks after the Count's departure, a mission led by Phillippe Chabot, sieur de Brion and Admiral of France, crossed the Channel for high-level talks in London. De Brion at once passed on Charles's suggestion of a French marriage for Mary – a suggestion which Henry had no hesitation in ascribing to the Emperor's malice and his intent to 'dissolve the amity' between François and himself. At the same time, the King resisted French proposals designed to involve him in the Habsburg–Valois vendetta. Instead, he put forward a proposal of his own. If François could obtain from Pope Paul a reversal of Clement's 'unjust and slanderous' verdict on the divorce, Henry would consider formally renouncing the title of King of France, still borne by the kings of England, and would also be willing to open negotiations for a marriage between the Princess Elizabeth and the Duke of Angoulême.[10] Thus the twelve-year-old duke achieved the distinction of becoming the first in a long line of Elizabeth Tudor's suitors and Elizabeth, at the age of fourteen months made her debut on the international political stage.

In spite of much outward cordiality, the French were disappointed by Henry's reluctance to be drawn into their net and by his evident determination not to give an inch in dealing with the Pope. According to Eustace Chapuys, de Brion left for home in a mood of disenchantment, and certainly his departure was followed by a somewhat ominous silence. Henry, who seems to have been expecting a prompt reply to his flattering offer, grew so impatient that de Morette, the resident French ambassador, began to avoid the Court, but it was not until the end of January 1535 that de Brion's secretary, Palamedes Gontier, returned to London to resume discussions. The King received him informally, leaning against a sideboard as Gontier opened the subject of the Angoulême marriage with a discreet enquiry about the prospective bride's exact legal status – a matter of some interest to her prospective father-in-law. François assumed that, having given Elizabeth the title of princess, Henry intended to assure it to her and treat her as his only heiress; but, said Gontier, his king felt that in the circumstances steps ought to be taken which would 'deprive lady Mary of any occasion or means of claiming the Crown'.[11]

Henry hastened to allay any French misgivings by explaining 'what had been done by Parliament' – that is, by the 1534 Act for the Establishment of the King's Succession. This was the Act which had ratified the divorce proceedings conducted under the aegis of Thomas Cranmer at Dunstable in May 1533. It declared Henry's marriage to Catherine of Aragon 'utterly void and annulled' and settled the succession on children born of the Anne Boleyn marriage, naming 'the Lady Elizabeth, now princess', as heiress presumptive. To make assurance doubly sure, it further laid down that the King's subjects were to 'make a corporal oath' to 'truly, firmly and constantly ... observe, fulfil, maintain, defend and keep ... the whole effects and contents of this present act' or incur the penalties of misprision of high treason.[12] This oath, Henry assured Gontier, had now been taken throughout the kingdom, adding pleasantly that everyone took Mary for the bastard she was. Elizabeth had been quickly proclaimed his sole heiress and there was no question of Mary ever becoming Queen or claiming any right to the crown. He went on to point out that, if François would only persuade the Pope to agree that his first marriage was null and void, all doubts would cease.[13] This was not strictly true, for the French had already been taking legal advice as to whether or not Mary could still be considered legitimate, even if her parents' marriage *was* invalid.[14]

Palamedes Gontier did not, however, feel it necessary to mention this to Henry, but turned instead to financial matters, indicating that the King of France would be obliged if the annual pensions being paid to England under the terms of the Treaty of Amiens were remitted as part of Elizabeth's dowry. The King of England 'took this ill'. Considering that he had, of his own accord, offered the heiress of a kingdom 'of most certain title, without remainder of querel to the contrary', to a younger son, all the obligation was on the French side and 'they ought rather to give him something than ask'. Such looking of a gift horse in the mouth, together with the long delay in giving him an answer, made him think 'there was a practice going on elsewhere'.[15]

Having got over these preliminary skirmishes, Gontier was passed on to the King's advisers, and during the month he spent in England the rough draft of a marriage treaty was drawn up and arrangements made for a further meeting between the representatives of both sides to be held at Calais at Whitsun, so that the Bishop of Faenza, papal nuncio in France, thought the matter could reasonably be expected to take effect.[16]

But, unknown to the Bishop, some devious cross-currents were moving beneath the surface. Thomas Cromwell, the King of England's hard-headed secretary and man of business, placed little long-term reliance on the French connection. Cromwell, who had already set in train the complicated administrative machinery for nationalising the resources of the Catholic Church in England, knew there was not going to be any accommodation with the Pope, that, in fact, the open hostility of the Pope could not be long delayed. He also knew that France, a Continental power with important interests in Italy, would never break her ties with Rome and that, if it came to a showdown, England could not rely on her support. By far the most logical alliance for England was still with the Emperor, and Cromwell, unhampered by illusions, ideals or old-fashioned notions of honour and filial piety, found it hard to credit that Charles could seriously mean to go on denying himself the obvious advantages of English friendship just for the sake of a surely expendable aunt and cousin. As early as February 1535, Master Secretary was remarking to Eustace Chapuys that it would be better to be talking of a marriage between the Spanish prince – the Emperor's eight-year-old son Philip – and the King's last daughter.[17] This unlikely suggestion was apparently intended as a joke, and the ambassador took it as such, but a month later Cromwell brought the subject up again – only to drop it hastily at the sight of Chapuys' frosty expression, saying wistfully that he supposed the Emperor would not hear of it out of respect for his cousin.[18]

Meanwhile, negotiations with France continued. The Calais meeting duly took place at the end of May, but ended in stalemate. The English commissioners, headed by the Duke of Norfolk, had been instructed to press their opposite numbers to agree that young Angoulême should come to England immediately to complete his education, although the formal betrothal would not be solemnised until Elizabeth was seven years old.[19] The French, not unnaturally, jibbed at the idea of parting with their bridegroom before the bride was of full marriageable age and, according to the Bishop of Faenza, François refused disdainfully to send his son to be a hostage in England.[20] But this was a negotiable point, and the rock on which the talks foundered seems to have been Henry's 'exorbitant demand' that François should make a public declaration binding himself to uphold the validity of the Anne Boleyn marriage against all comers.[21] The King of France was quite prepared to do his best to persuade the Pope to re-open the King of England's case with a view to revoking Clement's 'false and unreasonable' judgement on the divorce;[22] for such a revocation would not only place Henry under a heavy obligation to France but, more important, would also go a long way towards realising her king's dreams of detaching the papacy from its dependence on the Empire. But François could only move through conventional channels. He neither could nor would reject or even question the Pope's right of jurisdiction in matters of Canon Law. By July, therefore, the Angoulême marriage negotiations had petered out and the Anglo-French *entente* was showing distinct signs of strain.[23]

Fortunately for Henry, developments in Italy in the autumn of 1535 portended the imminent renewal of Franco-Imperial hostilities and considerably increased his opportunities for engaging in the exhilarating diplomatic sport of playing one great power off against the other. In October, Cromwell was telling Chapuys about attempts by certain 'malicious and badly-intentioned parties' to make mischief between their respective masters, and that Henry was thinking of sending 'a very great and most honourable embassy' to the Emperor to discuss a renewal of their old friendship and confederacy.[24] Cromwell had also reverted to his idea of an alliance cemented by the marriage of Elizabeth and the Prince of Spain, working the subject into conversation with elaborate casualness and always making the suggestion timidly, 'like one offering a coin to an elephant'.[25]

During the Christmas holidays Chapuys had a long audience with the King, who walked the ambassador up and down with an arm round his neck explaining how invaluable English support would be to the Emperor should war break out again in Italy. But, Henry went on, if Charles did not soon respond to his overtures, he would be obliged to listen to the French, who were overwhelming him with the most flattering offers.[26] When Chapuys tried to pin him down, saying that all the time he and Cromwell had been discussing the possibility of a new understanding no tangible proposal had been made, Henry himself spoke of the marriage of his 'little daughter'. Although Chapuys was too old a hand not to see through Henry's game, and found the thought of a marriage between the English kings' bastard and the Holy Roman Emperor's heir almost too preposterous to be mentioned, he nevertheless told his master that perhaps the proposal should not be rejected out of hand, in case England was driven back irretrievably into the French orbit.[27]

During the first half of 1536 the situation on both the international and the domestic fronts underwent a radical change. By the spring a French army had invaded northern Italy, and the Emperor had less time than ever to spare for England. In any case, the chief personal bones of contention between Henry and himself were now beginning to disappear. Catherine of Aragon died in January and, on 2 May, Anne Boleyn was arrested and taken to the Tower. A fortnight later she was arraigned before a commission of lords on a charge of treason against the King's own person. The result of the trial was, of course, a foregone conclusion and Anne was beheaded on Tower Green at eight o'clock in the morning of Friday, 19 May, 'when she had reigned as Queen three years, lacking fourteen days, from her coronation to her death'. But Henry was not content with merely killing the woman for whom he had so recently been prepared to turn the world upside down. Two days before her execution, 'at a solemn court kept at Lambeth by the Lord Archbishop of Canterbury and the doctors of the law, the King was divorced from his wife Queen Anne... and so she was discharged and was never lawful Queen of England'.[28]

The dissolution of the King's second marriage necessitated a second Act of Succession, passed in the summer of 1536, by which Parliament once again ratified a decision by Thomas Cranmer on Henry's matrimonial affairs and once again bastardised and disabled his heiress. The two-year-old Elizabeth thus joined her half-sister in social limbo, the natural consequence being a drastic reduction of her value in that area where sixteenth-century princesses were alone considered to be of value – the international marriage-market.

Such wholesale dissipation of his potential assets worried the King's more frugal advisers, and in the spring of 1537 an *aide-mémoire* drawn up for a council meeting noted that: 'The King has two daughters, not lawful, yet king's daughters, and as princes commonly conclude amity and things of importance by alliances, it is thought necessary that these two daughters shall be made of some estimation, without which no man will have any great respect to them'. As Mary, now twenty-one, would be 'more apt to make a present alliance', it was suggested that the King should either relegitimise her or else 'advance her to some certain living decent for such an estate, whereby she may be the better had in reputation'. A similar course could then be taken with regard to Elizabeth and in this way Henry might, by means of his elder daughter, 'provide himself of a present friend and have the other in store hereafter to get another friend'.[29]

Needless to say, no part of this ingenuous plan was ever carried out. It was probably never even discussed. The legitimacy or otherwise of the princesses was a touchy subject at the best of times, but especially so just then in the aftermath of the Pilgrimage of Grace. That October, Queen Jane Seymour succeeded (though it killed her) in presenting the King with a male heir unquestionably born in wedlock, but Henry continued to adopt an uncompromising take-it-or-leave-it attitude towards his daughters' suitors. In any case, now that he was a widower again, he had a far more tempting piece of merchandise to offer and at once embarked on an extensive programme of consumer research.

Although there is a strong flavour of *opéra bouffe* about the King of England's heavy-footed pursuit of love round the courts of Europe during the years 1538 and 1539 – a pursuit which finally netted the despised Anne of Cleves – his underlying purpose was serious enough. The King of France and the Emperor, both at least temporarily exhausted by their increasingly pointless and increasingly expensive hostility, were showing definite signs of coming to an understanding. Such an understanding might well lead to England's isolation; at a time of domestic unrest, ominously linked with the names of certain surviving members of the old royal house, it might well lead to something worse. Dread of the Catholic powers combining to attack the heretic island under colour of a papal crusade, in the expectation of internal support as well as of rich pickings for themselves, first became acute in the late 1530s and influenced English foreign policy for the rest of the century. Henry's marriage-mongering was therefore designed primarily to prevent a new alignment of the great powers or, failing that, to prevent his exclusion from any new Continental alignment.[30]

With this end in view, either a French or an Imperialist bride would do equally well, and the King's first choice fell on a Frenchwoman, the widowed Mary of Guise. But, when the lady was irritatingly snapped up by James of Scotland, Henry turned his attention to the Emperor's niece, the young Duchess of Milan – and certainly the far-reaching Habsburg family provided greater scope for the multiple marriage-schemes he now began to evolve.

The first suggestion was for a double wedding – Henry to the Duchess of Milan and Mary to Dom Luis of Portugal. This idea was presently expanded to include the other two Tudor children, Prince Edward being offered to the Emperor's daughter and Elizabeth either to one of his nephews, sons of the King of Hungary, or alternatively to a son of the Duke of Savoy.[31] Charles von Habsburg and Emmanuel Philibert, Prince of Piedmont, were later to become familiar figures in the Elizabethan matrimonial scene, but in 1538 not even Henry could expect his younger daughter – bastard of a notorious adultress – to be in much request among foreign royalty in search of eligible brides, and by October he was lumping Elizabeth together with his niece, Margaret Douglas, and Mary Howard, widow of his base-born son, in a special bargain offer – all three girls to be bestowed by the Emperor's advice 'upon such of the princes of Italy as shall be thought convenient'.[32]

Just how seriously Henry took schemes of this nature is hard to say, but in any case he was, as usual, asking too high a price for his goods. He had not been able to prevent Charles and François from signing a ten-year truce in the summer of 1538 and, predictably, neither monarch was now so interested in an English alliance. In 1539 the international situation became so threatening that Henry was forced to look for friends among the non-aligned German Lutheran princes, and by the end of the year found himself trapped in his distasteful fourth marriage.

But the crisis was short-lived. Cracks soon began to appear in the papering-over of Habsburg–Valois animosity, and by the beginning of 1541 France and the Empire were at loggerheads once more, thus once more opening up England's freedom of diplomatic manoeuvre. Since there were no longer any personal obstacles in the way of an Anglo-Imperial alliance and since, for both economic and sentimental reasons, English public opinion favoured the Emperor, France was now obliged to make the running if she wanted to avoid being left out in the cold. In June, therefore, François instructed his ambassador to assure the Duke of Norfolk that he had 'no greater desire than to live in perpetual amity with England'. If Norfolk showed any disposition to enquire how this amiable intention might be furthered, Charles de Marillac was to reply that he had heard that when the Duke was last in Calais 'some question of marriages' had been under discussion, and that these were the surest bonds to strengthen amity between princes. He could then add – quite casually, of course – that the King of England had a daughter, 'her who is held legitimate', and François a son, M. d'Orléans, to whom he intended to give the Duchy of Milan, and that this would be one of the greatest matches in Christendom 'by means of which great things could be accomplished both for France and England'. Marillac was to suggest that Norfolk might care to think the matter over, while at the same time being careful to maintain the convention that it was all his own idea, and one that he would not like his master to know he had even mentioned.[33]

There were two flaws in this interesting scheme, one being that François was under the mistaken impression that Elizabeth was still regarded as legitimate by the English. The other concerned the Duchy of Milan, the rival claims to which constituted one of the chief bones of contention between François and Charles. France plus Milan plus England would certainly have formed a powerful combination, but unfortunately Milan was currently firmly in the Emperor's possession. Another snag was the fact that M. d'Orléans was already married. But since his wife, Catherine de Medici, had so far proved barren there was talk of divorcing her.

It was August before the Duke of Norfolk gave the French ambassador his cue to broach the subject of the Orléans marriage and appeared so receptive to an initial approach that Marillac felt justified in asking how it could best be arranged and which of King Henry's daughters should be proposed for the honour. Although Mary was better qualified by age and seniority, no French prince – and especially not Henri d'Orléans, who was François' eldest surviving son and his heir – could ever marry a bastard, so perhaps it might be better to choose the younger sister in spite of her regrettable maternity. The Duke's reaction was immediate and for that reason, thought Marillac, unfeigned. The younger of the two was not to be spoken of, he said roundly. For one thing she was only seven years old, and her mother's reputation was such that 'it was quite decided to consider her illegitimate, as the Act of Parliament declared'. In any case, Norfolk refused to become involved. Anne Boleyn had been his niece and, if he attempted to advance Elizabeth's cause, he would be laying himself open to accusations of 'seeking to aggrandise his own house'.[34]

Such sensitivity seems a little curious in a man who had recently married another of his nieces to the King, but Norfolk was not, as he hastened to assure Marillac, opposed to a French alliance in principle. The Lady Mary was available, and the Duke readily undertook 'to forward matters so that a good end might be expected'.[35] Negotiations did, in fact, begin and dragged on for several months – always to be frustrated by Henry's rigid insistence on the immutable nature of Mary's illegitimacy. Not even by implication would he allow the annulment of his first marriage to be questioned.

Meanwhile the King was busy angling for an alliance with the Emperor, and in 1542 Elizabeth's name was again briefly linked with the Prince of Piedmont. Eustace Chapuys saw no objection to this. Such a connection, he thought, would help to detach England from France.[36] But the whole tide of events during the 1540s was taking England away from France, and an Anglo-Imperial treaty was concluded in February 1543. It was not, however, to be sealed by a marriage. Henry, it appeared, did not intend actually to part with his daughters if he could help it; they were too useful to him as bargaining-counters in the endless horse-trading of dynastic diplomacy, as bribes to be dangled in front of recalcitrant allies.

Mary, now in her mid-twenties, her youth slipping emptily away, had already realised that as long as her father lived 'there would be nothing to be got but fine words', and was bitterly resigned to being only the Lady Mary, 'the most unhappy lady in Christendom'.[37] Elizabeth, at nine years old and not yet understanding all the bleak implications of a spinster's fate, was old enough and intelligent enough to have begun to observe the developing pattern of her sister's life and her own. A sixteenth-century princess was conditioned to expect an arranged marriage at an early age, to serve her country's interests abroad with her own body. There was nothing new or remarkable about that. But to see herself being cynically hawked in the market-place without serious intention was another matter. It was not playing fair. If Elizabeth did indeed say to Robert Dudley about this time 'I will never marry', it may have been a child's statement of simple fact rather than of intent.

In 1543, Henry's younger daughter was once again featured in the shop-window as the centre of political interest moved to Scotland, where a crisis situation had been building up over the past two years. Scottish friendship with France, dating back to the early fourteenth century, had always been a source of inconvenience and sometimes danger to her southern neighbour. Henry VII had hoped to break the 'auld alliance' by marrying his daughter Margaret to King James IV, but even this did not prevent James in 1513 from adhering to the time-honoured custom of attacking through England's back door while English forces were engaged across the Channel.

At the beginning of the 1540s it looked as if the bloody lesson of Flodden Field had been lost on Margaret Tudor's son. As he grew to manhood James V turned his face obstinately towards France, choosing first one French wife and then another. Influenced by the powerfully pro-French Cardinal Beaton, he snubbed his English uncle's friendly overtures and rejected the anti-papal propaganda disseminated by Henry. Scotland remained a Catholic country, potentially if not actually hostile – a state of affairs made more than ordinarily explosive by the fact that the King of Scots stood very close to the English throne. The King of England was no longer a young man, and his health had begun to deteriorate. Prince Edward was still little more than a baby, and Henry had himself removed his daughters from the succession. If he could not soon separate James from his foreign friends and secure the vulnerable land-frontier, the danger from possible future consequences scarcely needed spelling out. In 1541 border incidents were already proliferating, and by the autumn of 1542 England and Scotland were at war.

Within a matter of weeks a dramatic series of events had changed the situation out of all recognition. The Scots had suffered total and humiliating defeat at Solway Moss, the melancholic James had turned his face to the wall and died, and a week-old baby girl had succeeded to the Scottish throne. Now, if ever, was the time for a bold stroke of dynastic diplomacy. A marriage between the five-year-old heir to the English throne and the infant Mary Queen of Scots would unite the two countries with England as the dominant partner and certainly seemed to offer the best chance of a permanent solution to the whole intractable problem of Anglo-Scottish relations. 'I would she and her nurse were in my lord Prince's house,' remarked one Englishman less than a fortnight after Mary's birth.

To begin with, at least, the omens looked favourable. The Scots were ready to make peace, the Franco-Catholic party had fallen into disarray, and in January 1543 the Scottish Council named James Hamilton, Earl of Arran, as regent or governor. Arran was generally considered to be well disposed towards England, but the Hamiltons were themselves of royal Stuart blood; Arran was, in fact, the heir presumptive, and it was known that he had hoped to marry the little Queen to his own son. It would, therefore, be necessary to offer him a consolation prize and, in April, Sir Ralph Sadler, the English diplomat sent by Henry to handle negotiations in Edinburgh, was instructed to tell him that the King had a daughter called the Lady Elizabeth 'endowed with virtues and qualities agreeable with her estate'. If Arran proved sincere in his friendship, Henry meant to condescend to her marriage with his son, and would 'bring up and nourish his said son' as a son-in-law at the English court.[38]

When these tidings were conveyed to him, reported Sadler, 'the Governor understanding the great honour your Majesty did offer unto him in that behalf, put off his cap and said, "he was most bound of all men unto your Majesty, in that it pleased the same, being a prince of so great reputation in the world, to offer such alliance and marriage with so poor a man as he is, for the which he should bear his heart and service to your Majesty next unto his sovereign lady during his life".'[39] Three days later Arran told Sadler that he would willingly 'accept and embrace' Henry's proposal, and on 6 May he sent the Earl of Glencarne and Sir George Douglas to London with instructions 'humbly to desire the King to accomplish the contract of marriage betwixt the Lady Elizabeth and James Lord Hamilton, son and heir apparent to us, James Earl of Arran, governor and second person of Scotland; not doubting but the King shall provide for the said lady and her part according to the state of such a princess'.[40]

Meanwhile, progress towards accomplishing the other and more important Scottish marriage-contract was less satisfactory for, with his customary insensitivity, Henry had presented a shopping-list of demands calculated to confirm the worst fears of a nation notoriously touchy and suspicious of English intentions. Although the treaty finally signed at Greenwich in July met the Scots rather more than half-way, the damage had been done and the pro-French faction led by Cardinal Beaton and the Queen-Dowager, Mary of Guise, was rapidly regaining its former ascendancy. Arran continued to feed Sadler with fair words, but he was not a strong character and his position had become untenable. In September, to Henry's unspeakable disgust, he threw in his lot with the Cardinal and a rare opportunity for creating a peaceful and united Great Britain had vanished into the northern mist.

The King of England spent most of the next eighteen months trying to win by fire and sword what he had failed to achieve at the conference table. In the spring of 1544 he sent the Earl of Hertford on a punitive expedition to Scotland and that summer embarked on a war with France which, although undertaken in conjunction with the Emperor, was chiefly designed to cut the Scots off from their Continental allies.

The capture on 14 September of the strategic port of Boulogne by the English army went some way towards gaining this objective by cutting the short sea-route to Edinburgh. Henry had personally superintended the siege of Boulogne, and its fall gave him a good deal of simple pleasure. To the French it was a serious loss which they immediately exerted their best efforts to recover. As early as October, Cardinal du Bellay was suggesting to William Paget that Henry might care to give his younger daughter to 'some Prince of France' together with Boulogne, and François might afterwards exchange other lands in France for it. Unsurprisingly Paget was not impressed by this hopeful plan. It would, he remarked, be a great dowry and offer no compensation for the cost of winning it.[41]

Henry clung to Boulogne, but by the beginning of 1545 found himself uncomfortably short of friends. He had fallen out with his Imperial ally and, since France and the Empire had made a separate peace, François would now be in a position to concentrate all his forces against England. Henry, therefore, turned once more to Germany, sending his unofficial envoy, Christopher Mundt, on a visit to the Landgrave of Hesse with instructions to propose an offensive and defensive alliance with the Protestant League. Mundt, and Walter Buckler who went with him, were to say that the King was surprised that none of the German princes had so far sought 'to enter with us by marriage or otherwise'. They were 'to set forth the qualities' of the King's two daughters – either of whom would, of course, be a catch 'for a prince of the greatest honour' – and suggest the King of Denmark's brother as a possible bridegroom.[42]

The King of Denmark, when this flattering offer was relayed to him, was polite but not notably enthusiastic – the Protestant League had problems enough of its own at that particular moment – and Henry, facing the prospect of a French counter-offensive, was obliged to mend his fences with the Emperor. All the old triple-marriage proposals were trotted out again – Mary to the Emperor himself, Prince Edward to the Emperor's daughter and Elizabeth to Philip of Spain. Elizabeth's claims in particular were pressed when Henry got wind of 'a practice in hand' for a French marriage for Philip.[43]

After a period of intense diplomatic activity the Anglo-Imperial *entente* was patched up, but no betrothals followed. The Emperor, who was just then gathering his forces for an onslaught on German Protestantism, seemed unaccountably uninterested in welcoming the Tudors into the great Habsburg clan, and when Henry died in January 1547 he left his daughters unsought, unpromised and fancy-free – their future a matter for speculation.

CHAPTER II

The Noblest Man Unmarried in This Land

ELIZABETH TUDOR was rising thirteen and a half when her father died. The portrait painted by an unknown artist some time between 1542 and 1547 shows a pale flat-chested girl in a red dress. Her carroty-coloured hair is parted in the middle and tucked smoothly under a French hood. Her eyes, dark and watchful in the immature but unmistakably Tudor countenance, give nothing away. She holds a book in her incredibly long fingers. Beside her another book lies propped open on a reading-stand. She looks the very image of the studious young lady whose 'maiden shamefastness' was considered so praiseworthy by sober Protestant divines like John Aylmer. She looks, in fact, as if butter wouldn't melt in her mouth.

Until 1547, Elizabeth's life had been spent almost entirely in one or other of the royal manor-houses which lay in a rough semi-circle to the north of London, sometimes sharing an establishment with her elder sister, sometimes with her brother. Apart from those infrequent occasions when she was summoned to court to play her part with the rest of the royal family in some state function, she had lived quietly in the country, working at her lessons, aware of the great world which lay on the periphery of her existence but not yet personally involved in it. Now all this was to be changed. The year 1547 marked the end of childhood – the beginning of a long life spent at the epicentre of the great world.

Henry had left his daughters in a peculiar constitutional position. Both remained bastards by Act of Parliament but, bastards or not, both had now been restored to their places in the succession. In 1536, Parliament had granted the King power to bequeath the crown by will in order to meet the then very real possibility that he might die without any legitimate heirs at all. The birth of Prince Edward had relieved the worst of this anxiety, but in 1544 the situation was still sufficiently uncertain to make a third Act of Succession seem a necessary precaution. In the event of Edward's death without heirs,

and failing any further heirs born of the King's sixth marriage, this
Act settled the succession first on Mary and then Elizabeth, subject
to conditions to be laid down in their father's will or by his letters
patent. In his will, a complicated and much discussed document,
Henry confirmed his daughters' rights to the reversion of the crown
on condition that neither of them married without 'the written and
sealed consent' of a majority of the surviving members of the Privy
Council appointed by the same will to rule during Edward's minority.
If either Mary or Elizabeth failed to observe this condition, she would
forfeit her chance of succeeding.[1]

Looked at from a personal point of view, both sisters were left in a
peculiarly uncomfortable position – both were orphaned and unmarried in a society where the Law, with few exceptions, regarded
women as the extension of either husband or father; both were
shadowed by the reproach of bastardy and yet both, by reason of
their royal blood and their father's will, might well become objects
of dangerous interest to practitioners of the sort of cut-throat politics
likely to prevail in a country suddenly bereft of strong leadership.

Of the two princesses, Elizabeth was the most vulnerable. Mary
was at least an adult, with an adult's experience and capacity for
judgement. Elizabeth, at thirteen, was still a child, although in the
eyes of the Law she had reached maturity and was of full marriageable age. Unlike her sister, she had no relatives, either at home or
abroad, with the power to exert themselves on her behalf. The Boleyn
family had disappeared as completely as if it had never been, and
Elizabeth's noble kinsfolk, the Howards, were in eclipse – the Duke
of Norfolk being in the Tower under sentence of death. Her natural
protector, of course, was her brother, but at nine years old King
Edward could scarcely be expected to provide much in the way of
support. For the time being, at any rate, effective power over the
government, over the King and the King's sisters lay in the hands of
the King's maternal uncle, Edward Seymour, Earl of Hertford, now
created Duke of Somerset.

The question of Elizabeth's immediate future had been settled by
the beginning of March 1547 when François van der Delft, the
current Imperial ambassador, reported from London that the Queen-
Dowager was shortly going to reside in the suburbs with Madam
Elizabeth, daughter of the late King. Madam Elizabeth, he added,
would remain always in the Queen's company.[2] On the face of it, this
seemed a sensible and humane arrangement. The Queen-Dowager
was the obvious person to take charge of the King's sister and

Katherine Parr, in many ways the most sympathetic of Henry's wives, had already proved herself a conscientious and affectionate step-mother. The household she established in the cheerful, modern, red-brick mansion overlooking the Thames at Chelsea was joined by nine-year-old Jane Grey, eldest of King Henry's English great-nieces, as well as by Elizabeth and offered all the facilities of an exclusive boarding-school. No one could reasonably have foreseen the danger that was to intrude itself into these decorous surroundings.

Trouble, inevitably in the circumstances, came in masculine shape. The Queen-Dowager was serious-minded, well educated and pious, an active patron of the New Learning and advanced Protestant thinkers. But, for all her formidable intellectual piety, Katherine was no prig. She had already been obliged to nurse three elderly hus-bands. Now, in her mid-thirties and still a very pretty woman, she considered she had earned the right to a little personal happiness, and some time in the late spring of 1547 she married Thomas Seymour, younger brother of the Duke of Somerset and another of King Edward's maternal uncles.

The newly wedded pair were old friends. Thomas had in fact been courting Katherine at the time when King Henry's eye was attracted by the charming Lady Latymer – a development which brought their relationship to an abrupt conclusion. As Lady Latymer, Katherine Parr had been a rich and desirable widow. As Queen-Dowager, she was even richer and still more desirable – a first-rate matrimonial prize for any younger son, even if he did happen to be the King's uncle. Nevertheless, a rumour soon got round that Thomas Seymour, always more noted for optimism than common sense, would have preferred one of King Henry's daughters to King Henry's widow. Elizabeth's governess, Katherine Ashley, falling into conversation with the bridegroom in the park at St James's, remarked that she had 'heard one say that he should have married my lady'. 'Nay', answered Thomas, 'I love not to lose my life for a wife. It has been spoken of, but that can never be. But', he went on, 'I will promise to have the Queen'. 'It is past promise,' said Mrs Ashley, who had evidently been keeping an ear to the ground, 'as I hear you are married al-ready.'[3]

Thomas Seymour had been named as an assistant executor of Henry's will, which gave him a seat on the Council. He had now been elevated to the peerage as Baron Seymour of Sudeley and presented with the office of Lord High Admiral, but he was very far from satisfied. It seemed to him the height of injustice that one brother should rule the country in vice-regal state, enjoying both the prestige of the title of Lord Protector and the material benefits accruing from custody of the King, while the other was excluded from all but a fraction of the sweets of power. It was a state of affairs which the Lord Admiral intended to alter just as soon as he was in a position to challenge the Protector on equal terms.

An eligible bachelor, his obvious first step was to make the best marriage available, and having failed – not very surprisingly – to get himself considered as a husband for Princess Elizabeth he wasted no time in renewing his attentions to Katherine Parr. The Dowager, unaware of her lover's treachery, needed little persuasion. It is true that she spoke of a two-years delay, but Thomas Seymour was not risking the loss of his second choice and made short work of her scruples about unseemly haste. All the same, their marriage was kept secret until Katherine had been able to see the King and explain that no disrespect was intended to his father's memory. Young Edward, who was genuinely fond of his stepmother and becoming increasingly dependent on his uncle's gifts of pocket money, was graciously pleased to give them his blessing and offer to be 'a sufficient succour' in their godly and praisable enterprises; but the Lord Protector considered this particular enterprise neither godly nor praisable and was 'much displeased' when the news leaked out.[4] However, no actual offence had been committed – it was not a crime to marry the Queen-Dowager – and by midsummer the Admiral had moved in with his wife.

The boisterous loud-voiced personality of Thomas Seymour blew like a gale through the cosy ultra-feminine atmosphere of the Queen's household, rapidly dispelling all resemblance to a girls' boarding-school. He took no interest in the New Learning or in advanced Protestant thought, his over-riding interest in the advancement of Thomas Seymour leaving very little room for anything else. Vain, greedy and shallow, he was, nevertheless, an extremely attractive man physically with a commanding presence and plenty of surface charm. The Admiral wanted to be liked – to be considered a good fellow, generous, open-handed, everybody's friend, was an important part of his image – but his total self-absorption made him a dangerous friend, especially to the weak, the foolish, the innocent and the in-experienced whom he both fascinated and exploited without ever actually meaning them any harm. He was to cause his wife great unhappiness and come close to ruining the Princess Elizabeth without actually meaning either of them any harm.

There was probably no deliberate malice behind his teasing pursuit of the Princess – all those early-morning romps in her bedroom at Chelsea and Hanworth and Seymour Place during the summer and autumn of 1547 were innocuous enough in themselves. At the same time, a moment's thought would have shown most men that such rowdy goings-on might easily be misunderstood and damage the reputation of a nubile young woman. Unfortunately, the Admiral was not given to looking at any situation from anyone's point of view but his own, and when Mrs Ashley attempted to remonstrate, he roared that by God's precious soul he meant no evil and would not leave it. The Lady Elizabeth was like a daughter to him, he added, conveniently forgetting that only a few months earlier he had been hoping she might be a wife to him.[5]

An Italian Life of Elizabeth, published in the seventeenth century and more remarkable for its imaginative than its historical qualities, prints a turgid correspondence between Seymour and the Princess, dated February 1547 and consisting of a formal proposal of marriage and an equally formal refusal. These letters are almost certainly without foundation in fact and it is unlikely that Elizabeth knew anything about the Admiral's intentions at that time. According to her own account, she first heard of them from Mrs Ashley, who unwisely told her that 'if my lord might have had his own will' he would have had her before he married the Queen.[6] This knowledge added extra spice to games of hide-and-seek round the bed-curtains, rousing all the nascent sexual awareness of an adolescent girl and giving her a delicious sense of power. One way and another it was a situation fraught with undesirable possibilities; but when Mrs Ashley, unable to control either the Admiral or her charge, went to the Queen for help Katherine was inclined 'to make a small matter of it'. However, she promised to chaperon her husband's marauding expeditions in future, and so she did – for a time at least.[7]

Whether it was her stepmother's intervention, or a consciousness of her new fourteen-year-old dignity, Elizabeth seems to have lost her taste for slap-and-tickle. When the household moved to Seymour Place in London, she took to getting up earlier, so that when the Admiral came surging in, still in his nightgown and slippers, 'to bid her good morrow', he would find the Princess up and dressed and 'at her book'.[8] Their relationship, inevitably, was changing, and what had begun as a joke in rather doubtful taste was now ceasing to be a joke of any sort.

There had been an ominous little episode at Hanworth, when the

Queen told Mrs Ashley that 'my lord Admiral looked in at the gallery window and saw my lady Elizabeth cast her arms about a man's neck'. The Princess denied this accusation tearfully, but Mrs Ashley knew there could be no truth in it, 'for there came no man but Grindal, the Lady Elizabeth's schoolmaster', and he was evidently quite unembraceable. All the same, the governess was worried and began to wonder if the Queen was becoming suspicious and had intended the story as a hint that she should take better care of her charge 'and be, as it were, in watch betwixt her and my Lord Admiral'.[9] Mrs Ashley was also warned by her husband, who told her several times 'to take heed, for he did fear that the Lady Elizabeth did bear some affection to my Lord Admiral'.[10]

All this illustrates clearly enough the kind of danger to which the bastardised and orphaned Elizabeth was exposed. During King Henry's lifetime no man would have dreamt of approaching either of his daughters – no man ever did dream of approaching Mary. But then Mary's mother had been a princess of impeccable virtue and lineage, and in the days before the divorce, when she had been the Princess of England, Mary's governess was Margaret, Countess of Salisbury, a lady of the highest breeding whose royal Plantagenet blood finally brought her to the block. Elizabeth's governess, on the other hand, had originally entered her service in 1536 as a waiting-gentlewoman. Katherine Ashley, *née* Champernowne, was a good-hearted woman devoted to her princess, but although she came from a perfectly respectable old Devonshire family she lacked – in an intensely status-conscious world – the authority and prestige of aristocratic birth. Even Katherine Parr, Elizabeth's official guardian, was neither noble nor royal in her own right. As the Lord Protector's wife spitefully remarked, she had been but Latymer's wife before King Henry raised her 'in his doting days', and was now married to a mere younger son. Katherine possessed intelligence, kindliness and much generosity of spirit but she did not, unfortunately, inspire the sort of dread necessary to protect a self-willed Tudor princess from predators like Thomas Seymour.

The volcano which had been rumbling below the surface of the Queen-Dowager's household for nearly a year finally erupted in the spring of 1548, when 'the Queen, suspecting the often access of the Admiral to the Lady Elizabeth's grace, came suddenly upon them, when they were alone (he having her in his arms). Wherefore the Queen fell out, both with the Lord Admiral and with her grace also.'[11] Katherine's anger is understandable. To find herself betrayed

by the husband she loved and the girl she had mothered was enough
to try her patience to its limit, particularly when she was five months
pregnant with her first child. The Queen found some relief by sending for Mrs Ashley and giving that lady a piece of her mind, but she
could not afford the luxury of giving way to her feelings for long.
Gossip, once started, would be unstoppable and a public scandal
would be appallingly damaging to all concerned.

Clearly, though, the two households could no longer remain under
one roof and arrangements were made for Elizabeth to pay an
extended visit to Sir Anthony and Lady Denny, old and trusted
friends of the Royal family, at their house at Cheshunt. The Princess
and her entourage set out immediately after the Whitsun holiday and,
thanks to Katherine's self-control and good sense, no one, except Mrs
Ashley and possibly the Dennys, who could be relied on to keep their
mouths shut, knew the real reason for the move.

The Queen and her stepdaughter parted on affectionate terms, and
Elizabeth's gratitude is manifest in her 'bread-and-butter' letter to
Katherine. 'Although I could not be plentiful in giving thanks for the
manifold kindness received at your Highness' hand at my departure,'
she wrote, 'yet I am something to be borne withal, for truly I was
replete with sorrow to depart from your Highness, especially leaving
you undoubtful of health; and, albeit I answered little, I weighed it
more deeper, when you said you would warn me of all evils that you
should hear of me; for if your Grace had not a good opinion of me,
you would not have offered friendship to me that way, that all men
judge the contrary.'[12]

Although any immediate danger of scandal had been averted, the
episode had left its mark and Elizabeth was ill that summer – the first
recorded instance of her suffering from even a minor indisposition. In
her later teens and early twenties she was to be afflicted by well-
documented and recurrent attacks of migraine, catarrh and nephritis,
but this particular illness is not described. It may have been the
result of emotional disturbance coinciding with puberty; but the
possibility that it was the result of a miscarriage – induced or otherwise – cannot be dismissed out of hand. We know – or, rather, we
can deduce – that at one time in her life Elizabeth's periods were
irregular and scanty, but there is no reason to suppose that she did not
develop normally. In the sixteenth century girls of fourteen were
generally considered fully mature – many were married by that age,
some were already mothers. We know, from the accounts of eye-
witnesses, that Elizabeth was physically attracted by Thomas

Seymour – it would probably not be too much to say that she believed herself in love. We know that Seymour was a man of strong appetites with few scruples about taking what he wanted. We are also told that he and Elizabeth found opportunities of being alone together. An experienced, self-indulgent man and a susceptible inexperienced girl can make an explosive mixture. It would not be unbearably surprising if they had lost control of themselves.

According to Mrs Ashley, the Princess 'was first sick about mid-summer' – that is, approximately six weeks after she reached Cheshunt – and it is perhaps not without significance that Katherine Ashley and Joan Denny were sisters. If Elizabeth was, or was feared to be, in the early stages of pregnancy, it is at least possible that between them the two matrons could have concealed her condition, and perhaps taken steps to end it.

All this, of course, is conjecture. We are never likely to know for certain whether or not Elizabeth remained *virgo intacta*, and on the evidence that exists she must continue to be given the benefit of the doubt. At the same time, it's worth remembering that, if she ever did lose her celebrated virginity, this was about the only period of her life when it might have passed undetected.

Whatever the nature of her illness in the summer of 1548, it persisted for some weeks and she was still 'sick in her bed' with Mrs Ashley in close attendance when news of Katherine Parr's death in childbirth reached Cheshunt. For Mrs Ashley this changed everything, and she at once began to tell Elizabeth that her 'old husband' was free again and she could have him if she liked. 'Nay,' said Elizabeth. 'Yes,' said Mrs Ashley, 'yes, you will not deny it if my Lord Protector and the Council were pleased therewith.' 'Why not?' persisted the governess, with splendid disregard for political realities. The Admiral had been worthy to marry a queen and was now 'the noblest man unmarried in this land'. Elizabeth continued to say 'nay, by her troth', but she could not quite conceal her interest. Playing the parlour game of 'drawing hands', 'she chose my lord and chased him away', and when Mrs Ashley told her 'that she would not refuse him if the Lord Protector and the Council did bid her' she answered 'yes, by her troth'.[13]

In the privacy of the household Elizabeth might allow herself the indulgence of blushing and smiling over the Admiral, and showing 'a glad countenance' when, as frequently happened, he formed the topic of conversation; in public her discretion was absolute – an example which Thomas Seymour would have done well to copy. But

Seymour was growing increasingly impatient of discretion, and in London that autumn gossip linking his name with the Princess had begun to reach government circles.

Riding with the Admiral 'towards the Parliament House' at the end of November, the Lord Privy Seal, Lord Russell, took the opportunity of tackling him on the subject, warning him bluntly that, if he 'made means' to marry either Mary or Elizabeth, he would be courting disaster. Taken off his guard, the Admiral hedged and 'seemed to deny that there was any such thing attempted of his part'; but a few days later, again finding himself next to the Lord Privy Seal in the procession to Westminster, Seymour took the offensive himself. It was convenient for the princesses to marry, he said, and it would surely be better if they found husbands at home instead of in some foreign place. 'And', he went on, 'why might not I, or another, made by the King their father, marry one of them?' Lord Russell told him. Any Englishman who attempted to marry either of the princesses would 'procure unto himself the occasion of his utter undoing'; but Thomas Seymour, 'being of so near alliance to the King's majesty', would be writing his own death warrant. The Tudor monarchs, though wise and noble princes, were noted for their suspicious minds. If one of his uncles married one of the heirs to his throne, young Edward would certainly take occasion to have that uncle in great suspect 'and, as often as he shall see you, to think that you gape and wish for his death' – a thought which once rooted in the royal head would grow and flourish. Then there was the financial aspect. Under the terms of their father's will, both Mary and Elizabeth were to receive lands to the value of £3000 a year and marriage portions of £10,000 in money, plate and goods. How far would that go, demanded Russell, to maintain a man's charges and estate, matching himself there? They must have the three thousand a year as well, said the Admiral. 'By God! but they may not,' said Russell. 'By God! none of you all dare say nay to it!' But old Lord Russell had the last word. 'By God! for my part I will say nay to it, for it is clean against the King's will!'[14]

After this, even the most optimistic suitor should have been convinced that he stood no chance of getting official blessing, but Thomas Seymour was not easily discouraged. He was, it seems, impossible to discourage. Certainly he would not be warned. Elizabeth had wisely refused to correspond with him; and Seymour, perhaps fortunately, was not much of a letter-writer. Instead, he used the Princess's steward, Thomas Parry, as a go-between; and when Parry came up to London shortly before Christmas he had a long session with the Admiral, who was showing a close, almost a proprietorial interest in Elizabeth's affairs. The Admiral wanted to know how many servants she kept, what houses and lands had been assigned to her, and whether her title to them had yet been confirmed by the King's letters patent. It had not, and the Admiral told Parry that she could get her lands exchanged for better lands, preferably 'westward or in Wales'. He went on to ask about her housekeeping expenses and to compare them with his own.[15]

Elizabeth had now left Cheshunt and was established with a retinue of about a hundred and forty people in the old bishop's palace at Hatfield. She wanted to come to London, said Parry, to see her brother, but Durham House in the Strand which had previously been at her disposal was being used as a mint and she had nowhere to stay. The Admiral at once offered the loan of Seymour Place, adding that he would like to see the Princess himself – perhaps something could be arranged when she moved to Ashbridge, which would be on his way when he went into the country.

Parry returned to Hatfield well primed with messages, and as his mistress appeared to receive them 'very joyfully and thankfully' he ventured to ask whether, if the Council approved, she meant to marry the Lord Admiral. 'When that shall come to pass,' said Elizabeth, 'I will do as God shall put into my mind. 'Anyway, what did Parry mean by asking such a question? 'Who bade him say so?' The steward retreated hastily, explaining that nobody had bade him say anything, but it had seemed as if my lord 'was given that way rather than otherwise'. Elizabeth then wanted to know if Mrs Ashley had been told about the Admiral's 'gentle offers' and ordered Parry to be sure to pass on everything that had been said, 'for I will know nothing but she shall know of it'.[16]

But Mrs Ashley had also been to London and had heard all the gossip about the Admiral's gentleness towards the Lady Elizabeth; how he would soon be coming to woo her and had even kept Queen Katherine's maids together, so that they would be ready to wait on his new bride. Mrs Ashley, though, was not quite so sanguine as she had once been. She had had an unpleasant quarter of an hour with the Protector's formidable wife, who had rebuked her for being too friendly with the Admiral and told her she was not worthy to have the governance of a king's daughter.[17] Somewhat depressed by this experience, she warned Elizabeth that it might not be possible for the Admiral to get his way 'till the King's majesty came to his own rule', for it looked as if the Protector and the Council 'would not suffer a subject to have her'. In fact, she had better not set her mind on the marriage, seeing the unlikelihood of it, but be content to hold herself at the appointment of my Lords of the Council.[18]

This was good advice; but all the same Mrs Ashley could not quite bring herself to give up her romantic dreams, and towards the end of the Christmas holiday she and Thomas Parry enjoyed a good gossip on the all-absorbing topic of the Lord Admiral and the Lady Elizabeth. Parry commented on the goodwill between them, which he had gathered 'both from him and her Grace also'. Oh yes, said Mrs Ashley, it was true, but she had had such a 'charge' from the Duchess of Somerset that she dared not speak of it. All the same, prompted by Parry, she did speak of it, and at length. She would wish the Princess to marry the Admiral 'of all men living' and thought he might bring the matter to pass at the Council's hands well enough. When Parry remarked that he had heard 'much evil report' of the Admiral, that he was not only a covetous man and an oppressor, but also a jealous man who had used the Queen very cruelly, Mrs Ashley flared up in defence of her favourite. 'I know him better than you do,' she exclaimed, 'or those that so report him.' He would 'make but too much of her Grace' and she knew it. 'He loves her but too well,' went on the governess, 'and has done so a good while.' It was the Queen, poor soul, who had been jealous, and Mrs Ashley told Thomas Parry all about Katherine Parr finding her husband with Elizabeth in his arms.[19]

It was less than a fortnight after this remarkable conversation that the bubble burst. On 17 January 1549 the Admiral was arrested at Seymour Place. Next day the government began to round up his cronies – including Katherine Ashley and Thomas Parry – while, at Hatfield, Sir Robert Tyrwhit arrived to extract a confession from the Princess Elizabeth.

When Elizabeth was informed that her governess and her steward had been arrested, she burst into tears and seemed 'marvellous abashed', but she did not confess. There was, apparently, nothing to confess. She had once written a note to the Admiral requesting a favour for one of her chaplains. She had asked him, through Parry, to help her recover the use of Durham House and he had kindly offered the loan of Seymour Place instead. When he suggested paying her a visit in the country, Mrs Ashley had written saying he had better not come 'for fear of suspicion'. Elizabeth had been annoyed about this and told her governess not to become involved in such matters, but there had never been the slightest question of a secret understanding with my lord. Mrs Ashley had never advised it – quite the contrary, in fact – and Elizabeth herself would never have considered any proposal of marriage without the full consent of the King, the Protector and the Council. She did not believe either Mrs Ashley or Parry had been engaged in any 'practice' to get her married without consent – certainly they had never told her they would do so.[20]

It was all very unsatisfactory. Robert Tyrwhit could see by the Princess's face that she was guilty, but he also perceived 'she would abide more storms ere she accuse Mistress Ashley'. 'I do assure your Grace, she hath a very good wit,' he wrote to the Protector, 'and nothing is gotten of her but by great policy.' During the weeks that followed he tried every trick of the interrogator's trade to break her resistance, and failed. The fifteen-year-old Elizabeth remained impervious to threats, was not deceived by promises or the blandishments of false friends, and reacted strongly to even more disagreeable methods. When Tyrwhit told her it was being said that she was already in the Tower and with child by the Lord Admiral, the Princess declared flatly that these were shameful slanders and, in a famous letter to the Protector, demanded that she should be allowed to come to court and 'show myself there as I am'.[21]

Tyrwhit himself, having practised unsuccessfully with my lady's grace 'by all means and policies' to persuade her to confess more than she had already done, was driven to the conclusion that there had been some secret promise between my lady, Mistress Ashley and the cofferer never to confess until death; but Thomas Parry and Katherine Ashley were not made of such stern stuff as the Tudor princess. Both cracked under pressure and, on 5 February, Tyrwhit was able to confront Elizabeth with their statements. The details of those frolics at Chelsea and elsewhere looked extraordinarily unfunny set down in black and white by some clerk's scribbling pen; none of it reflected much credit on those concerned, but it was not evidence of conspiracy. The Princess's servants had exposed her to embarrassment and a certain amount of moral censure; they had not implicated her in any treasonable activity, and this she was quick to realise. Apart from a few unimportant details, Tyrwhit got nothing further out of her.

The Admiral's activities were a very different matter. His undercover courtship of Elizabeth had been only one strand, albeit an important one, in the complicated web of subversion in which he was now enmeshed. Apart from the accusation that before he married the

Queen he had gone about to marry the Lady Elizabeth and since that time had 'by secret and crafty means... practised to achieve the said purpose of marrying the said Lady Elizabeth', there were thirty-two charges against him in the list drawn up by the Privy Council.[22] There can be no reasonable doubt that Thomas Seymour would have liked to marry Elizabeth, that he would have liked to overthrow his brother's government and had actively plotted to achieve both these ends; but whether it was fair to deduce that 'following the example of Richard III he wished to make himself King' is another matter.[23] The younger Seymour was a basically unstable character who had allowed personal jealousy to become an obsession. Such an inept conspirator scarcely represented a very serious danger to the State. He did, however, represent a serious nuisance which could no longer be safely tolerated, and by 5 March a bill declaring him 'adjudged and attainted of high treason' had passed all its stages in both Houses of Parliament.

At Hatfield, Elizabeth heard that my Lord Admiral's household had been dispersed, and knowing what that meant she began 'a little to droop'. Robert Tyrwhit reported that 'now she cannot bear to hear him discommended but she is ready to make answer therein; and so she hath not been accustomed to do, unless Mistress Ashley were touched'.[24] There could, of course, be only one end to the Admiral's story and, when news of his execution arrived, the Princess's only comment is said to have been: 'This day died a man of much wit but little judgement.' It was as apt an epitaph as any.

Elizabeth's emotional involvement with Thomas Seymour may not have gone very deep. Nevertheless, it had been a frightening and deeply shocking experience which she had faced with a courage and strength of will astonishing in a girl of fifteen. Now she buried the terror and the shock – at a cost of how much psychological damage can only be guessed – and began grimly to pick up the pieces. As it turned out, she was helped in the task of refurbishing her public image by external events. That autumn a *coup d'état* stage-managed by John Dudley, Earl of Warwick, toppled the Lord Protector more efficiently than anything the Admiral's amateurish efforts could have hoped to achieve. The new régime bore the Princess Elizabeth no personal animus and in December she paid a visit to court where, according to the Emperor's ambassador, she was received with great pomp and triumph and was continually with the King.[25]

The unfortunate episode of Thomas Seymour might be officially regarded as closed, but Elizabeth's future remained as uncertain as ever. In November 1550 the new Imperial ambassador, Jehan Scheyfve, picked up a rumour 'that my Lord of Warwick is about to cast off his wife and marry my Lady Elizabeth ... with whom he is said to have had several secret and intimate personal communications; and by these means he will aspire to the crown'.[26] Although Scheyfve was confident that his information had come from a 'safe source', there is no corroborative evidence to substantiate it. Brilliant, rapacious and essentially crooked, the Earl of Warwick had won his own way to the top and was to go to considerable lengths to stay there, but in 1550 he had more immediate problems on his mind, and there were more feasible bridegrooms in view for the Princess Elizabeth.

In the field of foreign affairs England was now reaping the sour fruit of Henry VIII's impetuous policies in Scotland, where his celebrated 'rough wooing' of the little Queen, unwisely pursued by Protector Somerset, had had the predictable result of driving the embattled Scots back into the 'auld alliance' with France. François had not long survived his old sparring partner the King of England, and Henri II – less absorbed by dreams of Italian conquest than his father had been – was readier to commit himself in the north. As he listened to the siren voices of the Duke of Guise and the Cardinal of Lorraine urging him to go to the aid of their sister the Scottish Queen-Mother and their niece the Queen of Scots, Henri could also reflect that Mary Stuart was a great-granddaughter of Henry VII, with an undeniable place in the English succession. The King, in fact, can scarcely be blamed for seeking to exploit a situation so fraught with interesting possibilities. In June 1548 a force of 6,000 French troops landed at Leith, and in July the French ambassador offered the Scottish Estate his master's unstinted protection against the English invader. In return, the Scots were to surrender their Queen, who would be taken at once to France and in due course be married to the Dauphin. The Scottish lords listened to the reassuring chink of French gold in their pockets, thought with satisfaction of English discomfiture, and agreed. On 29 July the five-year-old Mary went on board a French galley and was spirited away round 'the back of Ireland'. France and Scotland, not England and Scotland, had become one country, and in future England would have to live with the knowledge that her hereditary enemy would walk through her back door virtually at will.

Matters were not improved by the fact that England's nominal ally, Charles V, was currently engaged in a losing battle to control heretic

Germany and in no position to come to her assistance. Apart from this, relations between the allies had become increasingly strained over the English government's attempts to force the Princess Mary to comply with its new religious laws and, in March 1551, Jehan Scheyfve threatened the Council with the Emperor's grave displeasure if his cousin was deprived of the opportunity to hear mass.[27]

In the circumstances, the Earl of Warwick had little option but to cultivate the French, and the price of friendship was naturally high. Boulogne had already been ceded. Now England was obliged to relinquish all claims to the Queen of Scots as a bride for Edward VI. It was agreed that Edward should be betrothed instead to the French princess, Elisabeth of Valois, and in the summer of 1551, amid an ostentatious exchange of embassies and civilities, the Duke of Guise was putting forward possible suitors for the English Princess Elizabeth. His suggestions included his own brother and, according to Scheyfve, the Princess 'very hastily but with great care had her portrait painted just before the gentleman left for France, so that they might take the picture with them'. Such a marriage, the ambassador went on, would certainly go to prove that England and France intended to observe close friendship and alliance although, he was pleased to note, not a few Englishmen of rank were saying it was all too sudden and vehement to last.[28]

Another Guise proposal, made through the Florentine merchant Anthony Guidotti, was the Duke of Ferrara's son, 'one of the goodliest young men of all Italy'. Then there was the Duke of Florence's son, who was only eleven years old. 'If this party were liked,' wrote Guidotti persuasively, 'it were an easy matter to be concluded without any excessive dote.'[29] Yet another European prince whose name was being linked with Elizabeth's in 1551 was the King of Denmark's eldest son and, in November, Scheyfve heard that the Council was opening negotiations with the Danes, as it considered this match would be better than a French one 'because of religion and other reasons'.[30]

The Ferrara marriage came up again in March 1553 when Sir Richard Morysine, the English envoy in Antwerp, reported that he had been approached on the subject by Francisco d'Este, the young man's uncle. D'Este had asked for a description of the Princess, and Morysine replied tactfully that, even if God had made her a poor man's daughter, 'he did not know that prince that might not think himself happy to be the husband of such a lady'.[31] Morysine was also able to report that he had received a letter out of Saxony giving him to understand that Duke Hans Frederick's second son would, 'if he durst, bear a great affection to the Lady Elizabeth's grace'.[32]

But, as so often in the past, nothing came of any of these widely varied and mostly tentative proposals, and Elizabeth at nineteen remained an eligible spinster. England, hamstrung by the French presence in Scotland, her population restive and her currency devalued, did not cut a very impressive figure on the European scene during the early fifties, and the European princes preferred to await developments before committing themselves to firm alliances – so much depended on when, or if, Edward VI attained his majority. In the spring of 1552, just as he was approaching the dangerous age for Tudor boys, Edward had succumbed to a severe attack of measles. He seemed to make a good recovery and resumed his normal activities, but the damage had been done and by the autumn tuberculosis was already established. By the spring of 1533 he was dying and, in spite of an official news-blackout, London seethed with speculation.

The political power of John Dudley, now Duke of Northumberland, was still unchallenged and his influence over the King unbroken. His numerous brood of sons filled the Privy Chamber and people grumbled, though not too loudly, about Dudley greed and Dudley arrogance. The Lords of the Council grumbled to each other about the way in which the Duke – he was the first Englishman unconnected with the blood royal to bear such a title – summoned them daily to his house to wait upon his pleasure and reminded each other privately that his father had died a convicted traitor. Not that this was necessarily a social disgrace – the highest in the land quite frequently died as convicted traitors – but John Dudley's father had been a nobody, a low-born lawyer with a genius for finding ways of parting people from their money. John Dudley himself had no illusions about his unpopularity, or about his probable fate after Edward's death, and as soon as he realised that this would not be long in coming he began to put certain contingency plans into operation.

No one expected Northumberland to retire gracefully, but no one seemed very certain exactly what he intended to do. Jehan Scheyfve was in no doubt that the Duke and his party would try to prevent Mary from succeeding. 'They are evidently resolved to resort to arms against her,' he wrote, 'with the excuse of religion among others.' It was after this that the issue became clouded.

At Whitsun, M. de l'Aubespine, a secretary frequently employed by the French king on high-level diplomatic missions, arrived in

England. The reason for his visit was surrounded 'with the greatest mystery', but Scheyfve reported that it was being said he had come to offer the King of France's services to the Duke of Northumberland in the event of King Edward's death, and whether it might not be possible to make a closer alliance with England by arranging a French marriage for Elizabeth. Another story going the rounds was that, 'if the Duke of Northumberland felt himself well supported, he would find means to marry his eldest son, the Earl of Warwick, to the Lady Elizabeth, after causing him to divorce his wife . . . or else that he might find it expedient to get rid of his own wife and marry the said Elizabeth himself, and claim the crown for the house of Warwick as descendants of the House of Lancaster'.[33]

Although ideally Northumberland might well have chosen to use Henry VIII's Protestant daughter as his instrument in furthering the pretensions of the house of Dudley, his knowledge of the lady would certainly have told him that she was likely to prove a highly unsatisfactory cat's-paw. Elizabeth had always been careful to keep on good terms with the Duke, but there is no evidence whatever that she would even have considered linking her fortunes with a man so universally disliked and distrusted, or indeed that he ever approached her on the subject. Northumberland had no time to waste on persuasion, or divorce, and he had already settled on his victim. At Whitsun the hapless Jane Grey was married to the last remaining unmarried Dudley son, Guildford, and Edward was now being pressurised into making a new will – or rather into altering his father's will.

Failing heirs from his own children, Henry had settled the crown on the descendants of his younger sister, who had married the Duke of Suffolk – arbitrarily excluding the Stuart descendants of his elder sister. Edward's 'Devise for the Succession' arbitrarily excluded Mary and Elizabeth in favour of fifteen-year-old Jane Grey, granddaughter of Mary Tudor, Duchess of Suffolk.[34] The legality of the Devise was – to say the least – doubtful, but Northumberland was understandably less concerned with legality than with self-preservation, and when the King died, on 6 July 1553, Northumberland immediately had Jane proclaimed as Queen.

On paper the Duke's position looked unassailable. He controlled the capital, the fortress of the Tower with its armoury and mint, and the Council followed him like sheep – apparently hypnotised by his powerful personality. The rightful heiress was a lone woman of thirty-seven, in poor health, without friends, money or influence. No one believed she had a chance, not even the Emperor, who could only advise his ambassadors to try to influence Northumberland on Mary's behalf and to win his confidence.[35]

Neither the Emperor nor the Duke was in the habit of paying much attention to public opinion, and consequently the ignominious collapse of the *coup* and Mary's overwhelming victory took them almost equally by surprise. The English people had quite simply had enough of Northumberland and his kind. They rose in an unprecedented spontaneous demonstration of loyalty for the true Tudor line and of revulsion against the upstart tribe of Dudley, and the great Duke was swept away. It looked like a miracle. Mary herself – unfortunately, as it turned out – had no doubt at all that it was the personal handiwork of God.

CHAPTER III

Le plus beau gentilhomme d'Angleterre

THE sixteenth century was an age of queens, but Mary Tudor was England's first queen regnant (unless you count the long-ago Matilda of unhappy memory); and the islanders, delighted though they were over Mary's triumph, did not for a moment expect her to rule alone. Even before the Queen, travelling slowly down from East Anglia, had reached the capital, speculation as to the identity of the man she would choose to be her husband was already rife.

There was no doubt about the preference of all those who had an opinion on the subject – they wanted the Queen to marry an Englishman. One of the reasons put forward in King Edward's Devise to justify the exclusion of his sisters from the succession was that they might marry abroad and bring foreigners into the realm, an eventuality which could only 'tend to the utter subversion of the commonwealth'.¹ This was about the only point made by the Devise which struck any answering chord in the population as a whole. But, after all, why should the Queen marry a foreigner when there was an eminently suitable Englishman available? Edward Courtenay, grandson of Edward IV's youngest daughter and that monarch's only surviving male descendant, was surely the obvious candidate for the post of king-consort. 'There is much talk here to the effect that he will be married to the Queen, as he is of the blood royal,' reported the Emperor's ambassadors on 22 July.

The Courtenay family had in the past been given good reason to regret their royal blood. They'd been arrested in the November purge of 1538, when the threatening noises coming from the Catholic powers had prompted Henry and Thomas Cromwell to round up all the remaining offshoots of the Plantagenet tree they could lay their hands on. Edward Courtenay's father, the Marquis of Exeter, had been executed that December, together with his kinsmen Henry Pole and Edward Neville. His wife and twelve-year-old son were left in the Tower and, although Gertrude, Marchioness of Exeter, was presently 'pardoned' and released, young Edward had stayed in gaol for very nearly fifteen years – until the evening of 3 August 1553 when Queen Mary Tudor rode through the main gateway of his prison, the guns of the fortress booming a welcome, and raised him from his knees and kissed him and formally set him free.[2]

Despite the fact that no one yet knew for certain what the Queen's intentions were, Edward Courtenay had now become a figure of international importance and, as such, a focus of international interest. He had, it seemed, made good use of his captivity, devoting himself 'to all virtuous and praiseworthy studies', so that he could speak several languages and had also learnt to become proficient on 'various instruments of music'. There was in him, too, 'a civility which must be deemed natural rather than acquired by the habit of society' – the Imperial envoys were forgetting that the society to be found in the Tower was apt to include the best breeding in the land – and his bodily graces were in proportion to those of his mind.[3] No portrait of Edward Courtenay appears to have survived, but all foreign observers were agreed that he was uncommonly handsome. '*Le plus beau et plus agréable gentilhomme d'Angleterre,*' commented the French ambassador, Antoine de Noailles; and another Frenchman was to note in his memoirs: '*Il estoit l'un des plus beaux entres les jeunes seigneurs de son age.*'

At first glance, therefore, this beautiful, accomplished, well-mannered, high-born young man looked like the answer to any royal maiden's prayer and, from Mary Tudor's point of view, Edward Courtenay should have possessed other special advantages. He had remained faithful to the old religion, and there were long-standing ties of loyalty and affection between their families. The Marquis and Marchioness of Exeter had been close friends of Mary's mother – if Eustace Chapuys can be trusted, the Marquis had been ready to join an armed demonstration of sympathy for Queen Catherine during the early 1530s – and Mary was always conscious of an obligation towards those very few members of the aristocracy who'd been prepared to risk her father's murderous displeasure for her own and her mother's sake. The widowed Marchioness had now become one of the Queen's most intimate ladies-in-waiting, usually sharing her bedroom, but whether Mary was planning to extend a similar privilege to her friend's son was still a matter for conjecture.

It was, though, a matter which the Emperor, who was taking a close personal interest in his cousin's plans, wanted cleared up as quickly as possible. Charles V was naturally eager to grasp what might be a unique opportunity to forge a permanent link between England, Spain and the Netherlands; and, with this end in view, he was prepared to suggest his heir, Prince Philip, now a widower of twenty-six, as a bridegroom for Mary Tudor. Charles wasn't worried about other foreign competition, but he recognised that his son had a potentially dangerous rival in Edward Courtenay, and Simon Renard of the Imperial embassy was instructed to drop a hint to the Queen that such an inexperienced young man was scarcely a fit match for her. Renard might perhaps mention the rumours that Courtenay was already beginning to give himself airs and how it was being whispered that he'd been seen visiting houses of ill-fame in the city. At the same time, wrote Cardinal Granvelle, the Emperor's right-hand man in Brussels, the ambassador must be very careful not to go too far – at least until Mary's intentions were more clearly known – for, if she did take it into her head to have Courtenay, nothing would stop her, if she was like other women, and she would then always hold Renard's words against him.[4]

Simon Renard was far too shrewd a diplomat to risk jeopardising such delicate negotiations through lack of tact in the early stages, but by the middle of August he felt reasonably confident that the Queen 'had no wish to wed an Englishman'. 'As far as I can judge,' he told Granvelle on the fifteenth, 'she wishes his Majesty to suggest some one, believing he will name a person agreeable to her; and I am in hopes that if his Majesty were inclined to propose our Prince it would be the most welcome news that could be given to her.'[5] It was, however, necessary to be certain, and at the next opportunity Renard returned to the subject of Courtenay 'and the common rumour about his marriage to the Queen'. Mary brushed this aside. She had scarcely seen Courtenay since the day she had pardoned him and, in any case, there was no one in England she wanted to marry. Hadn't the Emperor, she asked, selected some suitable person yet? The Queen could hardly have given Renard a better opening and within a few minutes Philip's name had entered the conversation in the most natural way in the world. Seizing his opportunity, the ambassador began to expatiate on his Highness's great good sense, judgement, experience and moderation, adding hopefully that the Prince was already 'an old married man' with a seven-year-old son. Philip was actually a year younger than the despised Edward Courtenay, but Renard, knowing Mary's sensitivity about her own advancing age, contrived to skate round this awkward fact. It seemed, though, as if the Queen was hardly listening. She had never, she told Renard with

painful honesty, known that thing which was called love, 'nor harboured thoughts of voluptuousness'; she had never even thought of
marriage until now, when God had been pleased to raise her to the
throne. She left it all to the Emperor, whom she regarded as a father.
He would have to take the initiative and deal with the Council for
her, as she could not face the prospect of discussing such a delicate
personal matter with them.[6]

It was unfortunate, but not surprising, that Mary should have
disliked and distrusted so many of the men with whose help, for
better or worse, she now had to govern the country. Nearly all of
them were associated in some way with past humiliations; nearly all
had been prepared to bow before the recent violent wind of religious
change; and nearly all were more or less heavily compromised by
their connection with the Duke of Northumberland. The Duke
himself had paid the price of unsuccessful treason, but his erstwhile
accomplices remained. Since a novice queen could not afford to
alienate the Crown's most influential and experienced servants, she'd
been obliged to accept their apologies and explanations; but for advice
and support Mary turned, as she had always done, to her cousin
Charles, and Simon Renard, as her cousin's surrogate, was rapidly
becoming her closest confidant and friend.

To have won the Queen was a triumph for Imperial diplomacy, but
neither Renard nor his master was deluding himself that the Spanish
marriage would be easy to negotiate. Such a project would inevitably
stir up strong feeling both in England and elsewhere – elsewhere, in
this instance, meaning France. Antoine de Noailles was not one of
Mary's favourites – he had, after all, been another of Northumberland's cronies – and the Frenchman, excluded now from the inner
circle at court, had spent August trying to find out what the
Imperialists were up to. He got his first definite clue early in
September, when he heard from a friend in the royal household that
the Emperor had already formally offered his son to Mary. The news
was premature but it confirmed all de Noailles' forebodings. The sort
of alliance being planned between the Queen of England and her
Habsburg relations could only result in France's encirclement and it
was, therefore, the plain duty of France's ambassador to bestir himself
to prevent it.

De Noailles wasted no time. Having despatched a rather panicky
warning to Paris that Mary and Philip might be found in bed
together before anyone realised what was happening, he at once set
about opening channels of communication with Courtenay and his

friends, with leading members of the Protestant party – with any Englishman, in fact, with any influence to exert who could be guaranteed to oppose the importation of a foreign king. Using this varied assortment of allies, the ambassador began to organise a vigorous and highly effective anti-Imperialist scare campaign, but he also employed the more conventional diplomatic approach of waiting on the Lord Chancellor, Stephen Gardiner, Bishop of Winchester, to endeavour to impress on him the obvious practical and political disadvantages of a Spanish marriage. If, de Noailles pointed out reasonably enough, the Queen wanted a husband at her side to support her and perhaps give her children, then Philip could hardly be a more unsuitable choice. A prince with so many prior commitments abroad would not be able to stay in England, and Mary would probably be lucky if she saw him for as much as a fortnight in the whole of her life. Apart from this, she and the country would inevitably be dragged into the Emperor's unappeasable quarrel with France – a quarrel in which they had no interest and from which they could expect no profit.[7]

Stephen Gardiner found himself in the embarrassing position of agreeing wholeheartedly with everything de Noailles said, while at the same time distrusting him profoundly. As an Englishman, a patriot and a politician, the Chancellor instinctively recoiled from too close an involvement with any foreign power-bloc. As a Catholic who had spent most of the previous reign in prison for his religious beliefs, he was afraid that any chance of achieving a peaceful reconciliation with Rome, such as he and Mary both desired, would vanish overnight if once it became associated in the public mind with the taint of foreign interference. He knew the French would not hesitate to play on Protestant fears and prejudices in their efforts to kill the Spanish marriage, and he also knew that, once roused, the closely related passions of nationalism and religious fanaticism could quickly boil over into violence – already there had been some ominous anti-Catholic demonstrations in London.

But, until the Emperor came into the open, there wasn't a great deal Gardiner could do. He did, however, go to see the Queen, taking with him a group of pro-Courtenay councillors – Robert Rochester, Francis Englefield and Edward Waldegrave – to ask her to think seriously about marriage and naming Courtenay as a desirable and acceptable match. Gardiner was, on paper at least, her principal adviser and the other three were old friends, loyal and devout Catholics who'd stood by her and suffered with her in the past. But even in this company Mary's reserve held. Courtenay was very young, she remarked dismissively. Only time would show what he was made of.[8]

Renard, meanwhile, had been waiting for instructions. These finally arrived towards the end of September. He was to seek a private interview with the Queen and make the Emperor's offer of Prince Philip in strict confidence, at the same time asking her to 'set aside the ceremony and concealments which are practised by strangers when dealing with matters of this nature'. Charles wanted a plain answer from his cousin 'as to her own inclination' for, if she didn't like the idea, he would prefer it not to go any further.[9]

It was nearly another fortnight before Renard was able to act. In spite of his privileged position, it wasn't always easy to see the Queen in private. His colleagues at the embassy, including his predecessor Jehan Scheyfve, who was still in England, were inclined to be jealous; and Mary herself was busy with her coronation, which took place on 1 October, and with the opening of Parliament on the fifth. At last, on Tuesday the tenth, an assignation was made and a servant came late that evening to lead the ambassador to the Queen's inner sanctum at Westminster.

The moment the proposal had actually been spoken aloud, Mary's immediate and instinctive reaction was to draw back. She couldn't make up her mind so quickly. It was such an important step and would be for all her life. She didn't know how the people would take it – the Emperor knew what they were like – or whether the Council would consent. Then, she really knew very little about Philip. She had heard he was not so wise as his father. He was very young and, if he were disposed to be amorous, 'such was not her desire,' not at her time of life and having never harboured thoughts of love.[10]

Renard settled down patiently to reassure her, much as he might have gentled a nervous thoroughbred. Philip's nature was so admirable, so virtuous, prudent and modest as to appear 'too wonderful to be human', and this was no exaggeration. He was so stable and settled that he could no longer be considered young – he was nearly thirty, after all – and, besides, the Queen must remember that an older man might not be able to give her a child. The Emperor had 'maturely examined her requirements' and had been unable to think of a more fitting person. It would be a great marriage, too, both for herself and her country; Philip being so puissant a prince to whom the kingdom could turn confidently for protection and succour. Of course, certain people would have reasons of their own for disliking the match. 'The Queen and her Council', said Renard impressively, 'would do well to remember that she had four certain and open enemies; the heretics and schismatics, the rebels and partisans of the late Duke of Northumberland, the French and Scots, and the Lady Elizabeth, who would never cease to trouble her while they had the means, and even rise against her and her government.'[11]

Ever since his arrival in England, Renard had been keeping a watchful eye on the Queen's half-sister, who, he was convinced, was deep in the counsels and intrigues of the heretics and rebels. He also suspected the Princess of being in touch with the French ambassador, though he'd so far been unable to prove it. He warned Mary frequently, and unnecessarily, not to trust her sister and discussed wistfully with the Emperor the possibility of shutting Elizabeth up in the Tower or, alternatively, of persuading Parliament to disinherit her. A more immediately practicable solution to the problem of the Protestant heiress (Elizabeth was now accompanying the Queen to mass, but her suffering air robbed the gesture of much of its effect as far as the Catholic party was concerned) would be to marry her off to a reliable Catholic husband, and it was being suggested in some quarters that, if the Queen didn't want young Courtenay for herself, she might pass him on to the Princess.

This idea seems to have been circulating as early as the previous August, when the Imperial ambassadors were reporting, without naming their sources, that Elizabeth showed signs of taking a great interest in Courtenay.[12] But Courtenay himself, in conversation with the Queen early in October, had been careful to disclaim any desire for 'so exalted an alliance'. If the Queen wished him to marry, then he would much prefer 'some simple girl' to Elizabeth, who was a heretic, too proud and 'of too doubtful lineage on her mother's side'.[13] These words were evidently repeated – at any rate, Renard wrote on the nineteenth that Courtenay was in disgrace with the Lady Elizabeth 'for having spoken otherwise than she had looked for about *amourettes* said to have existed between them'.[14]

Ten days later, after much heart-searching and prayer, Mary gave Renard her solemn word in the presence of the Holy Sacrament that she would marry Philip and 'love him perfectly'.[15] The Queen's decision was, of course, a major step forward; but Renard and his ally on the Council, William Paget, now had somehow to win over the anti-Spanish councillors led by Stephen Gardiner, and it was in this context that the question of a marriage between Elizabeth and Courtenay began to be seriously discussed. As Paget explained to

Renard, although Parliament had willingly reversed Henry VIII's divorce from his first wife and relegitimised the Queen, this did not, contrary to all reasonable expectations, in any way affect Elizabeth's right to the succession – a right which, in Paget's opinion, would be very difficult to take away without causing the sort of trouble everyone was most anxious to avoid. Besides this, the next heirs, according to King Henry's will, were the Suffolk girls – Lady Jane Grey, currently in prison awaiting her trial for the treason of usurping the throne, and her younger sisters – all of them Protestants and none of them exactly likely to commend herself to the Emperor. Worse still, if Henry's will were disregarded and the normal laws of inheritance followed, the crown would go to Mary Queen of Scots, now a pretty and promising ten-year-old shortly to become the King of France's daughter-in-law.

If Mary Tudor were to have children, then naturally these difficulties would disappear of their own accord; but Mary Tudor would be thirty-eight before her marriage could be consummated and no one personally acquainted with her and her long history of ill-health could honestly rate her chances of successful motherhood at more than remote. William Paget knew better than to say this aloud, but he was surely thinking of the future – his own and England's – when he suggested that the next Parliament should be asked to confirm Elizabeth as heiress presumptive, on condition she married Courtenay. In the short term, as he pointed out to Renard, this would disarm the pro-Courtenay faction on the Council and satisfy Elizabeth's numerous supporters in Parliament and elsewhere. Elizabeth and Courtenay themselves would be conciliated, the nobility would be pleased, and popular opposition to the idea of the Spanish marriage would be allayed. Looking further ahead, dangerous uncertainty over the succession would be removed and, with any luck, French intrigue discouraged by this setback to their candidate's hopes.[16]

It sounded persuasive, but Renard remained unconvinced. To unite two such doubtful quantities at such a sensitive moment seemed to him to be taking a quite unacceptable risk. Another obstacle was Mary's unconcealed dislike and distrust of her sister. Elizabeth, she said flatly, was a heretic, a hypocrite and a bastard; it would be a disgrace to the kingdom to allow her to succeed on any terms.[17] Nevertheless, the scheme continued to be aired at intervals through the autumn, being finally vetoed by the Emperor in a letter dated Christmas Eve.[18]

Throughout that autumn, though, it was the Queen's matrimonial plans which were getting all the attention. 'In the beginning of November', commented a contemporary chronicler, 'was the first notice among the people touching the marriage of the Queen to the King of Spain', and the news struck dismay into the hearts of Courtenay's supporters. Renard heard that they were planning to ask Parliament 'to speak to the Queen about the match, begging her not to wed a foreigner and expressing a fear that if she does so the people simply will not stand it'.[19] The only Englishman who might, even at this late stage, have been able to make Mary see the sort of trouble she was storing up for herself was Stephen Gardiner, and it was particularly unfortunate in the circumstances that so little trust or communication should have existed between them. Mary could not forget that the Bishop had once been one of her father's most active agents in the matter of her mother's divorce; and Gardiner, faced with a stubborn emotional woman who had already given her confidence elsewhere, seems to have lost his nerve. Against Renard he could marshal his arguments with cogency and force; to Mary he could only object lamely, 'And what will the people say? How will they put up with a foreigner who will promise things he will not keep?' The Queen retorted that her mind was made up and, if her chancellor preferred the will of the people to her wishes, then he was not keeping *his* promises.[20] Stephen Gardiner was no longer a young man, he was already a sick man and, with his past experience of Tudor wilfulness in matrimonial matters, he was understandably uneager for a battle. He was also hampered in this instance by his known personal fondness for Courtenay, to whom he'd become much attached when they were in the Tower together. As the Queen snappishly remarked, was it suitable to expect her to marry someone just because the Bishop had made friends with him in prison?[21] Gardiner gave it up. His first loyalty was to his sovereign and, if she really wanted Philip, then he would abide by her choice.

Having vanquished the Chancellor, Mary proceeded to make short work of the Speaker of the Commons. Her marriage was entirely her own affair and it was no business of Parliament to attempt to dictate to her on such a personal matter. In any case, if they forced her to take a husband who would not be to her liking, they would cause her death, for she would not live three months and would have no children, and then, indicated the Queen, they would be sorry![22]

Gardiner's surrender and Mary's reception of the parliamentary delegation made it clear that all hope of preventing the Spanish marriage by constitutional methods was at an end; but opposition in the country at large was mounting steadily, and Antoine de Noailles had by no means given up hope that it might yet be possible to confound the Imperialists. The Princess Elizabeth had left court early in December for her country house at Ashbridge, and on the fourteenth of the month de Noailles told the King of France: 'From what I hear it only requires that my Lord Courtenay should marry her and that they should go together to the counties of Devonshire and Cornwall. Here it can easily be believed that they would find many adherents, and they could then make a strong claim to the crown, and the Emperor and the Prince of Spain would find it difficult to suppress this rising.'[23]

Elizabeth and Courtenay (he had recently been created Earl of Devonshire) should certainly have made a powerful combination. Indeed, the romantic appeal of such a handsome well-matched young couple, both of the English blood royal, ought to have been irresistible. But, wrote de Noailles, 'the misfortune is that the said Courtenay is of such a fearful and timid disposition that he dare not make the venture . . . There are many, of whom I know, who would be ready to give him encouragement and all help in carrying out some plan to his advantage, and I do not see what should hinder him, except his weakness, faintheartedness and timidity.'[24] The disappointing truth was that, for all his good looks, pretty manners and patrician breeding, Courtenay had turned out to be a poor creature, self-indulgent, irresponsible and vain, with a vicious streak beneath the charm; one who would agree amiably to the suggestions of his more strongminded friends and then carry tales to the Queen. He was obviously untrustworthy and in a crisis would undoubtedly lose such nerve as he possessed; but de Noailles, who had to work with the available material, continued to hope that, properly handled, he would make a useful tool.

As for Elizabeth, the ambassador seems to have taken her cooperation for granted, though on what grounds it's impossible to say with any certainty. It was highly unlikely that the Princess ever took him into her confidence. She was far too shrewd not to have seen through his flattering eagerness to promote her cause; not to have realised that, although France's immediate objective might be to stop the Spanish marriage at all costs, her long-term cross-Channel interests were bound up in the person of the young Queen of Scots. It would clearly have been pointless to try to create a party for Mary Stuart in the England of 1553 but, if Henry VIII's daughters could be goaded or tricked into destroying one another, then the prospects of seeing England and Scotland united under the sovereignty of his half-French great-niece would look a great deal more hopeful.

Elizabeth had long since learnt to keep her own counsel, yet it's difficult to believe that she was unaware of the plans being made for her future. Of the dozen or so gentlemen now busily engaged in conspiring to depose the Queen, to marry the Princess to Edward Courtenay and place them jointly on the throne, at least three were personally acquainted with her or with members of her household, and one of their leaders, James Crofts, assured de Noailles that he was 'very familiar' with the Princess and her servants. Crofts, who actually paid a visit to Ashbridge about this time, used Elizabeth's name freely in his communications to the ambassador, describing her determination to resist any attempt by the Emperor to marry her to one of his nominees and her hopes of gaining the crown, 'especially if the matters undertaken for her come to a successful end'.[25]

Whether Crofts was speaking with authority, or whether he was simply trying to convince the French that the conspiracy had a solid 'foundation', we have no means of knowing. We do know that Elizabeth strongly resented her sister's hostile and at times insulting treatment of her, and de Noailles may well have been right when he reported that 'she was most desirous of freeing herself from control', but this doesn't necessarily mean that she approved of the steps being contemplated by her friends. Certainly in later life she never showed the slightest sign of wishing to rule jointly with anyone and, if she was really hoping to gain the crown by force, the chicken-hearted Courtenay was surely the last person she would willingly have chosen for a partner. Not a scrap of reliable evidence survives to indicate that they ever corresponded, ever made contact at a personal level or indeed ever met at all, except formally and in public. It therefore seems pretty safe to assume that the *'amourettes'* said to have existed between them existed only in Simon Renard's imagination, and that Elizabeth's reputed eagerness to wed Courtenay and ride westwards with him was based on the wishful thinking of men like James Crofts. One thing is quite certain: the Princess had no intention of showing her hand unless and until the conspiracy had succeeded in its object of removing Mary. What she might have done then remains anybody's guess.

The rising intended to save England from the rule of the proud Spaniards who, as all right-thinking Englishmen knew, would ravish their wives, deflower their daughters, despoil them of their goods and lands, and then cut their throats, was to have been a four-pronged attack, with armed revolt in the west country, led by Peter Carew with Courtenay himself as figurehead; in Wales, led by James Crofts; in Leicestershire, under the command of Jane Grey's father, the Duke of Suffolk; and in Kent, under Sir Thomas Wyatt. The outbreak of violence had been planned to coincide with Philip's expected arrival in the spring of 1554, but things began to go wrong early in January, when the Council suddenly summoned Peter Carew to London. Carew defied the order, and Stephen Gardiner, worried about the way Courtenay's name kept cropping up in connection with reports of impending trouble in the west, and afraid that his young friend had been getting into bad company, took the opportunity of having a serious talk with him. The upshot, according to de Noailles, was that 'this young fool of a Lord Courtenay' promptly revealed everything he knew about 'the enterprise of Peter Carew and his companions'.[26]

But even before Courtenay's betrayal the conspirators, realising they'd lost the element of surprise, had decided to go ahead – it was a case of now or never. The movement in Devonshire had always depended heavily on Courtenay's presence, on the prestige of his name and his strong family connections with the area. Without him it died at birth, and Peter Carew was obliged to leave hurriedly for France. It was only in Kent that the rebel forces came anywhere close to success; and Thomas Wyatt's men, marching on the capital to the battle cry of 'We will have no foreigner for our King', came very close indeed to success. They failed because, in the last resort, the sober citizens of London found that old habits of loyalty and obedience to the sovereign – not to mention a natural repugnance at the thought of possible danger to their property – outweighed their detestation of the sovereign's affianced husband. The rebellion failed to prevent the Spanish marriage and served to confirm Mary and Gardiner in their belief that the heretics would stop at nothing to defeat the cause of true religion. It was the death of sixteen-year-old Jane Grey and might have been the death of Elizabeth Tudor.

Before the end of February both Elizabeth and Courtenay were in custody – he back in the Tower, she confined to her apartments at Whitehall. The 'Queen', wrote Simon Renard, 'is advised to have her thrown into the Tower, as she has been accused by Wyatt, mentioned by name in the French ambassador's letters . . . and it is certain that the enterprise was undertaken for her sake.'[27] Renard believed that unless Mary seized this heaven-sent opportunity to get rid of her

sister she would never be secure again, and he was therefore exasper-
ated to discover that 'the law as laid down by the English Parliament
did not inflict the capital penalty on those who had consented to
treason if they had committed no overt act'.[28]

By the middle of March he had begun to despair of the English.
Religion was unsettled, the Queen's own councillors were at odds, the
people fickle, treacherous and implacably hostile to foreigners. God
might have granted victory over the rebels this time, but disaffection
still seethed below the surface and it seemed to Renard that a suspicious negligence was being shown in high places over the business
of bringing Elizabeth and Courtenay to trial. It even looked as if
delays were being deliberately created 'in the hope that something
may crop up to save them'.[29]

Two days after writing this thoroughly gloomy despatch in which,
for the first time, he questioned the wisdom of allowing Philip to
hazard his precious person among the ungrateful islanders, Renard
was relieved to hear that the Council had at last taken the decision
to commit the heir to the throne to the most notorious prison in the
land.[30] But it was a decision taken only after heated argument and
in the teeth of vigorous opposition, and when Renard next saw the
Queen he took the opportunity of expressing his anxiety about the
whole security situation. Philip, he reminded her, was forbidden
by the terms of the marriage contract to bring an armed guard with
him and would therefore be entirely dependent on his wife for
protection. If anything were to happen to him, the consequences
would be very serious, and Renard felt in duty bound to lay his
doubts before the Queen so that, as he delicately put it, 'she might be
pleased to take every necessary step'. Mary did not pretend to mis-
understand her friend and mentor. She replied with tears in her eyes
that she would rather never have been born than that any harm
should come to his Highness, and promised to see to it that
Courtenay's and Elizabeth's trials were over before he arrived.[31]

Renard continued, in his own words, to work unceasingly to make
the Queen of England understand how essential it was to take every
precaution and to have the trials and executions of all criminals, especially Courtenay and the Lady Elizabeth, concluded before Philip's
arrival. Mary continued to assure him that she was doing everything in her power, and there seems no reason to suppose that she
would not unhesitatingly have sacrificed her sister had she been in a
strong enough position to do so. But Wyatt had not, after all, accused
Elizabeth, nor had James Crofts, although 'marvellously tossed'. Even

her servant William Saintlow, who had actually been seen with Wyatt's army, resolutely refused to incriminate his mistress. Elizabeth herself denied everything and, since she had written no letters, made no promises, had not apparently done anything, it looked as if there was no case for her to answer. The Council, an unwieldy and increasingly factious body, remained deeply divided on the subject of her future – or lack of it. 'What one advises, another opposes,' wrote Renard; 'one strives to save Courtenay, another Elizabeth; and such is the confusion that one can only expect the upshot to be arms and tumult.'[32]

Thomas Wyatt was executed on 11 April and, in his last moments, publicly exonerated both Elizabeth and Courtenay from any complicity in the rebellion. The news spread joyfully through the city and after that, of course, any attempt to bring the Princess to trial would have been the signal for a popular uprising far more serious than anything which had gone before. So, what was to be done with her? As early as the end of March, William Paget had begun to suggest that, if it turned out to be impossible to put Elizabeth to death, then the best way of arranging matters might be to marry her to a foreigner – the Prince of Piedmont was his candidate this time – and settle the succession on her and her husband if the Queen died childless – a proposition to which Renard thought it better to make no immediate reply.[33]

Meanwhile, some decision had to be taken. The Princess couldn't very well be set free at once (Renard believed that, if she were, the heretics would probably proclaim her Queen), but already she was being allowed out to walk in the Tower gardens and she couldn't be left in prison much longer. Courtenay's friends were working on the Queen to persuade her to pardon him and it seemed as if he, too, was going to get off scot free – although Renard remained convinced that, in his determination to shield his protégé, Stephen Gardiner had suppressed evidence which might have convicted both Courtenay and Elizabeth, and it's certainly true that an intercepted despatch of de Noailles', containing an account of Courtenay's crucial interview with the Chancellor in January, had conveniently gone missing.[34]

Eventually a face-saving formula was arrived at. It was agreed to send Courtenay to rusticate at Fotheringay Castle and, on 19 May, Elizabeth, demurely inscrutable as ever, departed for the disused royal residence at Woodstock under the escort of Sir Henry Bedingfield, a loyal and incorruptible Catholic gentleman from Norfolk, who was charged with the not very enviable task of keeping her out of harm's way and out of mischief until a more satisfactory solution to the problem of her future could be found.

The Princess's celebrated incarceration had lasted just under two months and, while it had undoubtedly been a frightening and upsetting experience, it may also have contained a few lighter moments. There's a longstanding tradition that she managed to see something of one of her fellow-prisoners – her old friend Robert Dudley who, with his three surviving brothers, still languished in the Beauchamp Tower under sentence of death for his part in the family's enterprising activities during the previous summer. Elizabeth occupied a room in the neighbouring Bell Tower and, in spite of the strict security precautions being enforced in the crowded fortress, it's not impossible that the two could have contrived to meet. The tradition which maintains that this was the time when they fell in love is a good deal more doubtful. They had known each other since they were children – as he climbed to power the Duke of Northumberland had missed no opportunity of introducing his numerous progeny to the attention of the royal family, and Elizabeth and Robert were almost exactly the same age. He was, therefore, no new figure of romance, and at a time when Elizabeth needed all her wits and her self-control for staying alive she was unlikely to have further complicated her situation or dissipated any energy on flirtation.

Whatever the truth of the matter, Elizabeth may well have drawn comfort from the knowledge of Robert's nearness, and there's nothing like having been in gaol together for cementing the bonds of friendship. When the Princess was sent to Woodstock, Robert remained behind – until the following October, when he and his brothers were finally pardoned and released and sent home with instructions to stay there and behave themselves. Home for Robert Dudley was with his young wife Amy and his father-in-law, John Robsart, on the latter's East Anglian estates. But the routine of country life had little to offer a restless ambitious younger son with his way to make in the world; and in 1557, when, as all opponents of the Spanish marriage had always predicted would happen, England was drawn into Spain's quarrel with France, Robert grasped at the chance to rehabilitate himself. He did well in the fighting at St Quentin, and in March 1558 was sent home with despatches for the Queen at Greenwich. The same month the attainder on the family was lifted. Robert and his brothers and sisters were 'restored in blood' – an important step on the way towards more dramatic manifestations of royal favour.

CHAPTER IV

No Alliance More Advantageous than That with the Duke of Savoy

HAVING postponed his arrival for as long as – or rather longer than – he decently could, Philip of Spain finally disembarked at Southampton on Friday, 20 July 1554, and to the crowds of curious sightseers who trampled over one another in their eagerness to catch a glimpse of him, the bloodstained ogre of the Protestant propaganda machine was revealed as a slim dapper young man, rather below average height with blue eyes and yellow hair and beard which, some observers considered, made him look like a Fleming.[1]

Philip had come primed with instructions to be affable and to show himself to the people, to be lavish with presents as well as with smiles, to 'caress the nobility' and take them hunting with him – in short, to make every effort to placate and propitiate the rude, heretical English.[2] To a prince very well aware of his importance as an international figure, and who was in the habit of concealing his natural shyness with strangers under a stiff reserved manner, such advice was no more palatable than the prospect of a middle-aged bride in a hostile country. But Philip was a dutiful son and realised quite as fully as his father the inestimable value of an alliance which would not only secure the sea-route to the Netherlands and help safeguard those wealthy Habsburg possessions against a predatory France but which might also, if all went well, permanently tilt the balance of power in Habsburg favour. If such an alliance was worth bedding a woman whom Philip sardonically described as his 'dear and well-beloved aunt', then it was certainly worth any amount of synthetic affability. He did his best – kissing all the Queen's ladies on the mouth after the English custom which, he tactfully declared, was a good one, laboriously learning a few words of the language and even, heroically, calling for some English beer and drinking it.[3]

The royal wedding took place in Winchester Cathedral on 25 July, the Queen in a trance of happiness keeping her eyes fixed on the sacrament throughout the hour-long nuptial mass. The fact that

Philip was the greatest match in Christendom had always mattered far less to Mary Tudor than the fact that he was of her mother's kin, a true Catholic who would help her bring her people back to Rome. All that mattered now was the fact that he was there beside her, that she was already hopelessly, helplessly in love. When the religious ceremonies were over, the couple adjourned to the Bishop's Palace for a sumptuous wedding breakfast eaten off gold plate to the strains of music. This was followed by dancing, in which Philip's Spanish gentlemen led the English ladies on to the floor and the King and Queen danced together 'after the German fashion'. Then, at last, after a quiet supper in their private apartments, Stephen Gardiner blessed the marriage bed and the newly wedded couple were left alone. 'What happened that night,' wrote an anonymous Spaniard in a letter home, 'only they know. If they give us a son our joy will be complete.'[4]

A few weeks later Mary brought her bridegroom to London, travelling in easy stages via Basing, Reading and Windsor, with Philip always at her side, ready to help her mount and dismount, unfailingly polite and attentive. 'Their Majesties are the happiest couple in the world and more in love than words can say,' gushed a member of Philip's suite, and the Spaniards were full of praise for their master's exquisite manners, for the Queen, although a dear good creature and a perfect saint, dressed badly, was older than they'd been led to expect and was not at all beautiful, being small and flabby with no eyebrows.[5]

To everyone's relief the entry into the capital passed off without incident. Renard reported that the people had been favourably impressed by Philip's appearance and their present opinion seemed to be that he was a handsome prince 'of benign and humane countenance and likely to turn out a good ruler'.[6] There was, inevitably, a fair amount of jealousy and backbiting. The Spaniards complained that they were being palmed off with inferior accommodation, were not allowed to do anything for their prince, were insulted when they ventured on to the streets and horribly overcharged in shops and inns; while the English grumbled that it was they who were kept kicking their heels in Philip's antechamber, that London was overrun by foreigners who made them feel like strangers in their own homes and that the Queen seemed to care nothing for her own subjects but only for Spaniards and bishops.[7] There were faults and nasty prejudices on both sides, and the atmosphere was often edgy and strained, but considering what had gone before things might have been a great deal worse.

There were two important developments on the political front that autumn – by the end of September, Mary believed herself to be pregnant and, by the end of November, England had once more become a Roman Catholic country. Both these interesting events were, in the long term, capable of altering the course of history. In the short term, both served to highlight the perennial problem of the Princess Elizabeth. Stephen Gardiner had never made any secret of his conviction that all attempts to eradicate English Protestantism would amount to no more than stripping the leaves and lopping the branches as long as the root of the evil – the heretical heiress presumptive – remained untouched. Back in the spring he had told Simon Renard that 'as long as Elizabeth lived he had no hope of seeing the kingdom in peace' and now he was insisting that a bill to bastardise and disinherit her should be introduced during the current session of Parliament. But there was little support for the Chancellor. Even Renard believed it would be a mistake to attack Elizabeth now – for one thing it would be bound to stir up trouble in the country and for another it might soon be unnecessary.[8] William Paget, always an influential figure, was taking the line that, since the Queen was with child, Elizabeth no longer mattered very much and the safest way of disposing of her would be to marry her off to 'some poor German prince'. The Emperor was inclined to agree – certainly marriage did seem the only possible solution – but with the stipulation that the poor German prince in question should have domains far enough inland to prevent his ever becoming a nuisance to England, and the Margrave of Baden was mentioned as a likely candidate.

Another idea might be to marry the Princess in Spain – to the Duke of Segorbe's son, for instance, whose lands were situated on the Mediterranean coast; but the obstacle here was that, being 'defiled' by heresy, Elizabeth or her servants might meddle in matters which the Inquisition would have to take seriously and the result would be scandal.[9] The thought of Elizabeth Tudor becoming a Spanish duchess and scandalising the Holy Office is sufficiently intriguing, but the Emperor was probably only thinking aloud – at any rate, nothing more was heard of this interesting scheme.

In the meantime, another suitor had decided to try his luck in person. Emmanuel Philibert, Duke of Savoy, was a poor relation of the Habsburg clan and, since losing his duchy in the everlasting dispute with France, had become entirely dependent on Habsburg patronage. To a professional soldier in reduced circumstances the prospect of marrying the English princess was naturally an enticing one, and in November 1554 the Duke was planning to sail to England and 'pluck the fruit of the hopes that are now blossoming there'.[10] He did, in fact, cross the Channel and seems to have stayed at Somerset Place, Elizabeth's London house. But he did not see the Princess, who was still at Woodstock, and left again shortly after Christmas a disappointed man.

Emmanuel Philibert, though, had his supporters. In the spring of 1555, Simon Renard prepared a long memorandum on English affairs for Philip, who was already beginning to wonder how soon he could get away, and inevitably a good deal of this document was concerned with the twin problems of Elizabeth and the succession. 'Supposing', wrote Renard, 'the Queen is not with child and dies without issue, there will certainly be strife and the heretics will espouse the cause of the Lady Elizabeth.' If Elizabeth was set aside, he reminded Philip again, the next heir would be the Queen of Scotland. But, if Elizabeth were to succeed, England would undoubtedly relapse into heresy and very likely into a new alliance with France – unless something was done to prevent it. 'If Elizabeth is married to an Englishman,' Renard went on, 'she will prevail upon her husband to adopt the new religion, even if he is a Catholic. If a foreign husband is found for her, it will be necessary to make sure that he is constant and faithful to your Majesty.'[11]

After nearly two years in England, Renard had come to realise that it would be virtually impossible to upset Henry VIII's will, and that Elizabeth's right to the succession would have to be recognised. Therefore, he argued, 'there would seem to be no alliance more advantageous for her than that with the Duke of Savoy'. It would be better than marrying the Princess in Germany or Spain, since the Duke could act as Philip's lieutenant in England, helping the Queen to cope with the burden of government during her huband's unavoidable absences. Then, when Philip returned, he might go over to Flanders and take Elizabeth with him, thus helping to promote international understanding. Renard believed that the marriage would be popular and that the sooner it was arranged the better. In any case, he urged Philip to see Elizabeth before he left the country and warn her to behave herself, in which case he might promise to remember her and to 'do what is suitable for her'.[12]

This last piece of advice, at least, the King took and, at the end of April, Elizabeth was summoned to Hampton Court, where the royal

c

household had gone to prepare for the Queen's confinement. Courtenay had been released from Fotheringay and sent to travel abroad – to the Imperial court in Brussels in the first instance, so that his activities could be supervised – but Philip wanted Elizabeth under his own eyes. He may have been motivated in part by natural curiosity, but he was also taking out insurance against an uncertain future. If Mary died in childbirth, a fate which frequently overtook young strong women, and if the baby (always supposing there was a baby) died with her, Philip and his small retinue of Spaniards would find themselves isolated among a hostile population. In such circumstances it would be useful to have a hostage, perhaps even an ally. The Venetian ambassador went so far as to remark that Philip's safety and security would depend more on Elizabeth than any other person, and it was being widely speculated that the King might be contemplating a marriage with his sister-in-law if the Queen were to die.[13]

Elizabeth, though, was still officially in disgrace and she arrived at court 'very privately', entering the palace by a back way, still under the escort of Sir Henry Bedingfield and accompanied by a mere handful of her own people. She remained isolated in her apartments for nearly another month but, according to French and Venetian sources, the King and Queen both saw her in private. According to the Protestant historian John Foxe, who provides a detailed account of the occasion, Elizabeth was summoned to her sister's bedroom late one evening towards the end of May and a reconciliation was patched up between them.[14] Foxe declares that Philip was present, hidden behind a curtain; but, whether this is true or not, the reconciliation and Elizabeth's return to at least a limited amount of favour had undoubtedly been engineered by Philip. A correspondent writing to Edward Courtenay in Brussels on 25 May was able to assure him that 'my Lady Elizabeth is at her full liberty' and that she had seen the Queen twice.

It was a restless uneasy summer. 'Everything in this kingdom depends on the Queen's safe deliverance,' wrote Renard in June and if, against all the odds, Mary did give birth to a healthy child, then the Habsburgs would have absorbed England as efficiently and cheaply as in the previous generation they had absorbed Spain, and the rich Burgundian inheritance of the Netherlands in the generation before that. So, at least, it appeared to most thinking Englishmen in the spring and summer of 1555 and the thought was not a pleasant one. Not even the most committed Catholic could summon up any enthusiasm at the prospect of seeing his country fall victim to yet another dynastic takeover bid by the Habsburg family. Small wonder, then, that Renard noticed some strange expressions on the faces of the people round him. Even those he had previously counted as allies now seemed to have 'a masked appearance'.[15]

Early in the morning of 30 April a rumour reached London that the Queen had been delivered of a male child during the night 'with little pain and no danger'. Despite lack of official confirmation the report was so circumstantial that it was generally believed. Church bells were rung through the city, bonfires lit in the streets and free wine provided for all comers. Whatever its implications, the birth of a prince was automatically an occasion for rejoicing. But rejoicing was premature, as were prophecies of doom. There was no prince, not even any sign of his imminent arrival. On 24 June, Renard reported that the Queen's doctors had proved to be two months out in their calculations and that she would not be delivered for another eight or ten days. July came in and still the empty cradle waited, but Mary stubbornly refused to give up hope. Sir John Mason in Brussels was ordered to contradict the now widespread gossip that the Queen was not pregnant at all and to assure the Emperor's court that she was near her time. The doctors and midwives were still talking about miscalculation and hinting that the Queen might not be delivered until August or even September, but only the pathetic Queen believed them.

By the beginning of August something had to be done to bring Mary back to reality and put an end to what was rapidly becoming an acute embarrassment. Apart from anything else, the Queen's long seclusion and her refusal to transact any business were bringing the work of government to a virtual halt. So, on the third of the month, the court moved away to the royal hunting-lodge at Oatlands where there would be no accommodation for the noble ladies who had flocked to the palace to support the Queen through her ordeal and who had been living there at her expense all summer. In order to save as much face as possible, it was given out that Hampton Court needed cleansing (and so it must have done after four months of crowded occupation), but everyone recognised the move for what it was – Mary's tacit admission of defeat. As the Venetian ambassador put it, the pregnancy seemed to have ended in wind. In fact, the amenorrhoea and digestive troubles which had afflicted Mary ever since her unhappy adolescence, together possibly with incipient cancer

of the womb, had combined with her desperate yearning to bear
Philip's child to produce this tragic self-deception.

Elizabeth did not accompany her sister and brother-in-law to
Oatlands, but she had every reason to be pleased with the way events
were moving. She had regained her fredom of action, and the fear of
seeing her inheritance fall to some little half-Habsburg intruder had
receded. She also now felt reasonably confident that she could rely on
Philip's protection. The Princess had not wasted those months at
Hampton Court. While Mary hid herself away in the stuffy foetid
atmosphere of the palace, often sitting on the floor for hours at a time
with her knees drawn up to her chin, Elizabeth had been busy laying
the foundations of a useful friendship with the prince of Spain. Two
years later, the retiring Venetian ambassador noted in his report to
the Doge and Senate that 'at the time of the Queen's pregnancy, the
Lady Elizabeth . . . contrived so to ingratiate herself with all the
Spaniards, and especially with the King, that ever since no one has
favoured her more than he does; for not only would he not permit,
but opposed and prevented the Queen's wish to have her disinherited
and declared a bastard by Act of Parliament . . . which, besides affection, implies some particular design on the part of the King with
regard to her'.[16]

Philip's designs with regard to Elizabeth could undoubtedly have
been summed up in a single question : how best could the English
heiress be made to serve Habsburg interests? With every week that
passed it was becoming more and more obvious that Elizabeth would,
in due course, succeed her sister, and now that he had made her
acquaintance, Philip could view the future in a rather more optimistic
light. The Princess appeared to have seen the error of her ways and
was behaving herself like a good Catholic. In spite of Simon Renard's
gloomy forebodings, Philip believed that this demure, flatteringly
deferential young lady might yet be turned into an asset. The right
husband would have to be found for her – that went without saying
– but there was no immediate hurry. Elizabeth would do nothing
without consulting the brother-in-law who had taken such a kindly
interest in her affairs and she was still full young, not quite twenty-
two. Besides, in August 1555, Philip had other things on his mind.
All sorts of problems urgently needing his attention were piling up
abroad and, in any case, he was itching to escape from the un-
congenial scene of his disappointing and unfruitful marriage. But
before he left England at the end of the month he took the precaution
of telling the Queen that he wanted Elizabeth to be treated with

consideration and, according to the French, followed this up by writing to Mary from Flanders 'commending the princess to her care'.

Elizabeth had gone down to Greenwich with the rest of the court to see Philip off and stayed there for about six weeks. She was still very much on her best behaviour, going to mass with the Queen every day; while Mary, mindful of her husband's instructions, was trying hard to conceal her 'evil disposition' towards Anne Boleyn's daughter under a mask of synthetic amiability. Both sisters probably found all this a considerable strain and, when the Queen returned to London in October for the opening of Parliament, Elizabeth seized the opportunity to apply for permission to go back to the country – permission which was eagerly granted.

The winter passed with no sign of Philip's return – and no sign, either, that he had made up his mind about Elizabeth's future. There were various reports of vague plans for sending her over to Spain but, although the Queen was said to be strongly in favour, fears of the outcry which would be caused by any attempt to take the heir to the throne out of the country caused them to be abandoned – at least, according to the Venetians.[17] There was a somewhat bizarre scheme to marry the Princess to Philip's son, Don Carlos, but – again according to Venetian sources – Elizabeth was now saying plainly that she would not marry 'even were they to give her the King's son'.[18] Since Don Carlos was only ten years old and rumoured to be not quite right in the head, this reaction seemed understandable. Rather more plausible were the reports that the Emperor was planning a match between the Queen of England's sister and his nephew Ferdinand of Austria. When the King of France heard about this, he threatened to marry his son's fiancée, Mary Queen of Scots, to Edward Courtenay – anything to prevent the House of Austria from establishing itself permanently in England.[19]

Edward Courtenay had now left Brussels and was on his way to Italy, but during the spring and early summer of 1556 his name was once more being linked with the Princess Elizabeth. In March details of the Dudley conspiracy – so called after one of its ringleaders, Sir Henry Dudley, a distant connection of the Duke of Northumberland – began to come to light. In outline, the plot 'to send the Queen's Highness over to the King and to make the Lady Elizabeth Queen and to marry the Earl of Devonshire to the said lady' bore a close family resemblance to the aims of the Wyatt conspirators. But, although their activities were symptomatic of a deep-rooted and widespread discontent with Mary's policies, plus strong resentment over the generally held belief that the Queen loved foreigners and hated Englishmen, Dudley and his friends (who included a number of distinctly gamy characters) never commanded any worthwhile support among the 'substantial gentry'. This levelheaded and influential section of the community reflected that the Queen was an ailing childless woman who had passed her fortieth birthday and made up its collective mind to wait for nature to take its course.

This was certainly the attitude being adopted by the heir to the throne; but as Giovanni Michiel of the Venetian embassy pointed out, 'never is a conspiracy discovered in which either justly or unjustly she or some of her servants are not mentioned'.[20] On this occasion four of Elizabeth's servants, including Mrs Ashley, her old friend and governess, were mentioned loudly enough to be arrested, but there was no question now of proceeding against the Princess herself. The country would not have stood for it and neither would Philip of Spain. Instead, two gentlemen of the royal household were sent down to Hatfield bearing a kind message from the Queen, assuring her sister of her continued goodwill and using 'loving and gracious expressions, to show her that she is neither neglected nor hated, but loved and esteemed by her Majesty'. Michiel added significantly that this had been very well taken by the whole kingdom.[21] All the same, Mary did seize the opportunity to reorganize the household at Hatfield. A 'widow gentlewoman' was installed to replace Mrs Ashley, and Sir Thomas Pope, 'a rich and grave gentleman, of good name both for conduct and religion', appointed to be the Princess's governor. Elizabeth accepted these changes with a good grace. Thomas Pope, a witty cultivated man, the founder of Trinity College, Oxford, made a pleasant enough companion and his presence would, she knew, act as a safeguard.

It was a long hot summer with everywhere the consciousness of sullen revolt simmering just below the surface. In July a Suffolk schoolmaster called Cleobury caused a local flare-up by attempting to impersonate Edward Courtenay and proclaiming 'the Lady Elizabeth Queen and her beloved bedfellow, Lord Courtenay, King'.[22] In the circumstances, therefore, the news of her beloved bedfellow's death that September probably came as a profound relief to Elizabeth Tudor. As for Edward Courtenay, although the conspirators declared he had not been privy to their plans, the last few months of his shadowed life had been shadowed still further by the repercussions of the Dudley affair. There were rumours that he'd been offered 30,000 crowns to go to France and rumours among the English dissidents being harboured by Henri II that he would soon be coming to join them. There were rumours that the Duke of Ferrara was working to persuade him to serve France against England; rumours of a Spanish plot to have him murdered; rumours that he was planning to return home and take up arms against the Queen. Everywhere he went the unfortunate young man's footsteps were dogged by rumour, by suspicion and by spies. 'You will do well to watch him [Courtenay] carefully and find out everything he is up to,' wrote Philip to his agent in Venice.[23] No wonder Courtenay lived so quietly, almost as if he hoped that by doing nothing, saying nothing, going nowhere he might become invisible to all those watching eyes. When death found the last of the Plantagenets in Padua, perhaps he was not sorry to be released.

The Spaniards made little attempt to hide their relief, and the Venetians wondered if Philip would now return to England. As Federico Badoer wrote rather enigmatically from the Netherlands, he might take this opportunity to 'better arrange such things as are desired by him, and which as yet he has been unable to obtain'.[24] Philip did not return, although Mary was still begging and praying him to come back to her; but, at the end of November, Elizabeth paid a brief visit to London. According to the gossip at the French court, the Queen had summoned her in order to press her to accept the Duke of Savoy. Elizabeth, it seems, had burst into tears and declared she would rather die. Whereupon the Queen, seeing that her sister 'still persisted in this opinion of not choosing to marry', had packed her off back to Hatfield with renewed threats to have her disinherited.[25]

Finally, in March 1557, Philip did return to England, bringing with him his sister and his cousin, the Duchesses of Parma and Lorraine. This promptly led to speculation that the ladies had come for the purpose of escorting 'Madama' Elizabeth back to Flanders to be married to the Duke of Savoy.[26] The French ambassador thoughtfully sent Elizabeth warning of this scheme, for which the Princess thanked him but declared again that nothing would induce her to consent to such a thing. In fact, the real purpose of Philip's visit was to embroil his wife's reluctant subjects in war with France. By the beginning of July, his mission accomplished, he was gone and Mary never saw him again.

But, in spite of all his other preoccupations, Philip had not forgotten about Elizabeth and during that summer he made what was probably his first really serious effort to settle his sister-in-law's future and the future of the English alliance. He instructed his confessor, Francisco de Fresneda, a man 'very dear to the Queen', to discuss the whole matter with her and to urge her to arrange Elizabeth's marriage with the Duke of Savoy without further delay. Fresneda was to explain how necessary this was for considerations of religion and piety, for the safety of the realm and to prevent all those evils which might ensue if Elizabeth, feeling herself slighted, were to choose a husband 'who might convulse the whole kingdom into confusion' – in other words, a husband hostile to the Habsburg interest.

Philip also wanted Mary to put an end to any remaining uncertainty about the succession by formally recognising Elizabeth as her heir, but here he came up against the blank wall of Mary's bitter obsessive jealousy of her half-sister. According to the Venetians – and their intelligence service was usually reliable – 'For many days during which the confessor treated this business, he found the Queen utterly averse to give Lady Elizabeth any hope of the succession, obstinately maintaining that she was neither her sister nor the daughter of the Queen's father, King Henry; nor would she hear of favouring her, as she was born of an infamous mother who had so greatly outraged the Queen her mother and herself.'[27]

It had long been an open secret among the diplomatic corps that the Queen's 'evil disposition' towards the Lady Elizabeth was due quite simply to the fact that Elizabeth was Anne Boleyn's daughter – a living reminder of Mary's sufferings at the time of her parents' divorce. Now this sad sick woman, faced with the realisation that her beloved husband was thinking only of a future in which she would have no share, was being asked publicly to admit that that future would belong to Anne Boleyn's daughter. She would not do it; and Philip, to whom the old feuds of the Tudor family were a mere irrelevance, was not unnaturally profoundly irritated by this new evidence of perversity on the part of his useless barren wife. But Philip was more than usually busy just then, with the French war and with taking over from his father – the old Emperor had decided to spend his last days in a monastery – so England would just have to wait, and once more the problem of Elizabeth was shelved.

Nevertheless, it continued to nag at the back of his mind, and it continued to nag at Simon Renard who, although he had left England in the autumn of 1555, still took a proprietary interest in English affairs. In March 1558 the ex-ambassador prepared another of his appreciations on the subject of the English succession, reminding Philip yet again of the undesirable consequences likely to follow Mary's death unless 'timely measures' were taken. Despite her careful Catholic observance, Simon Renard had never believed for a moment in the sincerity of Elizabeth's apparent conversion, and her principal supporters were all equally suspect. 'If she succeeds and marries an Englishman,' he wrote, 'religion will be undermined, everything sacred profaned, Catholics ill-treated, churchmen driven out, those monasteries which have been restored will again suffer, churches will be destroyed, affairs which had taken a favourable turn will once more be compromised . . . Moreover, the ancient amity, good neighbourliness and understanding that have so far been maintained, albeit with difficulty, between England and your Majesty's realms, will not only be impaired but disappear altogether.'[28]

Renard was still strongly of the opinion that the best – indeed, the only – solution to the problem was for Philip to find a husband for the Princess abroad and he still believed the Duke of Savoy was the only man who 'would appear to answer all requirements'. He was, however, very much afraid that his master had left it too late. Emmanuel Philibert himself had cooled off and was looking elsewhere for a wife, though he might still be attracted by the prospect of a seat on the English throne. As for Elizabeth, Renard had heard that 'she and the leading men of the realm would refuse a foreign match' and the Princess was in too strong a position now to be coerced. In spite of Mary's desperate last-ditch resistance, everyone knew that it was probably no more than a matter of months before Elizabeth Tudor became Queen of England.

Philip, of course, was not the only European sovereign taking an interest in her future, and in April the Protestant King of Sweden sent an ambassador to propose a marriage between the English heiress and his eldest son, Eric. The Swedes, however, were rash enough to address themselves to the Princess without first observing the formality of asking the Queen's permission – a breach of protocol which gave Elizabeth all the excuse she needed for sending the envoy about his business. All the same, when Mary got to hear about it, she worked herself into a great state of agitation, apparently afraid that Philip would blame her all over again for her opposition to the Savoy marriage and that he might take this opportunity to renew his pressure on her to come to a decision about her sister. Sir Thomas Pope was therefore instructed to speak to Elizabeth to try to find out what she really felt about the Swedish proposition and also if she had any plans about marriage in general. Elizabeth reiterated her settled preference for a spinster's life – an estate she liked so well 'as to persuade myself there is not any kind of life comparable to it'. As far as the Swedes were concerned, she could only say that she sincerely hoped she would never hear of them again. Probing a little further, Thomas Pope ventured to remark that he thought 'few or none would believe but that her Grace could be right well contented to marry; so that there were some honourable marriage offered her by the Queen's highness, or by her Majesty's assent'. But Elizabeth was not to be drawn. 'What I shall do hereafter I know not,' she answered calmly, 'but I assure you, upon my truth and fidelity, and as God be merciful unto me, I am not at this time otherwise minded than I have declared unto you; no, though I were offered the greatest prince in all Europe.' This was no way for a healthy young woman of twenty-four to be talking and, like a sensible man, Sir Thomas Pope didn't take such nonsense seriously for a moment. As he commented in his report, 'the Queen's majesty may conceive this rather to proceed of a maidenly shamefacedness, than upon any such certain determination'.[29] Whether or not Mary believed that Elizabeth meant what she said, she was calmer after hearing from Hatfield though, as Count de Feria, over from Brussels for a few months, told Philip, she continued to take a passionate interest in the affair.[30]

Poor Mary, she had always taken a passionate interest in marriages, in babies and christenings. If only things had been different she'd have been delighted to have found a husband for her sister, to have fussed over the details of her trousseau, given her good advice and stood godmother to her first child. But Mary Tudor had been called upon to face many sorrows, many injustices and disappointments; perhaps the one thing she could not have faced would have been to see Elizabeth make a succesful marriage and bear the children Mary had craved with all the strength of her starved and passionate nature. Even so, if she had guessed that many people suspected Philip was only waiting for her death to marry Elizabeth himself and that this was the cause of his curious lethargy in the matter of her future, Mary might have tried to force the girl into the arms of Emmanuel Philibert and she might even have succeeded.

Years later there was a piece of gossip going round that Philip had been heard to attribute his sufferings at the hands of Queen Elizabeth to the judgement of God because 'being married to Queen Mary, whom he thought a most virtuous and good lady, yet in the fancy of love he could not affect her; but as for the Lady Elizabeth, he was enamoured of her, being a fair and beautiful woman'. It seems highly improbable that the prudent Philip was ever heard to say anything of the kind, but it's not impossible that he had been physically attracted to his sister-in-law – and he was a man of strong physical appetites, however rigorously he learnt to suppress them. One way or another during the mid-1550s there were enough cross-currents of sexual jealousy, of guilt, desire and old bitter resentment in the relationship of this peculiar threesome successfully to militate against the pragmatic approach advocated by Simon Renard – to prevent the sensible arranged marriage of the English heiress to some Habsburg nominee ever getting beyond the discussion stage. And it's worth remembering that, if the project had been tactfully presented and pursued at all seriously during the period between the death of Edward Courtenay and the disastrous French war which finally wrecked Philip's credit in England, Elizabeth might have found it very difficult to stand out against the pressure which could have been exerted on her. A lot of ifs and a good deal of speculation, but the fact remains that a unique variety of circumstances, both political and personal, had combined to enable Elizabeth to reach her twenty-fifth birthday still single and still unfettered to any foreign interest.

By the early autumn of 1558 it was becoming obvious that Mary's illness was approaching its final stages. By 22 October the news reaching Philip in Flanders had become sufficiently alarming for him to send Count de Feria back to England. The Venetians heard that 'the matter to be treated by him is the marriage of Miladi Elizabeth, to keep that kingdom in any event in the hands of a person in his Majesty's confidence', and that the Count's instructions 'purport that he is to try and dispose the Queen to consent to Lady Elizabeth being married as her sister, and with the hope of succeeding to the crown'.[31] De Feria arrived in London on 9 November, but whatever instructions he may have brought with him were already out of date and he was received, as he put it, like 'a man who came accredited with the Bulls of a dead Pope'. Three days earlier Mary had finally given in and recognised Elizabeth's right to succeed her, and now she was sinking fast. It didn't take de Feria long to realise that there was nothing more he could usefully do at St James's and by 10 November he was travelling the already crowded road to Hatfield.

Elizabeth received him amiably enough and invited him to supper. She spoke gracefully of her gratitude for Philip's kind offices towards her in the past, but she would have no truck with his ambassador's attempt to persuade her 'that the announcement of her succession was not owing either to the Queen or to the Council, but to Philip'. Elizabeth Tudor made it plain that she owed her crown to no foreign monarch, not even to the nobility of the realm, although they had all pledged their loyalty, but to 'the attachment of the people of England, to whom', commented de Feria, 'she seemed much devoted'. The Princess and the ambassador went on to discuss the characters of various English notables who came up in the course of conversation and laughed together over the idea of her marrying the middle-aged Earl of Arundel, one of the more preposterous of her English suitors. De Feria took the opportunity of sounding her on the subject of marriage generally and was told she was aware that Philip had wanted her to marry the Duke of Savoy but that Mary's popularity had suffered by marriage with a foreigner. De Feria tried to offer the same sort of advice about caution and moderation that Simon Renard had once offered Mary, but the interview left him with a distinct impression that the queen-elect meant to be governed by no one. She was very vain, he wrote, and very acute and appeared to be an enthusiastic admirer of her father's methods and policies.[32]

Barely a week later Mary Tudor was released from her earthly troubles. As the news spread through London the church bells were rung and by afternoon the November dusk was being illuminated by bonfires as the citizens set tables in the streets and 'did eat and drink and make merry for the new Queen Elizabeth'.[33]

CHAPTER V

I Am Already Wedded to an Husband

THE NEW Queen Elizabeth made her state entry into London on 28 November, riding from the Charterhouse through streets gay with banners and lined with cheering crowds; the trumpets brayed before her, the City waits blew enthusiastically down their various instruments, church bells pealed and the Tower guns thundered a salute such as 'never was heard afore'. Elizabeth's popularity – especially with the Londoners – had been her chief source of strength in recent times, but she was not likely to have forgotten that, only five years before, these same crowds had given her sister an equally rousing welcome. Nor is it likely that she would have failed to realise how much of her own popularity was due to the general dislike of Mary's régime, or that beneath all the cheering, the pealing bells and the roar of the cannon there lurked a rather desperate optimism.

In the decade which had passed since King Henry's death England had suffered from the rule of greedy factious juntas and the weak, incompetent government of an inept and unlucky queen. The resultant dismal chaos – economic, political and social – filled most thinking men with gloom. 'I never saw . . . England weaker in strength, men, money and riches,' commented one; while another drew up a stark and succinct memorandum of the most urgent problems facing the new administration: 'The Queen poor, the realm exhausted, the nobility poor and decayed. Want of good captains and soldiers. The people out of order. Justice not executed. All things dear. Excess in meat, drink and apparel. Divisions amongst ourselves. Wars with France and Scotland . . . Steadfast enmity but no steadfast friendship abroad.'[1] Armagil Waad did not add – he scarcely needed to – that what England needed now was a strong and able ruler – someone with the personality to unite the nation and the tough-mindedness to re-establish the authority of the Crown; someone with the statesmanship to provide a period of peace and stability at home, while clearing up the economic mess, and restoring prestige abroad.

After their recent unfortunate experience of petticoat government by no means all Englishmen were convinced that the country would be any better off under another woman head of state, but Elizabeth was the last of King Henry's children and she looked like being the last hope of the Tudor dynasty. The bogey of a disputed and uncertain succession, caused by an unprecedented shortage of male heirs in the direct line, had overshadowed English political life for more than half a century and there can be very little doubt that, in the opinion of the vast majority of her subjects, by far and away the most valuable service their new Queen could render them would be to marry and bear sons – sturdy English sons to guard their future and their children's future.

In the circumstances, Elizabeth's matrimonial intentions were of the closest personal interest to her own countrymen, but the importance of the Queen of England's marriage extended far beyond the domestic sphere. England might currently be a trifle down-at-heel but she remained potentially a rich country and, in any case, nothing could alter the strategic value of her position on the map. In the struggle for supremacy between the two great European power-blocs, whoever commanded the English alliance would always keep the edge over his rival; and for Philip, with his extended and vulnerable lines of communication, a friendly or at least a neutral England continued to be an essential factor in his diplomacy.

On the face of it, the international situation at the end of 1558 should have favoured Philip. England was still officially at war with France, and France still harboured Mary Queen of Scots, almost sixteen now and married seven months previously to the Dauphin. The Queen of Scots had an undoubted claim to be regarded as heir presumptive to the English throne and, in the eyes of all those orthodox Roman Catholics who had never recognised King Henry's famous divorce, she had a strong claim to be regarded as the rightful Queen, rather than Elizabeth, born during the lifetime of her father's first wife. The King of France had gone so far as to have his daughter-in-law proclaimed Queen of England on Mary Tudor's death; young Mary Stuart and her husband were already quartering the English royal arms with their own, in what would appear to be a deliberately provocative gesture; while rumours were circulating that the French intended to urge the Pope to declare Elizabeth 'a bastard and a heretic and therefore ineligible to the Crown'.[2] Add to this the fact of a strong French presence in Scotland, still being ruled by Mary's mother, the Queen-Dowager; the loss of Calais, last outpost of

England's once great Continental empire, in the recent disastrous war; and it would seem that the English must of necessity turn to Spain for protection against the threat from France. So it would seem, and yet, on 21 November, de Feria wrote to Philip from London : 'The new Queen and her people hold themselves free from your Majesty and will listen to any ambassadors who may come to treat of marriage.'[3]

De Feria was only too well aware how important it was that 'this affair' should go through Philip's hands, but he foresaw difficulties 'except with great negotiation and money'. Negotiations, though, could not even begin until the identity of a Spanish candidate had been settled. The Duke of Savoy was now definitely a non-starter. According to de Feria, the English would not hear his name mentioned as they feared, reasonably enough, that 'he will want to recover his estates with English forces and will keep them constantly at war'. Archduke Ferdinand remained as a possible alternative but new complications had arisen here. Charles V had died in September and the German electors had chosen to confer the title of Emperor on his brother, father of the hopeful Ferdinand and the other, younger Archduke, Charles. It would never do for the Austrian Habsburgs to start getting ideas above their station, so if Ferdinand were lucky enough to be preferred it would have to be made perfectly clear that he was receiving 'the titbit', as de Feria put it, at his Spanish cousin's hands. And what of that highly eligible widower, Philip himself? The court at Brussels was buzzing with gossip about the King's intention to have 'Miladi' Elizabeth for himself but, cautious as ever, he showed no immediate signs of coming to the point – in spite of de Feria's confident assurances that if the Queen decided to marry out of the country 'she will at once fix her eyes on Your Majesty'.

Three weeks later the ambassador had become rather less optimistic. Already English affairs seemed to be sliding out of his grasp. The Queen was a sharp-witted young woman, but flighty and altogether too sure of herself. The government was now entirely in the hands of the heretical younger generation and all Queen Mary's reliable Catholic friends were being eclipsed. Spaniards were as unpopular as ever, and de Feria found himself cold-shouldered by the court, so that it was increasingly difficult for him to find out what was going on. He believed, shrewdly enough, that his best course would be to get a foot into the palace and see more of the Queen 'as she is a woman who is very fond of argument'. But, he went on, 'everybody thinks that she will not marry a foreigner and they cannot make out whom she favours, so that nearly every day some new cry is raised about a husband'.[4]

De Feria warned Philip that, in the present confused and excited climate of opinion, he could see no disposition, on the part of either the Queen or the Council, to consider 'any proposal on your Majesty's behalf'. All that could be done for the moment was to work on individual councillors to put them off the general ideas of marrying the Queen to an Englishman. Though, even when they had made up their minds to accept a foreigner, the ambassador believed they would look more favourably on Ferdinand than Philip 'because they think he will always reside in the country and will have no quarrel with France'.[5] As for Elizabeth herself, de Feria knew no more than the next man what her real intentions were, but he hoped it might be possible to reach her by appealing to her vanity. 'We must begin by getting her into talk about your Majesty,' he wrote, 'and run down the idea of her marrying an Englishman and thus to hold herself less than her sister who would never marry a subject.' It could be pointed out how badly it would look if she chose one of her own countrymen (and luckily there was hardly a man among them worth mentioning) when there were such great princes available. The Queen of England could also be reminded of the rival claims of the Queen of Scots and of her urgent need for a powerful male protector. But, having succeeded in putting her in a suitably receptive frame of mind, de Feria could proceed no further without instructions from his master. 'If she inclines to your Majesty,' he observed rather plaintively in a long despatch dated 14 December, 'it will be necessary for you to send me orders whether I am to carry it any further or throw cold water on it and set up the Archduke Ferdinand, because I do not see what other person we can propose to whom she would agree.'[6]

Philip, though, was not to be hurried – not even de Feria's cry that 'one fine day we shall find this woman married and I shall be the last man in the place to know anything about it' could stir him into precipitate action – and it was the second week of January before he finally made up his mind to declare himself. In a matter of such grave importance, as he solemnly reminded the ambassador, 'it was necessary for me to take counsel and maturely consider it in all its bearings before I sent you my decision'. But even now it was a decision so hedged about with misgivings and conditions and made with such obvious reluctance as surely to dispose of any sentimental notions that Philip was cherishing a secret passion for his late wife's sister. On the contrary, the King could see the 'many great difficulties' which would present themselves with horrid clarity and proceeded to enumerate them to de Feria with a certain gloomy relish. He would not be able to spend much time in England – with his increased responsibilities perhaps less even than he had spent before. Another Anglo-Spanish marriage alliance 'would appear like entering upon a perpetual war with France' – a war in which the French would possess a useful weapon in the person of the Queen of Scots. In addition to this, another English wooing would involve him in crippling expense at a time when his exchequer was 'so utterly exhausted as to be unable to meet the most necessary ordinary expenditure, much less new and onerous charges'.[7]

On the other hand, Philip, that most Catholic of monarchs, could not lose sight of 'the enormous importance of such a match to Christianity and the preservation of religion which has been restored in England by the help of God'. Elizabeth's regrettable unsoundness over religion was only too well-known, and ever since her accession de Feria had been bombarding his master with dire warnings about the growing power and influence of the heretical faction. So, in view of the ethical and political importance of keeping England in the Roman fold, the King of Spain was resolved to set aside all objections and 'to render this service to God and offer to marry the Queen of England'. In return for this honour the Queen would, of course, have to undertake to remain a Catholic herself and promise to 'maintain and uphold' the faith in her kingdom by whatever means might seem necessary to her husband. 'In this way,' remarked Philip more than a little smugly, 'it will be evident and manifest that I am serving the Lord in marrying her and that she has been converted by my act.'[8]

Whether, after her sister's recent experience, either Philip or de Feria seriously expected Elizabeth would accept such a proposal is impossible to say but, having received the instructions he had been agitating for, the ambassador made no immediate attempt to follow them up. Philip had been insistent that this delicate matter must first be broached to the Queen alone, and obviously a propitious moment would have to be chosen – especially as de Feria still had really no idea about what she was thinking. Elizabeth was currently very much occupied with her coronation and its attendant festivities and with preparations for the opening of her first Parliament, which was to take place at the end of January, and de Feria had seen her only once, 'in the little chamber leading out of the privy chamber'. He did not bring up the marriage question then because, although the Queen had chatted to him 'very gaily', she was suffering from a heavy cold and, in any case, he thought it would be wiser to wait until Parliament had raised the subject, which Elizabeth informed him they were planning to do.[9]

Parliament got down to serious business during the first week of February, and on the afternoon of the sixth a deputation of members and Privy Councillors, headed by the Speaker, waited on the Queen and presented her with a petition urging her to take some man to be her husband. The deputation did not presume to be specific about his identity but it did point out in some detail the advantages which would accrue – the principal one, of course, being that the Queen might by marriage bring forth children and thus ensure her own immortality, and this, the Speaker of the Commons assured her fervently, was 'the single, the onely, the all-comprehending prayer of all English-men'.[10]

There are two accounts of the Queen's reaction to this, the first of numerous encounters she was to have with her anxious Commons on the subject of marriage. William Camden, who had access to some useful sources of confidential information through his friendship with William Cecil, says she told the Speaker that as a private person she had always chosen to remain single and, now that responsibility for governing the country had been laid upon her, she felt it would be 'inconsiderate folly' to add the distractions of marriage to a public career. In any case, she already had a husband – the kingdom of England – and, to emphasise her point, the Queen took her coronation ring from her finger and flourished it before her audience. 'Behold (said she, which I marvell ye have forgotten,) the Pledge of this my Wedlock and Marriage with my Kingdom . . . And do not (saith she) upbraide me with miserable lack of Children: for every one of you, and as many as are English-men, are Children and Kinsmen to me.'[11]

The official version of the Queen's reply, its text worked over and finally approved by the Queen herself, was not released for another four days and contains no mention of this classic piece of Elizabethan byplay. But in essence the two accounts agree. The Queen had so far remained unmarried by deliberate personal choice and hoped to continue in that way of life with which she was so thoroughly ac-quainted. If time or circumstances or both should cause her to change her mind, then she would be at pains to select a consort who could be trusted to be as careful for the preservation of the realm and people as she was herself. But Elizabeth made it clear that she regarded this as being an area very much within her own province and one in which she would tolerate no outside interference, however well meant. As far as the succession was concerned, she reminded Parliament with characteristic hard-headedness that they could not be certain any children of hers would necessarily turn out well – on the contrary, they might 'grow out of kind and become perhaps ungracious'. For her own part, she would prefer to leave it to Providence, trusting that with God's help 'an heir that may be a fit governor' would make his appearance in due course. She herself would be quite content if, in the end, 'a marble stone shall declare that a Queen, having reigned such a time, lived and died a virgin'.[12]

This was not, on the face of it, a very satisfactory response to their petition and there was an abortive attempt by some members of the Commons to take the matter further by appointing a committee to discuss what authority should be vested in 'that person whom it shall please the Queen to take to husband'.[13] On the whole, though, this, the first of Elizabeth's 'answers answerless', was accepted with a good grace. No one, of course, took all that talk about living and dying a virgin in the least seriously, but the Queen was a young and desirable woman and she was entitled to be a little coy. Indeed, it was only right and proper that she should display a certain maidenly reluctance and, provided she didn't take too long over it, no reasonable man grudged her the opportunity to look around and survey the field.

Actually, when one got down to cases, the field was not all that extensive. As with Mary, most people would have preferred the Queen to marry at home, but in the spring of 1559 even the most enthusiastic xenophobe had to admit that the choice was limited to the point of virtual non-existence. Unless you counted the Earl of Arundel, an unimpressive widower in his late forties, or Sir William Pickering, diplomat and courtier and a great success with the ladies, there was really no one of suitable age and rank. The young Duke of Norfolk might have done (apart from being England's premier nobleman and only Duke, he was the Queen's cousin on her mother's side), but unfortunately he was already married. If only Edward Courtenay had not been so careless as to get himself carried off by fever in Italy, the story would have been very different. If Courtenay had survived, Elizabeth would have found it hard to evade matrimony. Probably she would not even have tried – the perils of refusing such an obviously pre-ordained match would have been too great – and the whole course of English history might have been changed.

But Courtenay was dead and it was no use regretting the might-have-been. The Queen of England would have to look further afield for a husband, and anyone with a knowledge of the political realities was more or less resigned to the prospect of a foreign consort.

By the middle of February, de Feria had finally got round to making Philip's proposal and had been put off with 'fair words'. Elizabeth never had the smallest intention of accepting the King of Spain – it would have been the fastest way she could have chosen of committing political suicide – but de Feria was determined not to give this tiresome chit of a girl the satisfaction of being able to boast that she had refused the greatest prince in Christendom. He therefore cut short her objections and evasions and protestations about not wishing to marry, and it was finally agreed between them that he would have 'no answer that was not a very good one'. There the matter rested, but the ambassador was not optimistic, for, as he told Philip, he knew that the heretics who surrounded the Queen would take every opportunity to turn her against the idea.[14]

There were two other envoys in London that winter with marriage in mind. The Swedes had wasted no time in renewing the suit of their crown prince, but they seemed to have no idea of the social niceties to be observed in such matters. When the Swedish ambassador was brash enough to press the Queen for a reply to the letter sent to her the year before – the same which had caused Queen Mary so much anguish – he was told pretty sharply that this was no way for one monarch to approach another, especially a lady, and especially over a proposal of marriage. The letter in question had been written to the Princess Elizabeth. If the King of Sweden still wanted to offer his son, then he must address himself to the Queen of England in proper form. Elizabeth did not know whether Prince Eric was prepared to leave his country to marry her, but she would not leave hers for any consideration in the world.[15]

The other hopeful matchmaker was Count von Helfenstein, sent by the Emperor ostensibly to deliver his master's congratulations to the new Queen on her accession, but more importantly to try to discover what the prospects might be for the Habsburg Archdukes. The Emperor, like Philip, was concerned about the future of the Catholic religion in England, for he had heard disquieting rumours that the Queen was imbued with 'the new views of the Christian faith'. If this were so, it would probably put Ferdinand out of the running, as he was unassailably orthodox – there was also the little matter of his morganatic wife, Philippine Welser. Charles, being

younger, was less set in his ways but his anxious father was naturally
reluctant to expose him to the dangers of heretical infection and
possible forfeiture of eternal salvation, unless, of course, the political
advantages looked really worth having; nor did the Emperor want to
risk offending Philip by seeming to poach on his preserves. Von
Helfenstein was therefore instructed to say nothing about a marriage
until he had seen how the land lay and had reported back to
Vienna.[16]

The Count landed at Dover on 20 February and was given full
V.I.P. treatment. He saw the Queen on the twenty-fifth when Elizabeth received him in her friendliest manner, asking after the health
of the Emperor and his family, enquiring about the state of affairs in
Germany, where Von Helfenstein himself came from, and whether
he had had an easy journey, so that the Good Count was quite bowled
over by her charms and wrote enthusiastic letters home in praise of
her prudence and poise, her great-mindedness and 'all other heroic
virtues'. He was also able to report that open curiosity was being
displayed in English political circles about the Archdukes. 'There was
no one there', he wrote on the day after his audience with the Queen,
'who did not, as vulgar parlance has it, prick up his ears and listen
with great admiration and, as it were, silent reverence when I spoke
or answered about the ages, the morals, the talents of Your Imperial
Majesty's sons, as on these points frank and exhaustive enquiries were
frequently made of me. For many thought that one of them would
soon become consort of the Queen and rule her and England.' The
broadest hints were dropped by the Earl of Sussex, who was acting as
the Count's host, and even by the Queen herself that if he had anything private to say to her this could easily be arranged. The Count,
obedient to his instructions, was careful not to commit himself but he
was certainly given every reason to believe that a proposal was both
expected and would be favourably received.[17]

As far as the religious question was concerned, von Helfenstein
had made zealous and painstaking enquiries, but had 'observed nothing that deviates from the old Catholic creed'. Mass was still being
said and fast-days kept, 'so there is great hope that, if they get a
Catholic King, all religious questions may easily be settled by
authority of the sovereign'. At the same time, the Count felt obliged
to admit that, despite all his subtlety, he had been unable 'clearly to
fathom' what the Queen's intentions were. 'From the very beginning
of her reign,' he wrote, 'she has treated all religious questions with so
much caution and incredible prudence that she seems both to protect

the Catholic religion and at the same time not entirely to condemn or outwardly reject the new Reformation.'[18]

The burning of heretics, which had cast such a pall of gloom over the latter part of Mary's reign, had of course ceased and there had been a few minor innovations; but, at the end of February 1559, England was still officially a Catholic country and Count von Helfenstein was by no means the only person unable clearly to fathom Elizabeth's intentions with regard to the highly sensitive issue of religion. The concensus of government opinion was in favour of making haste slowly, and the Queen herself would pretty certainly have preferred to settle for a return to royal supremacy and an order of service based on the 1549 Prayer Book – in other words, to a modified form of the national Catholicism evolved by Henry VIII. It was, however, already clear that this would not satisfy the militant Protestants. These were still very much in a minority, but they formed a well-organised and articulate pressure-group, represented in the House of Commons by an influential 'choir of M.P.s eager to demonstrate that they wished to return not to the days of Henry VIII but to those of 'the young Josiah' his son.

For a time the government firmly resisted backbench attempts to force through a more radical solution to the problem; and as Easter approached, and with it the expected dissolution of Parliament, it looked very much as though the militants were going to lose the battle. Then, at the last moment, the Queen changed her mind. She adjourned the session, and when it re-assembled on 3 April a settlement along the lines of the second Edwardian Prayer Book, in which the mass had finally been transformed into a service of communion or commemoration, was officially put forward. Elizabeth had been taken aback by the strength of feeling and the determination manifested by the radical element in the Commons, but other factors had contributed to her sudden change of front. For one thing, the surviving Catholic bishops had proved irritatingly obstinate, all of them voting against the Supremacy Bill in the Lords. This meant that the Elizabethan Church would have to rely on Protestant divines, many of whom had taken refuge in such havens of advanced thought as Strasbourg and Geneva during Mary's reign and none of whom were prepared to accept anything less than the 1552 Prayer Book – some, indeed, would have liked to go further. Another development which undoubtedly influenced the Queen was the fact that a peace treaty had now been signed between England, France and Spain at Cateau-Cambrésis.[19]

Elizabeth's own religious inclinations were conservative – when she told de Feria that she believed in a Real Presence and only dissented from two or three things in the mass she was probably speaking quite sincerely. Certainly she disliked bigoted Protestants every bit as much, if not more, than bigoted Catholics and she had no time at all for the Calvinist breed of minister – the very name of John Knox was anathema to her. But she was far too astute not to see the dangers of attempting arbitrarily to impose a universally unpopular settlement, not to understand that the days when the nation would unquestioningly accept the sovereign's ruling on matters of salvation had gone for ever. Too many people now had read the Bible for themselves and had tasted the emotional and intellectual thrills of scriptural interpretation. Elizabeth, first-born child of the English Reformation, naturally came down on the Protestant side but she had been pushed further than she wanted to go and, despite their famous victory, the radical party did not get things all their own way – there was some disappointment among the returning exiles over the Queen's lack of godly zeal and her insistence on the retention of so much of 'the scenic apparatus of divine worship'. Nevertheless, when Parliament finally dispersed at the beginning of May, England was indisputably a Protestant country and the Anglican order of service, in very much the same form as it exists today, had become the only legal form of worship.

All this, of course, put an end to the Spanish courtship – as early as March, Elizabeth, in a rather excitable conversation with de Feria, had declared that she could not marry Philip 'as she was a heretic' and Philip, no doubt privately much relieved, had not waited for a formal refusal. In April he took the opportunity of sealing the new peace treaty by marrying the French princess Elisabeth, and the English Elizabeth remarked with a wistful air that the King of Spain could not, after all, have been so very much in love with her if he was not prepared to wait even four months![20]

De Feria knew the Queen well enough by this time not to take her seriously, but Philip was almost morbidly anxious that Elizabeth should not regard his marriage as a slight, or take it into her head that everything was now over between them. On the contrary, he wrote, de Feria was 'to assure her positively that this will not be so, but I am and shall remain as good a brother to her as before and as such shall take very great interest in what concerns her, and will try to forward her affairs as if they were my own'.[21] Philip was still hoping to draw England into the Habsburg net and had finally made

up his mind to throw the full weight of his influence behind which-
ever of his archducal cousins seemed most likely to find favour. In a
letter to de Feria dated 12 April he painstakingly outlined the obvious
advantages of an Austrian marriage – advantages which the ambassador was to explain to the Queen at the earliest opportunity.
Since neither Ferdinand nor Charles possessed a state of his own, her
husband would be free to remain at her side and help her bear the
burden of government. She would also acquire a host of powerful
and affectionate relations who would welcome her into the family
with open arms and give her all the protection she was ever likely to
need; she would rise in the estimation of her own subjects and no
one, at home or abroad, would dare to molest or offend her.[22]
Naturally enough, it did not occur to Philip that the young Queen of
England might regard the business of government not as a burden
but as an absorbing challenge which she had no desire to share, or
that she might have reservations about the prospect of all those affectionate Habsburg in-laws. After so many months and years of pro-
crastination and indecision, the King had set his heart on this method
of solving the Elizabeth problem and de Feria was urged to do his
utmost to see that negotiations were brought to a speedy and successful conclusion.

De Feria himself, despite a gloomy conviction that the English and
their queen were already at least half-way along the road to perdition,
was prepared to concede that a marriage with Archduke Ferdinand
appeared 'not a bad expedient' – if not, indeed, the only possible one.
He accordingly made contact with Augustin Gyntzer, Count von
Helfenstein's secretary, who had recently arrived in London with
more friendly letters from the Emperor and a full-length portrait of
Ferdinand, assuring him of wholehearted Spanish support and offering good – and, one suspects, rather patronising – advice on the best
way to proceed. (De Feria was determined that, whatever happened,
the Germans should be given no opportunity to claim credit for
carrying off the prize independently.) The ambassador also went to
see the Queen, finding her as usual full of fair words and graceful
evasions of the issue. As he wrote to Philip on 18 April, 'to say the
truth I could not tell your Majesty what this woman means to do
with herself, and those who know her best know no more than I do.'[23]

In this same despatch, de Feria makes the first recorded public
reference to the scandalous affair of the Queen's increasingly close,
perhaps intimate, relationship with her old playmate Robert Dudley.
'During the last few days,' he observed, 'Lord Robert has come so

much into favour that he does whatever he likes with affairs and it is even said that her Majesty visits him in his chamber day and night. People talk of this so freely that they go so far as to say that his wife has a malady in one of her breasts and the Queen is only waiting for her to die to marry Lord Robert. I can assure your Majesty that matters have reached such a pass that I have been brought to consider whether it would be well to approach Lord Robert on your Majesty's behalf, promising him your help and favour and coming to terms with him.'[24] Ten days later, after a querulous complaint about the difficulty of trying to negotiate anything with a woman so naturally changeable, and about the blindness, bestiality and general lack of understanding displayed by those around her, the ambassador went on: 'They talk a great deal about the marriage with Archduke Ferdinand and seem to like it, but for my part I believe she will never make up her mind to anything that is good for her. Sometimes she appears to want to marry him, and speaks like a woman who will only accept a great prince, and then they say she is in love with Lord Robert and never lets him leave her.'[25]

About a week after this, on 8 May, the Acts of Supremacy and Uniformity, twin cornerstones of the Elizabethan Religious Settlement received the royal assent and de Feria could only conclude that England had fallen into the hands of a woman 'who is a daughter of the devil, and the greatest scoundrels and heretics in the land'. The ambassador was already agitating for his recall and thankfully received permission to take his leave of the devil's daughter as soon as Parliament had risen. De Feria was an experienced and normally skilful diplomat but there could be no disguising the facts that his current mission had been a dismal and humiliating failure. He had totally failed to influence the course of events, failed to make any headway in negotiating the all-important English marriage and, worst of all in his opinion, failed to prevent the triumph of the heretics. In short, a raw young woman in her twenties had made rings round him and all he wanted to do now was to remove himself and his bride (he had recently married Jane Dormer, one of the late Queen's favourite maids) from the contaminating atmosphere of the godless island and never, never think about English affairs again. In his last despatch from London, dated 10 May, he reported that William Pickering, who had been strongly tipped as a possible bridegroom for the Queen, had returned home after a prolonged absence on the Continent. Elizabeth made quite a fuss of him, seeing him privately while Lord Robert was away on a hunting trip, and according to de Feria the London bookmakers were giving odds of four to one that he would soon be king. 'If these things were not of such great importance and so lamentable,' commented de Feria, 'some of them would be very ridiculous.'[26]

In fact, there is absolutely no evidence to suggest that Elizabeth ever seriously considered Pickering as a husband. He was an attractive man and amusing company, but that was all. Pickering himself naturally made the most of his brief ascendancy, entertaining lavishly, dining in solitary state to the accompaniment of a band of musicians and generally throwing his weight about. The Queen grew rather bored with him, and after a few months he had faded from the scene. The Swedes were still at court, bestowing expensive presents on all and sundry and getting laughed at for their pains, and there was no sign yet of any formal proposal from the Emperor. 'Meanwhile,' wrote the Italian gossip Il Schifanoya, 'my Lord Dudley is in very great favour and very intimate with her Majesty.'[27]

My Lord Robert Dudley, mounted on a snow-white steed, had been among the first to pay homage to the new Queen at Hatfield the previous November and she had rewarded him with the post of Master of the Horse, his 'beauty, stature and florid youth' together with his skill in riding a managed horse being apparently powerful recommendations. Good horsemanship and a fine presence were certainly both recommendations for this office, but it was no sinecure. The Master of the Horse was responsible for keeping the court adequately supplied with transport; for the buying, training, breeding and welfare of riding and carriage horses, pack horses and mules, horses capable of dragging heavy wagons over impossible roads, horses which could be trusted in crowds and processions. Robert always took this side of the job very seriously and worked hard at it, but his public and ceremonial duties were equally important and, involving as they did close attendance on the Queen on all state occasions, even more congenial. As for Elizabeth, she never made any secret of the pleasure she took in Robert's company and by the summer of 1559 it was beginning to look as if the Queen – who could have taken her pick of the bachelors of Christendom – had chosen to set her heart on the one man she could not have.

CHAPTER VI

If the Emperor So Desires
Me for a Daughter

On Friday, 26 May 1559, Caspar von Breuner, Baron of Stubling, Fladnitz and Rabenstein, arrived in London with powers to make the Queen a formal proposal of marriage on behalf of the Emperor's youngest son, Archduke Charles – Ferdinand having now definitely scratched from the English matrimonial stakes.

Von Breuner showed no signs of wishing to act independently of Spain. On the contrary, he immediately sought the assistance and hospitality of the Spanish embassy and 'was so determined to stay that there was no resisting him'. Don Alvaro de Quadra, Bishop of Aquila, who had taken over Count de Feria's thankless task, quickly summed up the good Baron as 'not the most crafty person in the world' and, bearing in mind his master's anxiety for the success of the Austrian mission, decided he had better be on hand during von Breuner's initial encounter with Elizabeth.

On the following Sunday afternoon, therefore, the two envoys went together to the palace, where they found the Queen 'very fine in her presence chamber looking on at the dancing'. De Quadra presented the Baron, begging Elizabeth to hear him out and decide the matter with 'the wisdom and prudence which God had given her', before standing aside with the air of one determined to give a junior colleague every chance to show what he could do. As it happened, the ambassador was able to fill in the time by having a useful chat with William Cecil on the subject uppermost in both their minds. The Secretary of State seemed distinctly lukewarm over the Austrian match, thinking, so de Quadra believed, that Ferdinand was about to be proposed 'as he is the only one that these people have any knowledge of and they have quite made up their minds that he would upset their heresy'. After mentioning all the flattering offers which the Queen had been receiving lately, Cecil went on to express polite regrets that religious difficulties had made a marriage with Philip impossible to arrange and de Quadra seized the opportunity to dispel

any fears the Secretary and his friends might have that they had in-
curred his master's anger by their change of religion. He therefore
answered 'without any reproach or complaint', merely remarking
that what had been done certainly seemed 'very grave, severe and ill-
timed' and hoping that a reform of those abuses at the court of Rome
which had so scandalised the provinces would presently lead to a
reconciliation, for surely God would not allow so noble and Christian
a nation as England to remain separated in faith from the rest of
Christendom to its own grave peril.[1]

This deliberately conciliatory policy towards the schismatic island
was prompted in part by Philip's continuing need to keep the English
alliance in being, and in part by his optimistic conviction that before
long circumstances would force Elizabeth to marry into the Habsburg
family. The King of Spain was to cling to this conviction for nearly
ten years, but on that Sunday afternoon in May 1559 the prospects
were not bright and Caspar von Breuner emerged from the Queen's
presence in near-despair. Elizabeth was deeply honoured that the
Emperor, whom she regarded as her dear lord and cousin, had
deemed her worthy to marry one of his sons, and her own council
and loyal subjects were daily and hourly begging and exhorting her
to marry whom she would, so that they might hope for heirs. When-
ever it should be possible, she would not only fulfil their wish but, if
necessary, hazard her life in their service. She would also like to
oblige the Emperor and recompense his paternal love and friendship
with her own possessions and those of the Crown. But now, although
she had often been desired in marriage, she could swear by the salvation of her soul that she had never set her heart upon, nor wished to
marry, anyone in the world. She found her celibate life so pleasant
and was so accustomed to it that she would rather go into a nunnery or
suffer death than marry against her will. At the same time, she would
not like it to be assumed that she had forsworn marriage entirely.
She was only human and not insensible to human emotions and im-
pulses, and when it became a question of the weal of her kingdom, or
it might be for other reasons, she might change her mind.[2]

It was hardly surprising that the Baron, inexperienced in Elizabeth Tudor's normal methods of dealing with proposals of marriage,
should have despaired – and this was de Quadra's cue to intervene.
He accordingly went back to the Queen and seems for the first time to
have made it clear that Charles and not Ferdinand was the proffered
bridegroom. He did this, so he said, to clear the ground and find out
whether Elizabeth was sincere about not wishing to marry or

whether, as he suspected, was simply determined not to marry a Catholic. If de Quadra really expected to find out anything so definite, he was disappointed, but he did succeed in arousing the Queen's interest. She had probably already heard the rumours that Charles was not such a committed Catholic as the rest of his family – there had even been rumours that he might be thinking of leaving the Roman Church. All the same, she soon 'went back again to her nonsense and said she would rather be a nun than marry without knowing with whom and on the faith of portrait painters'. Someone had told her that Charles had an enormous head, even bigger than the Earl of Bedford's, and she was taking no risks. 'We continued at this for some time wasting words,' reported de Quadra, but the Queen was firm in her resolution not to marry, 'except to a man of worth whom she had seen and spoken to'. Did de Quadra think the Archduke would come to England so that she could have a look at him? De Quadra thought that no doubt the young man himself (Charles was just twenty) would come willingly, but whether the Emperor would agree to send his son on approval was something else again. 'I do not know whether she is jesting, which is quite possible, but I really believe she would like to arrange for this visit in disguise', wrote the ambassador. Finally von Breuner was recalled, and it was agreed that he and de Quadra should lay the Emperor's proposition before a committee of senior members of the Council. The Queen promised to listen to their advice, although she reiterated her resolve not to trust in portraiture and to 'see and know the man who was to be her husband'.[2]

The session with the Council took place on the following afternoon and seemed satisfactory, as far as it went – at least it made a welcome change to be dealing with sensible men who understood how these matters were arranged. But, when von Breuner saw the Queen again, it was obvious that no progress had been made. She did not wish to marry – at any rate, not yet. She might change her mind some time in the future or God, with whom all things were possible, might change it for her. It was not, as Elizabeth readily admitted, a satisfactory answer but she hoped the Emperor would accept it as honest and sincere. Von Breuner did not attempt to hide his disappointment and hinted a little stiffly that, in view of the encouraging reception given so recently to Count von Helfenstein, he thought the Emperor would be surprised and hurt. However, he would, of course, send his master a detailed account of what had passed and hoped soon to be able to tell him about it in person.

This was going too fast. The Emperor was in altogether too much of a hurry, complained the Queen. She would be writing to him herself and her letter and von Breuner's reports could quite well go by courier, so that the Baron could stay on in England for a while if he wished. It looked like a gleam of hope and during the course of two interviews, on 30 May and 3 June, the Baron did his utmost to get Elizabeth to say whether she wished to go on with 'this marriage business' or not, and whether there was really any point in his remaining. It was not for her, answered Elizabeth demurely, to dictate to the Emperor's ambassador. He must do as he thought best. She could not explicitly say that she would marry 'within a short time', or even if she would marry at all, for her heart had not yet spoken. Nevertheless, she contrived to make it clear that she wanted von Breuner to stay.[4]

Von Breuner himself did not know what to think. His instinct warned him that he was being made a fool of but, on the other hand, women, especially young women, were notoriously capricious. If Elizabeth was just playing hard to get – and surely she couldn't seriously mean to refuse the Archduke? – it would be criminal folly to risk losing such a prize by being over-hasty. So the Baron decided to persevere, encouraged by the fact that the Queen seemed to have taken a fancy to him. This was an impression which the Queen proceeded to foster and, during the ensuing week, von Breuner got the full treatment. After supper on 10 June he had taken a boat out on the Thames and encountered Elizabeth, who was also taking the air on what one assumes to have been a balmy summer evening. As soon as she saw the Baron, she summoned him over, invited him into the Treasurer's barge and then had her own boat rowed alongside and played to him on her lute. She invited him to breakfast next morning and out on the river again that evening in the royal barge, when she made him take the helm and was altogether 'very talkative and merry'. The talk, naturally, was all about Archduke Charles, Elizabeth asking endless questions but still harping on her determination to be wooed at first hand. Von Breuner tried unsuccessfully to argue her out of this unreasonable demand and continued to press her for a straight answer, which he didn't get. However, he was by this time so dazzled by the flattering attentions being showered on him that he hastened to assure the Queen that the Emperor would certainly not break off negotiations.[5]

Elizabeth had her reasons for wishing to prolong von Breuner's visit. The political situation in Scotland was once again boiling up to a crisis and the presence of the Imperial envoy on a matrimonial mission might become a useful weapon if things got really difficult. The Scottish Protestant party – the Congregation of Jesus, as it styled itself – had been growing in strength over recent years and was now in open revolt against the alien and Catholic rule of the Queen-Dowager, Mary of Guise. But, although the Congregation had been reinforced by the return of John Knox, that rugged enemy of Rome, to his native land, it was soon distressingly apparent that no amount of Calvinistic fervour would by itself be sufficient to dislodge the Regent and her garrison of French veterans from the fortress of Leith. The Lords of the Congregation had, therefore, appealed to the Protestant Queen of England for help.

Neither the Protestant Queen nor her Secretary of State needed reminding that here, at long last, might be England's opportunity to drive the French out of Scotland and put an end to the menace of the 'auld alliance' once and for all. But it was by no means as simple as it sounded. Elizabeth, not surprisingly, detested the revolutionary doctrine preached by the Scottish reformers that subjects had a positive duty to overthrow and spit upon any earthly prince who failed to obey the law of Christ – that is, of course, the law of Christ as interpreted by John Calvin and his disciples. Equally unsurprisingly, she cherished an implacable hatred for John Knox, whose anti-feminist opinions as expressed in his recently published *Blast . . . Against the Monstrous Regiment of Women* were enough to raise the hackles of any self-respecting female head of state. Apart from these considerations, and her instinctive reluctance to be seen lending aid and comfort to another sovereign's rebels, Elizabeth knew very well that to interfere in Scotland's internal affairs would be to invite retaliation from the greatest military power in Europe. The risk of such an adventure ending with a victorious French army poised on England's vulnerable land-frontier was too real to be disregarded.

At the beginning of July the situation was rendered even more explosive by the sudden death of King Henri II of France in a tilt-yard accident. The French throne passed to Henri's son François, an unhealthy child of fifteen, and François' wife, the sixteen-year-old Mary Queen of Scots; effective power passed into the hands of the Queen of Scots' maternal uncles, the Duke of Guise and the Cardinal of Lorraine, a pair of sharp-clawed predators who were not likely to stand aside while their sister, the Queen-Regent, was driven out of Scotland by a rabble of heretics. Once disembarked at Leith, a French expeditionary force would make short work of the Congregation of Jesus – and then what? Henri II, while naturally eager to wring the last drop of political advantage out of his daughter-in-law's claims to the English crown, had been on the whole a reasonable man with whom it was possible to do business. The Guise family had no such reputation. Would they be able to resist the temptation to fling their army across the border and down through the predominantly Catholic North Country into the undefended English heartland, seize and dispose of the bastard Elizabeth and add yet another kingdom to their niece's collection? The answer seemed only too probably that they would not. Small wonder, then, that Elizabeth, faced with her first major crisis after only eight months on her none-too-secure throne, should have hesitated to embroil herself openly with the Scots, hesitated indeed to do anything which might set a match to the powder-keg.

Certain things, however, she could do, and messages of encouragement and consignments of gold began to go north under conditions of the greatest secrecy. There was, of course, always another weapon available to Elizabeth Tudor. Bishop de Quadra heard that, when she was told François intended to have himself proclaimed King of England, she retorted sharply that she would take a husband who would give the King of France some trouble and do him more harm than he expected.[6] There was no secret about the identity of the husband in question. He was James Hamilton, Earl of Arran, the same to whom Henry VIII had offered to match his younger daughter back in 1543. The Scots leaders were pressing for a marriage between these two 'chief upholders of God's religion', both as a present bulwark against French aggression and as a possible future means of 'uniting England and Scotland together'; for after his father, now dignified by the French dukedom of Chatelherault, young Arran was the Scottish heir presumptive.[7]

Elizabeth, as usual, was not committing herself but she was taking a close interest in Arran's welfare. The Earl was currently abroad. He'd been living in France as a hostage for his father's good behaviour, James Hamilton senior being a notoriously untrustworthy character; but, when trouble broke out in Scotland, Arran had sensibly ignored a summons to Paris and was now in hiding in Switzerland. Elizabeth sent Thomas Randolph, an expert on Scottish affairs, to organise his escape, and in due course the Earl was successfully smuggled across the Channel disguised as a merchant. All this, naturally, was kept as quiet as possible, but rumours that Arran was already in either England or Scotland were circulating as early as the beginning of July, and de Quadra expected news of the marriage to break at any moment, for he believed the Queen would scarcely risk receiving the fugitive and offending the French at such a critical juncture unless the matter was settled and 'he was to be something more than a guest'.[8]

De Quadra should have known the Queen better. Arran actually reached London on 28 August and was secreted in William Cecil's house at Westminster. On the twenty-ninth he had a very private interview with Elizabeth at Hampton Court and two days later, still under Randolph's escort, he left for Scotland where, it was hoped, he would take over the leadership of the revolt and provide it with a popular figurehead. But no more was said about a marriage, and de Quadra cheered up again. It certainly looked to any reasonable diplomat as if Elizabeth must now accept Archduke Charles and a Spanish–Imperialist alliance to protect her against France – especially in view of the martial preparations going forward in that country. Elizabeth herself, well aware of the need to keep Philip friendly (and she had tried him fairly hard over the religious settlement), apparently felt it was time to offer the patient von Breuner some further encouragement and, on 7 September, de Quadra had interesting news for the Duchess of Parma in Brussels. It seemed that he and the Baron had had a visit from Lady Mary Sidney, one of the Queen's Bedchamber Women and sister of the favourite, Robert Dudley. According to Lady Sidney, now was the moment to press the Archduke's suit again. They must not mind what the Queen said, 'as it is the custom for ladies here not to give their consent in such matters until they are teased into it'. But, declared Lady Sidney, it would only take a few days and the Council would press the Queen to marry. The ambassador might be sure she would never dare to say such a thing if it were not true and she was acting now with the Queen's consent. Her Majesty would not raise the subject herself, but she definitely wanted the Archduke to come to England.[9]

Puzzled but impressed, de Quadra did a little checking. He had a word with Lord Robert, who assured him that in this as in all things he was at the disposal of King Philip to whom he owed his life – a tactful reference to his release from the Tower in the autumn of 1554. The ambassador also talked to the Treasurer of the Household, fat Thomas Parry, who had been with Elizabeth since before the days of the Seymour scandal and might safely be supposed to be fully in her confidence. Parry confirmed Lady Sidney's story, adding significantly that 'the marriage had now become necessary'. There was a

D

rumour going round about a plot to poison the Queen and kill Lord Robert while they were both being entertained by the Earl of Arundel at Nonesuch, and de Quadra believed that this and the threatening international situation had combined to force Elizabeth into a decision.[10] However, when von Breuner bustled happily down to Hampton Court to seek audience with the Queen, he got smartly snubbed for his pains. It wasn't until de Quadra saw her in London three days later that any progress was made.

After a long preliminary skirmish over old ground – she didn't want to marry the Archduke or anybody else, if she married at all it would only be to a man she knew, but she didn't want Charles to come to England as she would not bind herself even indirectly to marry him – de Quadra made one more effort to pin her down, remarking reasonably enough that if they could not arrive at some sort of compromise they were simply wasting words. Let her begin, he went on, with the premise that she had to be married, as that could not now be avoided, and since she would not marry a man she had not seen let her agree to the Archduke's coming on a visit without her being bound any more than she was at present; let the Emperor be told of this, so that if he decided to send his son on those terms it might be done without further loss of time. After some more beating about the bush there was a pause and Elizabeth suddenly said: 'Shall I speak plainly and tell you the truth? I think that if the Emperor so desires me for a daughter he would not be doing too much by sending his son here without so many safeguards. I do not hold myself of so small account that the Emperor need sacrifice any dignity in doing it.'

'By these words and her manner of saying them', wrote de Quadra, 'I understood that she made no difficulty as to the conclusion of the business but only in the procedure to bring it about.' This looked like a giant step forward, but it was clear that the initiative must come from the Emperor. On no condition would Elizabeth herself ask Charles to come. It was not fit for a queen and a maiden to summon anyone to marry her for her pleasure – she would rather die a thousand deaths. In the circumstances, de Quadra felt justified in saying that, once the Emperor was satisfied his son would be welcome and that a visit might be 'convenient and advantageous', he was sure the matter could be arranged. A little more persuasion and Elizabeth had admitted that she would be glad to see the Archduke and was asking what languages he spoke. There followed a very pleasant conversation on the subject 'in a vastly different mood from her other conversations about her not wishing to marry' and, if it had not been for the risk of arousing the suspicions of the standers-by, de Quadra would have kissed her hand. He was still on delicate ground, though, for when he began to ask if Charles should come in public or privately Elizabeth drew back. She didn't want to be pressed any further. The Archduke must do as he thought fit; she didn't want to know anything about it. It must be clearly understood that she had not asked him to come, and she repeated several times that she was not committing herself to marriage and had still not yet resolved to marry at all. But this, as de Quadra triumphantly pointed out, was after she had agreed to the visit. He did not think these protestations need cause any alarm, as they were 'certainly nothing but ceremony'. He conceeded that he might easily be deceived himself, but went on, 'I do not believe that Lady Sidney and Lord Robert could be mistaken, and the latter says he never thought the Queen would go so far.'[11]

In any case, she really had no choice. Everyone knew she could not afford to delay her marriage much longer (most people believed it would take place by Christmas) and, whatever she said, by consenting to receive the Archduke at all Elizabeth *was* committing herself. Vain and fickle she might be, but not even she would have the gall to bring an Emperor's son half-way across Europe on a wild-goose chase and risk giving such mortal offence to the House of Habsburg. De Quadra quite realised it could be objected that, given these premises, all this uproar about seeing the Archduke before making up her mind was pointless – the Queen might just as well accept the inevitable and start negotiating the marriage treaty without wasting any more valuable time. 'I can only answer', he wrote, 'that in pure reason that is so, but, as she is a woman, and a spirited and obstinate woman too, passion has to be considered.' However tiresome to the logical masculine mind, feminine whims and fancies could not be ignored and would have to be pandered to if the main objective was to be achieved. De Quadra felt certain that the arguments in favour of sending Charles to London on Elizabeth's conditions far outweighed anything that could be said in favour of his staying away. Once the bridegroom-elect was actually on the spot the Queen would not be able to dismiss him, even if she wanted to – popular demand and pressure from the Council would be too strong – and in a long and detailed despatch the King of Spain's ambassador urged the Emperor to take the risk.[12]

Charles von Habsburg was by no means the only suitor competing for the Queen's favour that autumn. The King of Denmark's ambassador was parading about the court wearing a crimson velvet heart pierced by an arrow embroidered on his gown 'to demonstrate his King's love for Queen Elizabeth'; and Eric of Sweden, apparently impervious to discouragement, had sent his younger brother, the Duke of Finland, to plead his cause. The Duke landed at Harwich towards the end of September and turned out to be a pleasing young man, 'very courteous and princely, and well spoken in the Latin tongue'. He was free with his money too, and once he had got over an initial tendency to 'high looks and pontificiality' took enthusiastically to English ways. The Queen seemed to like him – he was often at Court and always well received. Some people began to whisper that he might be successful in a courtship on his own account, but 'how he shall speed, God knoweth and not I,' sighed William Cecil. The Scots had by no means given up hope for their candidate, the Earl of Arran, and a couple of outsiders, the Duke of Holstein and the Duke of Saxony's brother, hovered optimistically on the fringes of the crowd.

The Secretary of State, surveying this 'controversy of lovers' with a jaundiced eye, was moved to remark to his friend Ralph Sadler that he 'would to God the Queen had one and the rest were honourably satisfied'. The Queen would not have agreed. The present situation suited her very nicely, and when the French ambassador visited her one Sunday afternoon early in November he found her with the Duke of Finland on one side and the Emperor's ambassador on the other watching a tournament in which Lord Robert Dudley and her cousin, Henry Carey, were challenging all comers.

Antoine de Noailles had sought an audience to urge the Queen not to be alarmed by the reinforcements being sent to Scotland. His master was obliged to assist the Queen-Regent in her present predicament, but the ambassador would swear on oath that the King of France had no unfriendly intentions towards England. Elizabeth conceded that the Regent might feel herself threatened but thought the King of France was exaggerating the danger. He must not be surprised if, in view of the warlike preparations he was making (which seemed to her far greater than the occasion warranted), she mobilised her fleet and put the coastal defences in a state of readiness, for this was always the custom when England's neighbours armed.[13] The conversation remained perfectly affable in tone and, although de Noailles had well-founded suspicions about Elizabeth's undercover dealings with the Scottish rebels and her part in engineering the Earl of Arran's escape, there was no getting past her blandly smiling guard. When it came to playing diplomatic poker, Elizabeth Tudor, even in her twenties had no equal – a fact which was already becoming recognised in international circles. If she was worried by the various problems currently besetting her – the increased French presence in Scotland and how best to counter it, England's acute military and financial weakness, the necessity of making up her mind to marriage and all the extra difficulties that was going to bring in its wake – she concealed her anxiety admirably. The court was very gay that second winter of the reign and the Queen, at the centre of a hectic social whirl of banquets, balls and hunting parties, appeared to have no concern in the world except to enjoy herself.

But no one could fail to notice (no one did fail to notice) that, while she was ready to be civil to the Duke of Finland, to go to considerable trouble to have a private interview with the Earl of Arran, to flirt rather absentmindedly with William Pickering and to discuss with every indication of seriousness the possibility of marriage with Archduke Charles, it was the tall, arrogantly handsome figure of Lord Robert Dudley who was most often to be seen at her side. Not surprisingly this was now giving rise to a good deal of ill-natured gossip, and Sir Thomas Challoner, *en poste* in Brussels, had heard enough to cause him to write worriedly to his friend William Cecil that, although he counted the slander most false, a young princess could not be too careful 'what countenance or familiar demonstration she maketh more to one than another'.[14] He would not say so, even in a private letter to a trusted confidant, but Thomas Challoner, a man of sense and experience, was clearly very much afraid that Elizabeth, whose future as a wife and mother was of such vital importance to England ('for without posterity of her highness what hope is left unto us?'), might be wasting her time and ruining her good name by having an affair with a married man.

Rumours of a similar nature had been reaching the Emperor in Augsburg, and Caspar von Breuner received instructions to make searching enquiries into this matter, which was of close personal interest to the Habsburg family. But, despite his best efforts, he did not succeed in making any very startling discoveries. 'I have employed as my agent', he reported on 6 August, 'a certain François Borth, who is on very friendly terms with all the ladies of the bedchamber and all other persons who have been about the Queen and have brought her up since childhood. They all swear by all that is holy that her Majesty has most certainly never been forgetful of her honour. And yet it is not without significance that her Majesty's Master of the Horse, my lord Robert, is preferred by the Queen above all others, and that her Majesty shows her liking for him more markedly than is consistent with her reputation and dignity.'³⁵

Von Breuner had picked up a story that Katherine Ashley, now the Queen's 'most intimate Lady of the Bedchamber', had recently fallen at her old pupil's feet and implored her in God's name to marry and put an end to all these disreputable rumours, 'telling her Majesty that her behaviour towards the said Master of the Horse occasioned much evil-speaking'. A curious echo here of ten years before – of another time when Mrs Ashley had feared that her lady would be 'evilly spoken of'. Elizabeth, it seems, had replied that if she showed herself gracious towards her Master of the Horse 'he had deserved it for his honourable nature and dealings'. According to von Breuner's account, she had gone on to say that she failed to understand why anyone should object, 'seeing that she was always surrounded by her ladies of the bedchamber and maids of honour, who at all times could see whether there was anything dishonourable between her and her Master of the Horse'. 'If,' declared the Queen with a touch of defiance, 'if she had ever had the will or had found pleasure in such a dishonourable life . . . she did not know of anyone who could forbid her; but she trusted in God that nobody would ever live to see her so commit herself.' Von Breuner heard that Lord Robert was married to a fine lady 'from whom he has always had nothing but good', but ever since the Queen's accession he had never been away from court, and the fact that they were constantly together under the same roof was, in the Baron's opinion, feeding suspicion.¹⁶

Elizabeth might insist that she and Robert Dudley were just good friends, and nobody had yet been able to prove the contrary, but suspicion remained and gossip was growing uglier. In November, Bishop de Quadra informed King Philip that he had been told 'by a certain person who is accustomed to give me veracious news that Lord Robert has sent to poison his wife. Certainly,' continued the ambassador, 'all the Queen has done with us and with the Swede, and will do with the rest in the matter of her marriage, is only keeping Lord Robert's enemies and the country engaged with words until this wicked deed of killing his wife is consummated.'¹⁷ De Quadra was in a rage, for he now believed that he had been deliberately tricked by the Queen and her favourite. He'd noticed that Lord Robert was 'slackening in our business' and that Lady Sidney, hitherto so encouraging, had begun to avoid his company. He had therefore gone to the Queen to try to find out what was going on. The Archduke, he told her, might be already on the road and, since all her conditions had been complied with, he thought it was time he and von Breuner were given some assurance in the matter. But Elizabeth would only repeat yet again that she was not thinking about marrying, although she might change her mind when she saw the Archduke. De Quadra, determined not to be put off any longer, said that this hardly justified her implicit invitation, whereupon the Queen remarked airily that she only wished to meet Charles and get to know him in case she felt inclined to marry at some future time. It was at this point that the ambassador lost his temper and began to quote Lady Sidney, but if he expected to disconcert Elizabeth Tudor he was disappointed. Some member of her household may have said such things, she agreed calmly, and no doubt with good intentions, but without any commission from her.[18]

It's not surprising that de Quadra should have been angry. Not merely had six months' patient stalking of the quarry apparently gone for nothing, but he himself had been made to look a fool. He exonerated Mary Sidney, who had, he thought, been her brother's dupe – a suspicion borne out by a distinct coolness between them at this time – but he was now more than ready to hope for the worst as far as the Queen and Lord Robert were concerned: he'd been told some amazing things about their intimacy which he would never have believed, only he found Lord Robert's enemies on the Council were making no secret of their evil opinion of it. Lord Robert had numerous enemies by this time, especially among the older aristocracy who favoured the Austrian match, and the Duke of Norfolk had been heard to say that if the favourite 'did not abandon his present pretensions and presumption he would not die in his bed'. De Quadra was of the opinion that this general hatred of Robert would continue, 'as the Duke and the rest of them cannot put up with his being King'.[19] As for the Queen, the ambassador did not pretend to understand her and had given up all hope of her affairs.

Caspar von Breuner, who finally left England in December, thought that much of Elizabeth's stubbornness and generally wilful behaviour was to be blamed on her unfortunate upbringing, 'for sometimes she was regarded as legitimate and at other times not . . . She has been brought up at Court, then sent away, and to crown all she has even been held captive.' Now that she had finally come to the throne, 'like a peasant on whom a barony has been conferred', she had become so puffed up with pride that she imagined she was without peer and might do as she pleased. 'But herein she errs,' wrote the good Baron severely, 'for if she marry the said my lord Robert, she will incur so much enmity that she may one evening lay herself down as Queen of England and rise the next morning as plain Mistress Elizabeth.'[20]

Both de Quadra and von Breuner were convinced that the Queen had been deliberately using them 'and the other envoys who are sojourning here on matrimonial business' partly as a threat to scare the French and partly as a shield against her own subjects. 'For, as long as we are here,' remarked von Breuner shrewdly enough, 'she can put off the vulgar mob who daily beg and implore her to marry, with the plea that she must have leisure to occupy herself with the requests of so many potentates, to the weal and advantage of her realm.' Certainly it was blindingly obvious by the last weeks of 1559 that Elizabeth had no serious intentions towards any of her current crop of suitors. But what *were* her intentions? No one seemed to know. Did she really mean to remain a spinster? Or could two successive Spanish ambassadors have been right when they declared she was only waiting for her lover's wife to die to marry him?

Few men were ever more consistently vilified in their own lifetimes than Lord Robert Dudley. Outside his immediate family circle, his contemporaries, almost without exception, loathed and detested him – a loathing which cannot be entirely explained away by jealousy – and people simply could not understand what the Queen saw in this upstart son of a convicted traitor. The historian William Camden, who knew them both, could only offer a tentative astrological explanation – that the undoubted conjunction and affinity of their minds was caused by 'a hidden conspiracy and consent of their stars'.

Actually, of course, Robert possessed a number of attributes calculated to appeal to Elizabeth. He was very good-looking – 'tall and singularly well-featured and all his youth well favoured, of a sweet aspect but high-foreheaded'. He dressed well too, and knew how to display himself to the best advantage, making a splendid ornament for the court. This was useful when there were foreign visitors to be impressed and always important in an age when outward show had so much inner and symbolic value. Looks mattered to the Queen, and she had high standards of male beauty, but looks were not everything. Robert was a fine athlete, excelling in all the popular manly sports and war-games; and Elizabeth, like her father, always loved a man who *was* a man. She told von Breuner in the early days of their acquaintance that she would expect her husband to take part in warlike exercises and not 'sit at home all day among the cinders'. Robert was a good dancer – also very important to the Queen, who loved dancing. He was intelligent and had been well-educated, though Roger Ascham once regretted that he took more interest in Euclid's pricks and lines than in the classics. He was amusing company, witty, sophisticated, accustomed all his life to moving in the highest social and political circles. But perhaps what mattered most was the fact that he and Elizabeth had grown up together, talked the same language, shared the same jokes, the same background and experience – had even been in gaol together. With Robert, as with no one else, Elizabeth could drop her guard, relax, unwind and be herself. And Elizabeth, who lived so much of her life strung up to concert pitch, needed someone she could relax with.

She rewarded her old friend generously during that first year. In May 1559, Robert, together with the Duke of Norfolk, the Marquis of Northampton and the Earl of Rutland – three senior peers of the realm – was made a knight of the Garter. He was given 'a capital mansion' known as the Dairy House down at Kew, as well as other landed property and several sums of ready cash to meet current needs. He became Lieutenant of Windsor Castle and also got an extremely valuable licence to export woollen cloth free of duty. The Queen was apparently indifferent to gossip. If she enjoyed the company of her Master of the Horse in her off-duty hours and wanted to present him with some solid tokens of her regard, that was her business. Thirteen months on the throne had changed Elizabeth from the repressed, unhappy creature, nervously picking her way through the traps and pitfalls – political, religious and matrimonial – which had crowded her footsteps during her sister's reign into a spirited, vital young woman, increasingly confident of her ability to govern and determined to choose her own friends and arrange her private life without interference.

CHAPTER VII

Lord Robert Would Be Better in Paradise

By February 1560 there could be no disguising the fact that the Austrian marriage project was moribund. Despite all de Quadra's persuasive efforts of the autumn, the Archduke had not set out on his journey – no Habsburg ever did anything in a hurry. A number of people, including Count von Helfenstein who had returned to London in January in a final effort to breathe new life into the negotiations, thought this was a pity. The King of Bohemia and the Duke of Bavaria both spoke out in favour of the visit being made – the latter had even offered to accompany Charles and to contribute 100,000 crowns towards his travelling expenses. But the Emperor was determined to extract some sort of undertaking from Elizabeth before allowing his son to leave for London, and the result was deadlock. The Duke of Finland, on the other hand, was getting ready to go home and, although brother Eric threatened to come courting in person, no one believed there was the least likelihood of a Swedish marriage. De Quadra believed that the Queen's tricks were finding her out, for if both her Austrian and Scandinavian suitors deserted her 'not only will the French despise her but her own people as well and, in the event of the Scotch business turning out badly for her, as it probably will, she will be left helpless'.[1]

It was certainly true that 'the Scotch business' did not look particularly promising at the beginning of 1560. The Earl of Arran had proved a serious disappointment, both as a military commander and as leader of a popular-front movement – he was, in fact, already showing signs of the mental instability which later became hopeless insanity – and the Congregation's repeated failure to make any noticeable headway against the forces of the Queen-Regent was driving Elizabeth into more and more open intervention on their behalf. An English fleet under the command of William Winter had sailed for the Firth of Forth in December to blockade the port of Leith, and the Duke of Norfolk was on his way north with orders to levy an army in preparation for a possible assault by land. Robert Dudley, however, remained at home, still in high favour, and de Quadra heard he had been boasting that 'if he live another year he will be in a very different position from now. He is laying in a good stock of arms,' went on the ambassador, 'and is every day assuming a more masterful part in affairs. They say that he thinks of divorcing his wife.'[2]

Considering she was destined to become the heroine of an internationally reverberant scandal, exceedingly little is known about Amy Dudley, born Amy Robsart, only legitimate child and heiress of a substantial Norfolk landowner. She and Robert probably first met in July 1549 when he was campaigning in East Anglia with his father at the time of Jack Kett's rebellion. Amy was then eighteen, Robert about a year younger, and there is some evidence that they fell in love – at least, William Cecil believed they did and he was in as good a position to know as anyone. They were married in June 1550 with King Edward VI among the wedding guests, for these were the years of Dudley ascendancy, but there is no record even then that Amy ever enjoyed any share of her in-laws' new grandeur. Country bred, barely literate and utterly unused to high society, she seems to have made no attempt to keep up. Was she perhaps content to worship her godlike husband from afar, grateful for such crumbs of his company as he chose to bestow on her? When the crash came she visited him in the Tower, and during the period of eclipse between his release from prison and the outbreak of the French war in 1557 he was able to live comfortably enough down in Norfolk on John Robsart's money. But the life of a country gentleman was emphatically not for Robert Dudley, and the moment an opportunity presented itself he was off again into the wide dangerous world where he was so much at home. There were no children to keep the marriage together and in any case such a union, based on nothing but physical attraction, was probably foredoomed to failure. Certainly by the beginning of 1559 any passion on Robert's side was long spent. With a new, perhaps unimaginably glittering future opening before him, his wife had become an encumbrance to be kept out of sight and as far as possible out of mind.

Not that there was ever an open breach between them. The fact that Amy never came to court was of little significance by itself. The wives of the Queen's officers were not encouraged to put themselves forward and there was no accommodation for them in the overcrowded royal residences – unless, of course, they happened to hold some position in their own right. The unusual thing about the young

Dudleys' domestic arrangements was the fact that they had no home of their own. Most of the principal court officials rented a town house where they could join their wives and entertain their friends in their off-duty hours. Most rising men would also have acquired a country place where they could play the local magnate and lord it over their less fortunate neighbours. Robert did neither of these things. He remained in constant attendance on the Queen, as he was more or less forced to do if he wanted to keep the life-giving sunshine of her favour, while Amy lived as a kind of superior paying guest with various friends or connections of her husband. She spent most of 1558 and 1559 at Denchworth near Abingdon in the house of a Mr Hyde, brother-in-law of Anthony Forster who was Robert's 'treasurer' or steward. It's possible that she preferred this kind of life, which relieved her of all housekeeping responsibilities, and there's no suggestion that she was ever in any sense a prisoner. The account books show that she moved around quite freely. She came up to London once or twice to see Robert, and he paid an occasional flying visit to Denchworth. She was attended as befitted a lady of rank and spent quite a lot of money on clothes. Sometime before midsummer 1560 she moved from Denchworth to Cumnor Place, which lay just off the main road between Abingdon and Oxford and had been leased by Anthony Forster from William Owen, son of the late George Owen, at one time physician to the royal family. Cumnor, once a monastic building, was not large and, as well as the Forsters, Mrs Owen was still occupying part of it. So when Lady Robert Dudley moved in with her servants, her personal maid Mrs Pirto, and a Mrs Odingsells, the widowed sister of her former host Mr Hyde who had apparently come along to keep her company, space must have been at a premium. It hardly seems a very suitable arrangement for the wife of such a prominent man, but whether Amy went to Cumnor because she wanted to, or whether she simply fell in with a plan made by other people, is one of the many points on which we have no information.

Round about this time the situation in Scotland was finally beginning to resolve itself. The Duke of Norfolk had crossed the border at the end of March and, although the attack on Leith mounted on 7 May resulted in ignominious failure, other factors were now working in England's favour. For one thing, the French were experiencing the first stirrings of the civil unrest which was later to tear the country apart; storms in the North Sea the previous winter had scattered or destroyed many of the ships carrying reinforcements to the

Regent, and the government in Paris, reluctant to risk a direct confrontation with the English fleet in the Forth, felt itself unable to send any further assistance. The garrison at Leith was therefore starved out, and the death of that doughty warrior Mary of Guise took all the remaining heart out of the fight. France was ready to discuss terms, and William Cecil went north to represent Queen Elizabeth at the conference table.

Cecil was away for two months and during his absence the Queen's relationship with Robert Dudley is often said to have reached some sort of mysterious climax. In fact all that actually seems to have happened is that Elizabeth took advantage of the Secretary's sojourn in Scotland to enjoy a brief holiday from business herself and was out all day and every day hunting and riding with, naturally, her Master of the Horse. Like all the Tudors, Elizabeth was fanatically addicted to fresh air and exercise, and under Robert's tuition she was developing into a keen and fearless horsewoman. Indeed, as Robert told the Earl of Sussex, she was planning to send into Ireland 'for some hobbys for her own saddle, especially for strong, good gallopers which are better than her geldings'. Gossip, of course, continued unabated, and old Annie Dow of Brentwood got into trouble with the magistrates for spreading stories that Lord Robert had given the Queen a child. But people had been gossiping about the Queen and Lord Robert for more than a year now; there was nothing new in that. All the same, when Cecil returned to court at the end of July he was, for the first time, seriously alarmed about the Dudley affair – although his concern was probably caused not so much by the Queen's attitude to Robert Dudley as by her attitude to William Cecil.

Cecil had come home pardonably pleased with himself, for in the course of several weeks of hard bargaining in Edinburgh he had succeeded in extracting a series of important concessions from the French commissioners acting on behalf of the young Queen of Scots and her husband. It had, for example, been agreed that all French troops would be evacuated forthwith and the fortifications at Leith and Dunbar dismantled. It was also agreed that the government should be handed over to a Scottish Council, while England and France once more solemnly pledged themselves to observe a policy of non-interference. Finally, the French undertook that Mary would in future abstain from using the title and insignia of Queen of England. The religious question was carefully avoided but, as Cecil had confidently anticipated, the Scots wasted no time in adopting a Calvinistic form of Protestantism now they were free to do so and, whatever Queen Elizabeth's opinion of the Calvinists might be, even she must admit that they would make more desirable next-door neighbours than the French Army. It was never wise to be too sure of anything in Scottish affairs, but it did really look as if the foundations of a durable peace had been laid and the bogey of invasion from the north banished for good.

The Treaty of Edinburgh was a personal triumph for William Cecil and he could reasonably expect, if not a hero's welcome, at least some form of grateful recognition for his services. Instead the Queen virtually cut him dead and, to make matters worse, it looked as if he was going to be out of pocket as well. Exactly why Elizabeth treated her unfortunate Secretary in this unkind fashion is not very clear, but she may have been rather piqued by his success. Cecil had, from the beginning, been an enthusiastic advocate of intervention in Scotland and it was Cecil who had carried the policy through against all the Queen's misgivings. Events had proved him right and the Queen wrong, a situation no Tudor liked to be found in, and she probably just wished to make it understood that Cecil need not think he was infallible. But Cecil himself, who had not yet learnt to understand all his mistress's little ways, was deeply distressed and had no hesitation in laying the blame at Robert Dudley's door. There was, not surprisingly, no love lost between the Secretary and the Master of the Horse. Each feared and resented the other's influence, and each would have liked to dislodge the other from his privileged position in the Queen's confidence.

On 30 August the court moved down to Windsor and it was there, some time during the weekend of 7–8 September, that William Cecil chose to unburden himself to, of all people, the Spanish ambassador. De Quadra told the Duchess of Parma, in a letter dated 11 September, that after exacting many pledges of strict secrecy, Cecil said the Queen was conducting herself in such a way that he thought of retiring. 'He said it was a bad sailor who did not enter port if he could when he saw a storm coming on, and he clearly foresaw the ruin of the realm through Robert's intimacy with the Queen, who surrendered all affairs to him and meant to marry him. He said he did not know how the country put up with it, and he should ask leave to go home, although he thought they would cast him into the Tower first. He ended by begging me in God's name to point out to the Queen the effect of her misconduct, and persuade her not to abandon business entirely but to look to her realm; and then he repeated twice over to me that Lord Robert would be better in Paradise than here.'

Cecil also told de Quadra that 'Robert was thinking of killing his wife, who was publicly announced to be ill, although she was quite well and would take very good care they did not poison her'.[3]

It is generally assumed that this remarkable outburst was a piece of calculated indiscretion on Cecil's part; that, knowing Elizabeth would be unlikely to listen to him in her present mood, he had turned to de Quadra in the hope that an outsider might be able to bring her to her senses and persuade her to bring her faithful Secretary in out of the cold. This seems as good an explanation as any, for Cecil seldom said or did anything without a reason. De Quadra, naturally fascinated by what appeared to be an authentic glimpse behind the scenes, made suitably shocked noises and promised to speak to the Queen, though he felt bound to remark that she had never taken his advice in the past. But, before the Bishop could intervene, the bombshell had burst. According to de Quadra, the very day after his conversation with Cecil the Queen told him as she returned from hunting 'that Robert's wife was dead or nearly so' and asked him not to say anything about it. Some people have taken this to infer that Elizabeth told King Philip's envoy about Amy's death before it occurred, thus tacitly admitting guilty knowledge of murder. But, if that were the case, de Quadra is curiously uninformative about dates. We know he arrived at Windsor on Friday the sixth and wrote to Brussels on the following Wednesday, by which time the Queen had 'published' the news; but the ambassador nowhere gives the date of his interesting little chat with William Cecil. However, since the messenger from Cumnor reached the Castle during the morning of Monday, 9 September, it can reasonably be placed at some time during Sunday the eighth – the very day of the tragedy.

By a rather odd coincidence a member of Lord Robert's entourage, a kinsman of his named Thomas Blount, had left Windsor that Monday morning bound for Cumnor. Blount had not gone far before he encountered one Bowes, riding for his life in the opposite direction, who told him that their lady was dead 'by a fall from a pair of stairs'. A little surprisingly Blount did not turn back for further instructions but, leaving Bowes to break the news at Windsor, he continued on his journey. Nor did he hurry on to reach Cumnor that day. Instead, he put up for the night at Abingdon because, as he presently informed his master, he was desirous to hear 'what news went abroad in the country'. While he was at supper he therefore called for 'mine host' and, without revealing his identity, asked 'what news was thereabout'. The landlord was naturally full of 'the great misfortune'

which had befallen only three or four miles from the town – how my
Lord Robert Dudley's wife was dead by falling down a pair of stairs.
He was unable to supply any details and when Blount remarked that
'some of her people that waited on her' should be able to say what
had happened, he was told no, apparently not, for they were all at the
fair in Abingdon 'and none left with her'. Her ladyship, it seemed,
had risen up early and 'commanded all her sort to go to the fair and
would suffer none to tarry at home'.[4]

It sounded rather an odd story, but Thomas Blount would soon be
making his own enquiries on the spot and just at the moment he was
more interested in what was being said about Amy's death than in
any second-hand information the landlord could give him. What was
mine host's own opinion, he asked, and what was 'the judgement of
the people'? Some were disposed to say well and some evil, answered
mine host cautiously. For himself, he judged it a misfortune because
it had taken place in an honest gentleman's house.[5]

Blount had needed no telling that, in the circumstances, 'the judgement of the people' was going to be all-important and the same
thought was uppermost in the mind of the newly bereaved widower
at Windsor, who wrote frantically to his 'Cousin Blount' on the
Monday evening: 'The greatness and suddenness of the misfortune
doth so perplex me until I do hear from you how the matter standeth,
or how this evil should light upon me, considering what the malicious
world will bruit, as I can take no rest. And, because I have no way to
purge myself of the malicious talk that I know the wicked world will
use, but one which is the very plain truth to be known, I do pray you
as you have loved me, and do tender me and my quietness, and as
now my special trust is in you, that you will use all the devices and
means you can possibly for the learning of the truth, wherein have
no respect to any living person.'[6]

But truth was to prove an elusive commodity. In his first report
from Cumnor, Blount could only tell Lord Robert that the tale he
had already heard from Bowes and from the landlord of the inn at
Abingdon was confirmed by the household and by Amy's maid, Mrs
Pirto, who, according to Blount, 'doth dearly love her'. Everyone
agreed that her ladyship had insisted on sending all her servants out
on the day of her death 'and was so earnest to have them gone to the
fair, that with any of her sort that made reason for tarrying at
home she was very angry'. She had even quarrelled with Mrs Odingsells, who at first refused to go because Sunday was no day for a
gentlewoman to be seen gallivanting in the town. Amy had answered

The young Elizabeth,
aged about 14.

Thomas Seymour.

Erik of Sweden
by Steven van der Meulen.

Archduke Charles of Austria.

Left, Henry of Anjou.

Below, François, Duke of Alençon by Clouet.

ANNO ÆTATIS
SVÆ 31

Elizabeth, 'the Ermine Portrait'.

The Earl of Leicester
in his mid-forties,
artist unknown.

His second wife Lettice Knollys.

Elizabeth in old age, by an unknown artist.

Robert Devereux, Earl of Essex.

that Mrs Odingsells could do as she liked, but all her people should go and 'was very angry'. This was obviously considered uncharacteristic behaviour, and Blount remarked, 'Certainly, my lord, as little while as I have been here, I have heard divers tales of her that maketh me to judge her to be a strange woman of mind.' He had talked to the devoted Pirto, who should surely have known her mistress best, and went on: 'In asking Pirto what she might think of this matter, either chance or villainy, she said by her faith she doth judge very chance, and neither done by man or by herself.' Her lady, said Pirto, 'was a good virtuous gentlewoman, and daily would pray upon her knees'. Nevertheless, Pirto did let fall the possibly significant information that she had more than once heard the dead woman pray to God to deliver her from desperation. Blount pounced on this – then she might have had 'an evil toy' on her mind? 'No, good Mr Blount,' cried Pirto, 'do not judge so of my words; if you should so gather I am sorry I said so much!' It was not conclusive, of course – 'it passeth the judgement of man to say how it is' – but, all the same, Blount evidently believed that suicide could not be ruled out.

Robert had been insistent that the coroner's jury should be chosen from 'the discreetest and most substantial men . . . such as for their knowledge may be able to search thoroughly the bottom of the matter, and for their uprightness will earnestly and sincerely deal therein'. Blount was now able to tell him that the jury was already chosen and its members seemed to be 'as wise and as able men, being but countrymen, as ever I saw'. 'And for their true search,' he went on, ' . . . I have good hope they will conceal no fault, if any be; for as they are wise, so are they, as I hear, part of them very enemies to Anthony Forster. God give them, with their wisdom, indifferency, and then be they well chosen men.'[7]

This sounded a trifle ominous, but for the moment there was no more to be done. The Queen had sent Robert away to his house at Kew while the matter of his wife's death was investigated, and while the country thrummed with shocked speculation over this melodramatic climax to eighteen months of scandal-mongering the widower waited in painful suspense, being measured for mourning clothes and writing more anxious letters to Thomas Blount at Cumnor: 'Until I hear from you again how the matter falleth out in very truth, I cannot be in quiet.' He sent an urgent message to the jury that they were to do their duty without fear or favour and 'find it as they shall see it fall out'. There is no record that Robert ever expressed even a passing regret over his wife's death or showed any interest in Blount's guarded references to her 'strange mind'. He was quite simply obsessed with the necessity of proclaiming his own innocence by making it clear that he had nothing to hide and would welcome the fullest possible enquiry.[8]

Sometime during that frightening week Robert had received a visit of condolence from no less a person than Mr Secretary Cecil and wrote to him afterwards: 'I thank you much for your being here; and the great friendship you have showed toward me I shall not forget . . . I pray you let me hear from you what you think best for me to do (for the sooner you advise me, the more I shall thank you). Methinks I am here all this while as it were in a dream, and too far from the place where I am bound to be . . . I pray you help him that sues to be at liberty out of so great a bondage. Forget me not, though you see me not, and I will remember you and fail you not.'[9] Why it was that William Cecil had chosen to throw out a lifeline to the man he apparently regarded as his most dangerous enemy and whom he had recently been accusing of contemplating the murder which perhaps had now been committed, is something else which is by no means clear. But Cecil, a practised exponent of the art of political survival, was always a careful man who believed in taking out as much insurance as possible.

The Secretary's show of friendship had been a gleam of light and Robert received further comfort from Blount's second report, written on Friday, 13 September. It seemed that, although they had taken great pains to learn the truth, the jury – somewhat to their regret, in Blount's opinion – could find 'no presumptions of evil'. 'And,' Blount went on, 'if I judge aright, mine own opinion is much quieted; the more I search of it, the more free it doth appear unto me. I have almost nothing that can make me so much as think that any man should be the doer thereof, as, when I think your lordship's wife before all other women should have such a chance, the circumstances and as many things as I can learn doth persuade me that only misfortune hath done it and nothing else'.[10]

The inquest, as Blount had predicted, presently returned a verdict of misadventure and, on 22 September, Amy was buried in the church of St Mary the Virgin at Oxford with all the funereal pomp and ceremony due to her position. Officially the incident was closed, but few people believed that 'the very plain truth' or anything like it had been uncovered. How did Amy Dudley die? Had she been murdered by Robert's hired assassins – poisoned first, it was whispered, or stifled, and then arranged with a broken neck at the foot of that fatal staircase to make her death look like an accident? Had she committed suicide, driven to despair by the knowledge of her mortal illness, her husband's callous neglect and the terrible rumours which must have reached her? Or was the jury's verdict a true one after all? Modern medical research has revealed that in fifty per cent of cases of advanced breast cancer secondary deposits are present in the bones. The effect of such deposits in the spine is to make it extremely brittle – so brittle that the slightest stumble, even, as in Amy's case, the mere act of walking down a flight of stairs, could result in a spontaneous fracture of the vertebrae.[11] This suggestion, first put forward by Professor Ian Aird in 1956, is now generally accepted as the most likely explanation of the mystery and would certainly account for the curious fact that, although she had apparently suffered a fall violent enough to break her neck, the dead woman's headdress was undisturbed. But it still doesn't explain Amy's unusual behaviour on the day of her death. Why was she so determined to be alone that Sunday? Had she been planning to take her own life, or could she perhaps have been expecting a visitor? The question marks remain and, while it is only fair to remember that not one shred of hard evidence was ever produced to implicate Robert in murder, perhaps it is hardly surprising that in the autumn of 1560 the idea that such a suspiciously convenient death could have been accidental was greeted with widespread and cynical disbelief.

Nevertheless, by the end of September Robert was back at court, a free man in every sense of the word, and the world at large waited fascinated to see what would happen next. Bishop de Quadra, that disillusioned observer of the island scene, was not committing himself. He was not sure if the Queen intended to marry Robert at once or even if she would marry at all, as he did not think her mind was sufficiently fixed. But, as he told the Duchess of Parma, 'with these people it is always wisest to think the worst'.[12]

In France they were not merely thinking the worst, they were gleefully anticipating it, and the young Queen of Scots, so it was said, had exclaimed: 'So the Queen of England is to marry her horse-keeper, who has killed his wife to make room for her!' A remark which pretty well summed up opinion at the French court and elsewhere. Nicholas Throckmorton, Elizabeth's ambassador in Paris, was frantic with anxiety. 'I wish I were either dead or hence,' he wrote on 10 October, 'that I might not hear the dishonourable and naughty reports that are made of the Queen and the great joy among the French princes for the success they take it they are like to have in

England – not letting to speak of the Queen and some others that which every hair of my head stareth at and my ears glow to hear. I am almost at my wits' end and know not what to say. One laugheth at us, another threateneth, another revileth the Queen. Some let not to say : "What religion is this that a subject shall kill his wife and the Prince not only bear withal but marry with him?" If these slanderous bruits be not slaked, or if they prove true, our reputation is gone forever, war follows and utter subversion of the Queen and country.'[13]

At home, there was one man prepared to disregard gossip and scandal and all those nasty low-minded foreigners – a man prepared to keep his eye on the object, on the urgent and fundamental reason for the Queen's marriage. Thomas Radcliffe, Earl of Sussex, loathed Robert Dudley and could hardly bring himself to be civil to him in public, but he wrote to William Cecil that October: 'I wish not her Majesty to linger this matter of so great importance, but to choose speedily; and therein to follow so much of her own affection as [that] by the looking upon him whom she should choose, her whole being may be moved by desire; which shall be the readiest way, with the help of God, to bring us a blessed Prince.' If there had been other 'rightful inheritors' Sussex would not have advised such a desperate course, but seeing that Elizabeth was the country's 'ultimum refugium', and that 'no riches, friendship, foreign alliance or any other present commodity can serve our turn without issue of her body', he was ready to put aside his own feelings and prejudices and urge that 'if the Queen will love anybody, let her love where and whom she lists . . . And whomsoever she shall love and choose, him will I love, honour and serve to the uttermost.'[14]

Sussex found no supporters for this humane and generous attitude. Not even for the sake of a blessed prince would the English tolerate an upstart and a wife-murderer as their king, and Nicholas Throckmorton could hardly bring himself to contemplate the disastrous consequences of a Dudley marriage – 'the Queen our Sovereign discredited, condemned and neglected; our country ruined, undone and made prey'.

Throckmorton, writing to Cecil on 28 October, seems to have been genuinely afraid that the matter might be 'already determined, and so far past as advice will not serve', and yet two weeks earlier Cecil had told de Quadra that the Queen had now definitely decided not to marry Lord Robert.[15] Had she, at any time since the beginning of September, really considered it seriously? It is impossible to be absolutely certain, but the overwhelming probability is surely that she had not. If Amy had died peacefully in her bed, the Queen's decision might just conceivably have been different. But Amy dead as the result of a mysterious 'misadventure' presented just as insuperable an obstacle as Amy alive, and the verdicts of a dozen coroner's juries would not alter that. In any case, did Elizabeth need to marry Robert when she could have everything she apparently wanted from him – his daily companionship, his undivided attention and devotion – without marriage? Might there not, in fact, from the Queen's point of view, be a good deal to be said for keeping things as they were? As consort Robert would acquire independent power and status, as well as certain ungainsayable rights. As favourite, however much latitude she chose to allow him, he must in the last resort remain her creature, her servant and plaything.

This, of course, presupposes the situation which Elizabeth's contemporaries found so incomprehensible and which was admittedly an unusual one – an intimate relationship between a virile young man and a nubile young woman which yet was not based on physical love. For the answer to the question whether Elizabeth and Robert Dudley were lovers in the obvious sense is that they were almost certainly not. Such a thing could not have been concealed in the climate of the late fifties and early sixties when every aspect of the Queen's personal affairs was attracting the closest scrutiny of matchmaking ambassadors. Gossip that 'Lord Robert did swyve the Queen' and that she had borne him a child naturally continued, but there is not a shred of evidence to support it and Bishop de Quadra, who like all envoys of first-rate powers maintained a network of paid informers within the royal household, had seen no sign of such a thing and did not believe it.

As the weeks passed with no further alarming developments the crisis began gradually to go off the boil; but Nicholas Throckmorton, in his anxiety that the Queen should fully understand what foreign reaction to a Dudley marriage would be, sent his secretary, young Mr Jones, over to England to convey an urgent personal warning. Jones saw Elizabeth towards the end of November and reported that when he came 'to touch near the quick' the Queen stopped him. ' "I have heard of this before," quoth she, "and my ambassador need not have sent you withall," ' She then went on to explain that the whole matter of Amy Dudley's death had been carefully investigated 'and found to be not that which was reported'. Lord Robert had been at court at the time 'and none of his people at the attempt at his wife's house [which sounds rather as though Elizabeth suspected foul play of some kind]; and it fell out as should touch neither his honesty nor her own honour'.[16]

Jones was considerably reassured as a result of this interview. He thought the Queen did not look well – 'surely the matter of my Lord Robert doth much perplex her,' he told Throckmorton, 'and is never like to take place'. Talk of it had abated and, although Robert was still in high favour, favour should not, it seemed, be taken for granted. The Queen had promised him the earldom of Leicester, an honour which he greatly coveted, but Jones heard that when the letters patent for the creation were brought for Elizabeth's signature she had taken her penknife and 'cut them asunder', saying that the Dudleys had been traitors for three descents. Robert sulked and reproached her for her unkindness, but Elizabeth was in a teasing mood and would not relent, though she patted his cheek and said playfully, 'No, no, the bear and ragged staff [a reference to the Dudley crest, filched from the Neville family] are not so soon overthrown.' All the same, when some of Robert's friends urged her to marry him, she would only 'pup with her lips' and say she could not marry a subject; that would make her no better than the Duchess of Norfolk, for men would come asking for my lord's grace. It was pointed out that she could make her husband a king, but 'no,' said the Queen, 'that she would in no wise agree to'.[17]

And there the matter rested. William Cecil, now back in his accustomed place at the Queen's right hand, told Throckmorton at the end of December that, 'whatsoever reports and opinions be, I know surely that my lord Robert himself hath more fear than hope, and so doth the Queen give him cause'. But Robert had by no means given up hope and, in January 1561, de Quadra received a visit from his brother-in-law, Henry Sidney. After a good deal of beating about the bush Sidney finally came to the point which was, of course, a Dudley–Tudor alliance. Since de Quadra knew 'how much inclined the Queen was to the marriage' he was surprised that the ambassador had not thought of suggesting to King Philip this opportunity of winning Lord Robert's support for, if a hand were extended to him now, 'he would thereafter serve and obey your Majesty like one of your own vassals'.

De Quadra received this remarkable proposal with a good deal of reserve. What he had so far heard of the matter, he told Sidney, was of such a character that he had hardly ventured to write two lines to Spain about it nor, for that matter, had either the Queen or Lord

Robert said a word to him that he could write. He had no means of guessing the Queen's thoughts and, although his master was always anxious to be helpful, his advice had been consistently disregarded in the past. Sidney was obliged to admit this was true but, reported de Quadra, he went on to say 'that if I was satisfied about the death of Robert's wife, he saw no reason why I should hesitate to write the purport of this conversation to your Majesty, as, after all, although it was a love affair yet the object of it was marriage ... As regards the death of the wife, he was certain that it was accidental, and he had never been able to learn otherwise, although he had enquired with great care and knew that public opinion held to the contrary.'

Henry Sidney then began to drop broad hints that Elizabeth was anxious to take steps to remedy the religious disorders in the country, a task in which Lord Robert would willingly help her. But now, with popular suspicion so strong against him, so that 'even preachers in the pulpits discoursed on the matter in a way that was prejudicial to the honour and interests of the Queen', their marriage and any subsequent easing of the Catholics' position had become politically impossible. If, however, the Queen could be assured of the King of Spain's support, things would be very different and she and Robert would do everything they could to restore religion without delay.

De Quadra regarded Sidney as an honest and sensible man, but felt obliged to remind him of 'what happened with his wife in the matter of the Archduke when the Queen had deceived both of us'. The ambassador was determined not to be caught a second time. All the same, he told Philip: 'I have no doubt that if there is any way to cure the bad spirit of the Queen, both as regards religion and your Majesty's interests, it is by means of this marriage, at least while her desire for it lasts.'[19]

On 13 February, Sidney came to see de Quadra again, bringing Robert with him. Robert was in his most winning mood. He repeated everything his brother-in-law had said and promised that, if only Philip would advise the Queen to marry him, he would be the King's servant for life. De Quadra was still wary. He was not going to risk involving his master in what might easily turn out to be some kind of trick – not at least without more definite information. But what he could do was to see Elizabeth again and urge her yet once more to marry and settle down. Then, if Robert's name should come up, he would speak of him 'as favourably as he could wish'.[20]

This interview took place two days later and the Queen responded coyly to de Quadra's kite-flying. 'After much circumlocution,' he wrote, 'she said she wished to confess to me and tell me her secret in confession, which was that she was no angel, and did not deny that she had some affection for Lord Robert for the many good qualities he possessed, but she certainly had never decided to marry him or any-one else, although she daily saw more clearly the necessity for her marriage, and to satisfy the English humour it was desirable that she should marry an Englishman, and she asked me to tell her what your Majesty would think if she married one of her servitors.' De Quadra replied that he did not know and had not thought of asking, but he felt sure the King would be pleased to hear of her marriage, whoever she chose, as it was so important for the welfare of her kingdom. He also felt sure that Philip would be happy to hear of Lord Robert's good fortune, as he had always understood that the King had a great affection for him and generally held him in high esteem. The Queen, commented de Quadra, 'seemed as pleased at this as her position allowed her to be'. She said that when the time came she would speak to de Quadra again and would do nothing without Philip's advice and approval.[21]

The ambassador got the impression that she would have liked to go even further but, although he felt he had been right to allow her 'this little pleasure and hope', he did not relax his guard. In spite of Robert's repeated assurances that it was only 'timidity' and fear of what people would say which was holding Elizabeth back, and his solemn promises that once their marriage had taken place every-thing, including religion, would be placed in Philip's hands, de Quadra was not convinced. He had a nasty feeling that the whole ploy might in some way be designed to discredit Philip and the Catholic cause. Certainly he had seen no signs as yet of any relaxa-tion in the official attitude towards his co-religionists. On the con-trary, he reported that the sees of the dispossessed Catholic bishops had now been given to the greatest heretics, 'which is a very bad sign for the fulfilment of Lord Robert's promises'. In fact, the English Catholics were becoming disturbed by de Quadra's apparently grow-ing friendship with Lord Robert, so that the ambassador, who main-tained discreet contact with their leaders, felt obliged to reassure them privately that he was working in their interests and towards a restora-tion of the old faith.

Several weeks passed with no further developments, and de Quadra told Philip that Robert was 'very aggrieved and dissatisfied that the Queen should defer placing matters in your Majesty's hands' and had even fallen ill with annoyance! Then, about the middle of March,

William Cecil paid a visit to the Spanish embassy. It would be of great assistance to the Queen, he said, if the King of Spain could be persuaded to write to her advising her not to delay her marriage any longer and suggesting that, if she could not bring herself to accept any of her foreign suitors, she had better choose a gentleman of her own country whom Philip would befriend. This was all very well, but when de Quadra tried to find out if Cecil was speaking with authority or simply putting forward a plan of his own the Secretary hedged. The Queen was a modest maiden and reluctant to get married at all. It would not help to try to force her to propose these means and expedients herself, 'which would make her look like a woman who sought to carry out her desires and went praying people to help her.'[22]

Cecil went on to explain that, since Elizabeth was resolved not to do anything without the goodwill of her subjects, she wanted Philip's letter as an excuse for calling together a representative committee from both Houses of Parliament to lay the matter before them 'and with the accord of these deputies to arrange the marriage with Robert'. To present Robert Dudley to Parliament as the King of Spain's candidate would surely be the fastest way to kill the project stone dead, and de Quadra knew that Robert himself was violently opposed to such a course. 'The sum of it all', wrote the ambassador on 25 March, 'is that Cecil and these heretics wish to keep the Queen bound and subject to their will and forced to maintain their heresies.'[23]

This was quite possibly the very impression that Elizabeth intended to create. Exactly who was fooling whom in the elaborate charade being acted for de Quadra's benefit during the early part of 1561 is not entirely clear, but its underlying purpose was undoubtedly political and not unconnected with the reconvening of the Council of Trent. After a ten-year adjournment, this Great Council of the Church was about to make one last effort to repair the fractured unity of Christendom, and Pope Pius IV had made known his intention of inviting the Queen of England to send representatives to the negotiating-table. Elizabeth, acutely conscious of her country's vulnerable and isolated position, had always been careful in her dealings with the European Catholics never to seem to shut the door entirely on the possibility of reconciliation; while the Vatican, prompted by Philip, had so far been equally careful not to say or do anything which might antagonise her too severely. But if she refused to admit Abbé Martinengo, the papal nuncio now on his way to England bearing a papal olive-branch, it would be tantamount to a formal declaration that she had not only shut but finally locked the door on Rome. Certainly de Quadra regarded the reception of the Abbé as an important test of the Queen's good faith. The ambassador had no real idea what the outcome would be, but he thought there was still a chance that, with Philip's support, Elizabeth might be prepared to make a stand and free herself from 'the tyranny of the heretics'. Robert had recently been given new and more salubrious quarters next to the Queen's at Greenwich – a gesture which had apparently restored his health and spirits – and de Quadra himself took lodgings at Greenwich so as to be on hand when the nuncio arrived.[24]

Then, suddenly, the whole house of cards collapsed. During the second week of April there was a series of arrests among prominent Catholic sympathisers in London and, to his unspeakable annoyance, the Spanish ambasador found that he was being accused of complicity in a dangerous Catholic conspiracy against the Queen. Even worse, it was now being openly said that Philip had promised to help Elizabeth to marry her lover if she would agree to turn Catholic – just the kind of damaging talk de Quadra had been most anxious to avoid. The Queen soothed him slightly by assurances that she personally did not hold him responsible, but the nuncio's visit was off. In present circumstances it could only be regarded as provocative and might lead to unacceptable disturbance and disquietude. Besides, England could not agree to take part in the General Council as at present constituted. If a genuinely representative assembly, open to all Christian princes and independent of the Pope, were ever to be held in the future, then the Queen would be pleased to send ambassadors and learned men to explain and defend the Anglican viewpoint.[25]

Elizabeth's own sympathies always inclined towards the conservative and traditionalist, and her well-known prejudice against Calvinist or Puritan bigotry was often interpreted as undue leniency to the Catholic faction; but at the same time it is surely unthinkable that she ever for one moment seriously contemplated a return to Rome. It is equally unthinkable that Elizabeth Tudor ever for one moment even considered the abject course of begging Spanish protection to enable her to make a marriage which would have caused the deepest offence to every section of her own people. It therefore looks very much as if she deliberately took advantage of Lord Robert's consuming ambition and lack of any particular religious conviction to gain a political point. In short, that she tricked him into believing that she might for his sake be persuaded to surrender her freedom of action and to forfeit her subjects' love and respect.

Elizabeth was all her life a politician to her fingers' ends and it would have been entirely typical of her to use her nearest and dearest as a political weapon if she thought it necessary for her country's good. This was a fact which her nearest and dearest would simply have to live with. Elizabeth seldom or never gave anything for nothing. She was investing a good deal of emotional and material capital in Robert Dudley and she demanded a full and fair return. If this sometimes involved being made to look like a knave and a fool, then he must accept it as the price of his unique position as the Queen's 'brother and best friend'.

CHAPTER VIII

Without a Certain Heir,
Living and Known

In spite of their recent disappointment, Robert's dreams of winning the crown matrimonial and de Quadra's of using him to detach the Queen from the 'gang of heretics' who surrounded her proved remarkably tenacious of life. On 24 June, Robert gave a grand water-party on the Thames. De Quadra was among the guests and at one point during the afternoon found himself alone with Robert and Elizabeth on the deck of the vessel from which they were to watch the festivities. 'They began joking,' he wrote, 'which she likes to do much better than talking about business. They went so far with their jokes that Lord Robert told her that, if she liked, I could be the minister to perform the act of marriage and she, nothing loath to hear it, said she was not sure whether I knew enough English.' The ambassador let them have their fun and then tried to talk some sense into them. If they would only listen to him, they could extricate themselves from the tyranny of councillors like Cecil and his friends, and restore the country to peace and unity by reinstating the Catholic religion. (Like all Philip's envoys, de Quadra tended to overestimate the strength of Catholic feeling in England.) Once this was done, he went on, they could be married as soon as they liked and, with the King of Spain behind them, could snap their fingers at anyone who dared to object. De Quadra told Philip that he intended to persevere along these lines, for by keeping in with the Queen he would 'not only maintain her friendliness towards your Majesty, but have still some hopes of persuading her'.[1]

The Queen did not disillusion him. The longer Philip could be made to believe that her amorous desires might eventually overcome her fear of the heretics and lure her back into the orthodox fold, the better she would be suited – especially at a time when there might well be more trouble brewing north of the border. The young King of France had died the previous December and Mary Queen of Scots, a widow at eighteen, would now become a matrimonial prize second only to the Queen of England. This in itself was worrying, and so was the fact that Mary was about to return to her own kingdom, for who could tell what havoc the pretty creature might create among the volatile Scottish warlords? Who could tell how many simple men might begin to reflect, once she was back in their midst, on their queen's claims to her neighbour's throne and be 'carried away with vain hope and brought abed with fair words'? Mary herself was eloquent in her desire to be friends with her 'good sister and tender cousin' Elizabeth, but she was still refusing to ratify the Treaty of Edinburgh and Elizabeth was not impressed by fair words.[2]

The end of the summer brought the Queen another tiresome and possibly dangerous complication nearer home, when it came out that Lady Catherine Grey — heiress presumptive if the provisions of Henry VIII's will were to be regarded as binding — had married the Earl of Hertford without observing the courtesy of informing her sovereign lady. The matrons of the court had for some time been casting suspicious glances at Lady Catherine, and by August she was 'certainly known to be big with child' — a mishap which, in William Cecil's opinion, was a proof of God's displeasure. For the unhappy Lady Catherine, however, God's displeasure was of less immediate concern than Queen Elizabeth's, and of that the proof was unmistakable.

Elizabeth had never cared much for any of her Grey cousins and had never bothered to conceal her poor opinion of the Protestant heiress — a fact already noted with interest in certain quarters. Now she was furious at this evidence of flagrant deceit, disrespect and perhaps worse. Although it was no longer a punishable offence merely to marry a member of the royal family without the sovereign's consent, the Queen, with her own experience of the intrigues liable to surround the heir to the throne still fresh in her memory, suspected there was more to this tale of romance than met the eye. The young couple were therefore hustled into the Tower, pending an investigation of the circumstances surrounding their marriage, and Elizabeth's temper was not improved when Lady Catherine presently gave birth to a healthy son.

The affair occupied a good deal of attention during the autumn, but exhaustive enquiries failed to reveal anything more sinister than a quite astounding degree of irresponsibility on the part of the newly-weds. All the same, the Queen took a lot of convincing. Catherine's choice of husband had been particularly tactless, for Lord Hertford was a Seymour, son of the late Lord Protector Somerset, and the Seymours, as Elizabeth had good cause to know, had a long record of political ambition, besides being closely connected with the royal house. Elizabeth also knew that Catherine had a considerable following, that a number of influential people (including William Cecil) would have liked to see her officially recognized as the heiress presumptive. She was, after all, an Englishwoman born, a Protestant, and now she had proved her ability to bear sons. But anything which touched on the succession touched the Queen on her most sensitive spot. It was a matter which she regarded as coming entirely within the royal prerogative and over which she would tolerate no interference – even well-meant interference.

No evidence of conspiracy having come to light, Elizabeth proposed to deal with Catherine Grey by having her marriage declared invalid (or non-existent) and her infant a bastard. Since the clergyman who had performed the secret ceremony at Hertford's house the previous December had disappeared without trace and the only other witness, the bridgegroom's sister, Jane, had since died, this did not seem likely to present any insuperable difficulty – especially as Catherine had characteristically lost the only piece of documentary evidence she had possessed, a deed of jointure given her by her husband. The case was handed over to the ecclesiastical authorities and the culprits remained in gaol where, thanks to the indulgence of their guards, they later compounded their offence by producing another son.[3]

Any inclination Elizabeth might have felt to forgive her cousin's indiscretions was not increased by the fact that there was widespread sympathy for the plight of the young Hertfords. Their romantic story had touched the imagination of a sentimental public and it was generally held that their inability to prove their marriage was more their misfortune than their fault. Besides, it was argued, the solution to the difficulty lay in the Queen's own hands. She had only to do the obvious sensible thing – get married and start a family herself – and any threat to her security posed by Catherine Grey would vanish like snow in summer.

But there was no sign that the Queen intended to do the obvious sensible thing. On the contrary, for there were not even any negotiations currently in progress. Archduke Charles had gone into cold storage; Elizabeth had long since refused the Earl of Arran, to the annoyance and disappointment of the Scottish Protestants; and she had now finally sent Eric of Sweden, the most persistent of her foreign suitors, about his business in a bluntly worded letter which admitted of no misunderstanding.[4]

Lord Robert, on the other hand, was still her constant companion and the horrid possibility of a Dudley marriage was by no means a dead issue. Robert himself revived it in January 1562 by renewing his request that the King of Spain should be asked to write to the Queen in his favour. This time there were no large promises about restoring the Catholic faith, but Robert did drop a hint that the French were making him 'great offers'. De Quadra replied that, since Elizabeth already knew his king was anxious to see her wedded and had a high opinion of Lord Robert, it seemed unnecessary to ask him for a personal letter. There was no doubt about Philip's goodwill – the problem, observed the ambassador, lay rather in persuading the Queen to act and he offered to raise the subject with her again.

When de Quadra saw Elizabeth she told him that, whatever the world might think, she was 'as free from any engagement to marry as the day she was born'. However, she had quite made up her mind not to accept any man she did not already know and realised this might mean she would have to marry an Englishman, 'in which case she thought she could find no person more fitting than Lord Robert'. She would like all friendly princes, but especially Philip, to write advising her to take Robert so that, if she ever felt disposed to it, people could not say she had married him to satisfy her own desires but instead had followed the advice of her princely friends and relatives. This, she added hastily, was what Robert wanted. She asked nothing for herself but did not see that Philip risked anything by complying with Robert's request, even if the marriage never took place.

But de Quadra had smelt a large rat. He believed all this anxiety to extract a letter from Philip was simply so that it could be used for propaganda purposes to show the English Catholics that the King of Spain no longer cared about their fate; that he was prepared to countenance the Queen's marriage, even to such a dubious character as Robert Dudley, just to keep her sweet and without demanding any preconditions on their behalf; that, in short, Philip was ready to remain friendly with the heretic régime under almost any circumstances. The ambassador, therefore, tried to turn the matter off 'in a joking way', telling Elizabeth not to dilly dally any longer but satisfy Lord Robert at once, as she knew how glad his king would be.[5]

Reports that the Queen had followed de Quadra's advice were current during the summer, and in June there was an especially circumstantial story going about that she and Robert had been secretly married during a visit to the Earl of Pembroke's house. (Pembroke was by way of being a friend of Robert's.) It was all over town that the wedding had actually taken place – and not only in town. The Queen herself told de Quadra with a certain amount of glee that her own ladies had asked her if they were now to kiss Lord Robert's hand as well as hers. She also told him, 'with an oath', that if she had to marry an Englishman it would only be Robert, and Robert was saying the Queen had promised to marry him, 'but not this year'.[6]

And so it went on. De Quadra got into trouble with the Council for passing on the secret-wedding story, an accusation he indignantly denied. He had never told anyone that the Queen was married, he said, and was only sorry that he could not do so truthfully. De Quadra was not alone in this regret. Many serious-minded Englishmen were becoming increasingly disturbed by the Queen's obstinate, apparently frivolous refusal to look ahead. She would be twenty-nine on her next birthday – more than time she settled down. Indeed, if she was to have children, there was really no time to be lost.

While the serious-minded continued to worry about the future in a general way, and to tell one another that something ought to be done to settle the succession, the reality of the danger which threatened England's security was dramatically brought home even to the most thoughtless. During October the Queen was in residence at Hampton Court when she succumbed to a virulent strain of smallpox which had already infected several of the ladies of her circle. The rash would not come out, Elizabeth's fever mounted and she was soon desperately ill. Cecil, summoned from London at midnight, reached the palace in the small hours of the sixteenth, and as the Queen lay unconscious, perhaps dying, the Council went into emergency session to discuss the horrifying crisis which faced the country.

According to de Quadra, out of the fifteen or sixteen members present, 'there were nearly as many different opinions about the succession to the Crown'.[7] In fact, the Council seems to have been split more or less down the middle. One group, which almost certainly included William Cecil, wanted to follow King Henry's will and name Lady Catherine Grey; others, 'who found flaws in the will', pressed the claims of Henry Hastings, Earl of Huntingdon, who could boast double descent from Edward III and was known to be a reliable Protestant. The Earls of Bedford and Pembroke supported Huntingdon, and so – although they were not council members – did the Duke of Norfolk and Lord Robert Dudley. Huntingdon was married to Lord Robert's sister Catherine, and de Quadra thought that Robert would be ready to back his brother-in-law by force of arms. A third and smaller group, led by the old Marquis of Winchester who had already survived the alarums and excursions of three reigns, urged against too much haste and suggested referring the matter to a committee of jurists, who could examine the rights of the various claimants and advise the Council accordingly. No one, it seemed, within the precincts of Hampton Court had mentioned the name of Mary Queen of Scots, and de Quadra reported that the Catholics, too, were divided – some favouring the Queen of Scots, others preferring her aunt, Margaret Lennox, who had been born in England and was considered to be 'devout and sensible'.[8]

While the Council was still deliberating, Elizabeth recovered consciousness and, in her confused and feverish state, begged the anxious throng at her bedside to make Robert Dudley protector of the kingdom, with a title and an income of £20,000 a year. She swore, in what she believed might be her last moments, that although she loved and had always loved Robert dearly, 'as God was her witness, nothing improper had ever passed between them', and asked that the groom who slept in his room should be given a pension of £500 a year. 'Everything she asked was promised,' reported de Quadra, 'but will not be fulfilled.'[9]

Only one thing emerged with any certainty out of the terror and confusion of that dreadful day; if the Queen had died – and she was 'all but gone' – she would have left a vacuum which would rapidly have filled with political anarchy, with bitter faction-fighting and most probably civil war. To the unspeakable relief of the Council, the nobility and the country at large, the Queen recovered. She even escaped the dreaded disfigurement of smallpox and within a surprisingly short space of time she was up and about again and once more in full command. But the nation had had a fright it would not soon forget and, before the end of November, de Quadra heard that groups of gentlemen were meeting under the auspices of the Earl of Arundel to discuss the succession. When Elizabeth heard about this she was furious and was said to have wept with rage. She summoned Arundel and they appear to have had a first-class row, the Earl telling her that, if she wanted to govern the country by passion, he could assure her that the nobility would not allow it. The succession was a matter which affected them vitally and they had every right to be concerned.[10]

As well as a mutinous nobility, Elizabeth now had to face another Parliament – something she would have avoided if she possibly could, knowing what opportunities that would provide for bringing organized pressure to bear on her. Unhappily she could not avoid it.

She needed money. The Scottish adventure of 1560, although it had given value for money, had been expensive and now England was involved in another, equally expensive but far less well-judged foray on behalf of the French Huguenots. So the writs went out in November and, by the second week of January 1563, the members were gathering at Westminster with one thought uppermost in all their minds.

The first indication of the general mood came even before the official opening of the session, in the sermon preached at Westminster Abbey by Alexander Nowell, Dean of St Paul's, during the preliminary church service. Dr Nowell, never one to mince his words, reminded his hearers that, just as Queen Mary's marriage had been a terrible plague to all England, so now the want of Queen Elizabeth's marriage and issue was like to prove as great a plague. 'If your parents had been of your mind, where had you been then?' he demanded of the Queen sitting below him in the congregation. 'Or what had become of us now?' This was plain speaking and the Dean went on to ram his point home. 'When your Majesty was troubled with sickness, then I heard continual voices and lamentations, saying: "Alas! What trouble shall we be in? ... For the succession is so uncertain and such division for religion! Alack! what shall become of us?"' [11]

What indeed? And the fears of the nation, as reflected by its elected representatives, were succintly expressed in a petition presented to the Queen by the Speaker of the House of Commons on 28 January. They foresaw with awful clarity 'the unspeakable miseries of civil wars, the perilous intermeddlings of foreign princes with seditious, ambitious and factious subjects at home, the waste of noble houses, the slaughter of people, subversion of towns ... unsurety of all men's possessions, lives and estates' if the sovereign were to die without a known heir, and pointed out that 'from the Conquest to this present day the realm was never left as now it is without a certain heir, living and known'. [12] The Commons still wanted Elizabeth to marry, of course, but it was significant that, since the 'great terror and dreadful warning' of her illness, the emphasis of their anxiety had shifted. Whether she married or not, they wanted the succession to be settled — now.

The Lords' petition, delivered a couple of days later by the Lord Keeper, Nicholas Bacon, still put marriage first and begged 'that it would please your Majesty to dispose yourself to marry, where it shall please you, to whom it shall please you, and as soon as it shall please you'. But their lordships, too, were acutely worried about the succession and understandably so in a society where, as they grimly reminded the Queen, 'upon the death of princes the law dieth'. All the continuity of order and government depended on the peaceful transition from one reign to another, for with the death of the sovereign Parliament was automatically dissolved and could only be summoned again by the authority of the Crown. Nor would there be any council, judges, magistrates or royal officials of any kind – their commissions, too, automatically expired with the Crown. Without a known heir, ready and waiting to take over, the country would lapse into chaos where 'strength and will' must rule, with all the suffering, bloodshed and destruction that implied. It was a prospect calculated to terrify the stoutest hearted and the Lords ended with an urgent plea for immediate and serious consideration of the problem, so that 'good effect and conclusion may grow thereof before the end of the session of this Parliament'.[13]

Replying to the Commons, Elizabeth told them that she knew she was as mortal as the next woman. There was no need to keep reminding her about it. Nor was there any need to remind her of her responsibilities. She knew that she must seek to discharge herself of the 'great burthen' God had laid upon her. She quite understood the members' anxiety and did not take it amiss, but they could hardly expect an off-the-cuff answer 'in this so great and weighty a matter' which would need much thought and 'further advice'. In any case, they surely knew her well enough by now to trust her to look after them and to be 'neither careless nor unmindful' of their future welfare. 'And so I assure you all', she concluded 'that, though after my death you may have many stepdames, yet shall you never have a more natural mother than I mean to be unto you all.'[14]

If de Quadra is to be trusted, the Queen expended less tact on the Lords. According to him, she was very angry 'and told them that the marks they saw on her face were not wrinkles, but the pits of smallpox, and that although she might be old God could send her children as he did to St Elizabeth, and they [the lords] had better consider well what they were asking, as, if she declared a successor, it would cost much blood to England'.[15]

In spite of the depth of feeling on the subject, the succession was not openly debated, nor, in spite of a good deal of private agitation, was it officially referred to again until Parliament was prorogued at Easter. Then, in the presence of both Houses, Nicholas Bacon read a message from the Queen, written in her own hand and containing what might be construed as a conditional promise to get married in the not too distant future. Elizabeth still preferred spinsterhood for herself 'as a private woman, yet', she went on, 'do I strive with myself to think it not meet for a Prince. And if I can bend my liking to your need, I will not resist such a mind.' As regards the succession, she would not be drawn, taking refuge behind a baffling smoke-screen of words whose only discernible meaning seemed to be that the Queen did not feel the time was ripe for a decision. 'But', her latest 'answer answerless' concluded, 'I hope I shall die in quiet with *nunc dimittis*, which cannot be without I see some glimpse of your following surety after my graved bones.'[16]

A large part of Elizabeth's lifelong reluctance to have a named heir was rooted in her own experience during Mary's reign, but that was not the whole story. Always the keynote of her political philosophy was to keep things fluid – never, if humanly possible, to allow a situation to coalesce to the point where a decision had to be taken. People who made decisions also made mistakes, they limited their own freedom of action and they drove other people into making decisions – and mistakes. In the matter of the succession the Queen believed, and she was probably right, that any attempt to 'solve' the problem would have encouraged rather than disarmed faction and controversy. Perhaps more to the point, she did not regard it as a matter which was properly open to arbitrary settlement. The crown was not, after all, a piece of real estate to be bestowed according to personal or political convenience. The issue might have been clouded by religious passion and by King Henry's unfortunate will, but no one could deny that, out of the dozen or so persons of royal descent alive in the 1560s, Mary Queen of Scots had far and away the strongest hereditary claim to be recognised as heiress presumptive.

Elizabeth herself never denied it. She had already told the Scottish Secretary of State, William Maitland of Lethington, in private conversation that she considered Mary, her cousin and next kinswoman, to be her natural and lawful successor. 'I for my part', she said, 'know none better, nor that myself would prefer to her.' But she would not, despite everything Mary and Maitland could say or do to persuade her, agree to make the Queen of Scots her heir 'by order of Parliament'. When Maitland had urged that settling the succession on Mary would only cement the friendship between the two queens, Elizabeth promptly disabused him of any such sentimental notion. 'Think you that I could love my winding sheet?' she asked with brutal frankness. She had no illusions about the 'natural inconstancy' of men and nothing could shake her conviction that, the moment 'a certain successor' had been named, every restless, discontented or disappointed spirit in the kingdom, everyone with a real or imagined grievance, would turn towards the heir as towards the rising sun 'in hope then to be in better case'. 'So long as I live,' declared Elizabeth Tudor, 'I shall be Queen of England. When I am dead, they shall succeed that have the most right.'[17]

There, in the autumn of 1561, the matter had rested and there the Queen would infinitely have preferred to leave it. Her instinct was to do nothing, to go on gambling on her own survival until such time as a natural solution to the problem presented itself. But in the spring of 1563 things looked rather different and Elizabeth was undoubtedly troubled over what to do for the best. She could sympathise with her people's fears about the future and was far from insensitive to the pressure being exerted on her. Perhaps, too, her recent brush with death had shaken her more than she cared to admit. One thing was certain – if any way out of the present *impasse* were to be found, it would have to involve the Queen of Scots. Nothing, it appeared, was ever going to persuade Elizabeth even to consider the claims of any other contender in the succession stakes.

Mary was twenty now and had been a widow for just over two years. This was not a state of affairs likely to continue for ever and a great deal, if not everything, would depend on the identity of her second husband. There had been talk of a Spanish or Habsburg alliance for the Scottish Queen – the name of that useful stand-by Archduke Charles had been mentioned, and so had Philip's psychopathic son Don Carlos – but Elizabeth did not think Mary would marry to disoblige her, or at least not while she still had any hope of cajoling her into changing her mind about the succession. So, if a suitable, really trustworthy husband could be found, then maybe something could be arranged. Elizabeth had evidently begun to think along these lines quite early in the year, for it was in March, while Parliament was still sitting, that she first broached the matter to Maitland of Lethington, who happened to be in London again.

The plan itself – that Mary should agree to accept a consort of Elizabeth's choice in return for a promise of recognition as Elizabeth's heiress – might indeed have offered a possible solution, or at any rate a basis for negotiation. Unfortunately, Elizabeth's choice appeared so preposterous as to put the whole scheme right out of court from the start. De Quadra, who had the story from the Scottish Secretary himself, passed it on to Philip in a despatch dated 28 March. It seemed that the Queen had told Maitland 'that if his mistress would take her advice and wished to marry safely and happily she would give her a husband who would ensure both, and this was Lord Robert, in whom nature had implanted so many graces that if she wished to marry she would prefer him to all the princes in the world'. William Maitland was a shrewd politician and practised diplomat, but the very thought of that shop-soiled and controversial widower, Robert Dudley, sharing the throne of Scotland caused him to gag almost visibly. All the same, he managed to respond with a nicely barbed compliment. It was certainly a great proof of the love the Queen of England bore his queen if she was willing to give her a thing she prized so much, but he felt sure that Mary, even if she loved Lord Robert as dearly as Elizabeth did, would not wish to deprive her cousin of the joy and solace she derived from his company. Elizabeth did not take the hint. It was a pity, she mused, that Ambrose Dudley (Robert's elder brother, now restored to the dignity of Earl of Warwick) did not possess Robert's charm and good looks, for then she and Mary could each have had one of them. This was too much for Maitland. If the Queen of England could make tasteless jokes on such a serious subject, then so could he. Elizabeth had better marry Robert herself 'and then when it should please God to call her to himself, she could leave the Queen of Scots heiress both to her kingdom and her husband' – that way Lord Robert could hardly fail to have children by one or other of them.[18]

Maitland could not believe that Elizabeth was serious, but apparently she was – at any rate, she kept returning to her bizarre suggestion. Thomas Randolph, the English agent in Edinburgh, was instructed to let Mary know that, if she would leave her marriage in Elizabeth's hands, the Queen would be as good as a mother to her and at last, in the spring of 1564, Randolph, much to his embarrassment, received orders to propose Lord Robert officially to the Queen of Scots.

Mary's public reaction was polite but unenthusiastic. Was it comformable to Elizabeth's promise to treat her as a daughter, to offer to match her to a subject? she asked. Supposing Elizabeth were to get married herself and have children, what would Scotland have gained then? However, she promised to think the matter over and discuss it with her advisers.[19] In private, she was highly sceptical and more than inclined to take offence. If the proposal had been accompanied by a guarantee of recognition of her right to the reversion of her cousin's throne, the Queen of Scots might have swallowed her natural umbrage at being offered her cousin's discarded lover – the notorious horsekeeper no less. But it was never Elizabeth's way to give guarantees and Mary could not rid herself of the suspicion that she was being hoaxed, that this was some kind of tease designed to make her look foolish before the world and perhaps spoil her chances of making a more worthy marriage. Mary was not alone in her suspicions and many people since have found it extremely difficult to accept that Elizabeth ever really meant to part with her favourite man – and not merely part with him but hand him over to another woman, younger, prettier and her most dangerous rival.

Had she ever meant it seriously? Where Elizabeth is concerned it is never wise to be too certain of anything and her thought processes could be as convoluted as her prose style. But the original idea, born out of a genuine dilemma, had obviously been worth exploring. It would at least demonstrate that the Queen was not shutting her eyes to the problem, that she was honestly trying to find a solution; it would show the Scots that she was prepared to take a constructive interest in their queen's future and it might buy valuable time. Such a marriage would remove the threat of another foreign power establishing itself on England's back doorstep and would bring the youthful Mary firmly under English control. In the last resort what mattered to Elizabeth was the security of her throne and the peace and unity of her realm. If she could have been assured that her peculiar plan would achieve these ends, there is no real reason to assume that she would not have gone through with it, whatever the personal sacrifice involved.

She certainly continued to behave as though she meant it. When the Scottish courtier and diplomat James Melville came south in September 1564, Elizabeth told him that, if she had ever wanted to take a husband, she would have chosen Lord Robert. 'But being determined to end her life in virginity, she wished that the queen her sister should marry him, as meetest of all other and with whom she could find in her heart to declare the queen second person rather than any other.' For, she explained, if Mary were matched with Robert Dudley, 'it would best remove out of her mind all fear and suspicion to be offended by usurpation before her death; being assured that he was so loving and trusty that he would never give his consent nor suffer such thing to be attempted during her time'.[20] Robert was at last to get his peerage, to make the Queen of Scots 'think the more of him', and Melville had to stay and witness his investiture as Earl of Leicester and Baron Denbigh. The new earl conducted himself with very proper gravity and decorum throughout the ceremony but the Queen, helping to put on his robes, rather spoilt the solemn effect by putting a hand down his neck 'to tickle him smilingly'.[21]

Discussion of the marriage continued in a rather desultory fashion. Maitland and some others were coming round to the idea, but Mary remained lukewarm and, although she professed herself willing to be guided by Elizabeth over her choice of husband, it was clear that the Queen of Scots would not commit herself until she had seen the colour of the Queen of England's money. In other words, she wanted a definite undertaking, signed and sealed, about the succession. But Elizabeth, who preferred to deal obliquely, in hints, allusions and tacit understandings, would not oblige.

Given the fog of distrust which hung heavily between the two sides, there was probably never much real chance of reaching an agreement, and another obstacle lay in the attitude of the bridegroom-elect. The Earl of Leicester was not at all grateful for the kind plans being made for his advancement. On the contrary, he viewed them with consternation. He did not in the least wish to marry the Queen of Scots and be banished to the barbaric north. He wanted to stay at home and marry the Queen of England and, if Mary can be believed, he wrote to her secretly some time that winter to tell her that the project was nothing but a trick intended to discourage other suitors.

Nevertheless, another suitor was about to make his appearance on the scene. Henry Stuart, Lord Darnley, was Mary's first cousin – his mother, Margaret Lennox, being the daughter of Margaret Tudor's second marriage who had herself married into a collateral branch of the Stuart family. Mary and Darnley were therefore doubly related and the young man, through his combined Tudor, Stuart and Hamilton ancestry, stood very close to both the English and Scottish thrones. The cousins' names had been briefly linked during the first weeks of Mary's widowhood, and the Countess of Lennox, an ambitious and doting mamma, had been scheming unsuccessfully to make a match between them ever since. Queen Elizabeth knew this and it has always been something of a mystery why, in the circumstances, she allowed Lord Darnley to travel to Scotland in February 1565 – apparently accepting the not very convincing excuse that his presence there was necessary for the settling of some family business. In fact, so odd did it seem that some people later wondered if Elizabeth had had a sinister purpose. It is pretty well impossible now to unravel the dense cocoon of intrigue enveloping the whole affair, but it seems highly probable that Robert Dudley was working with the Lennox family behind Elizabeth's back and that it was he who talked her into letting Darnley go.

The Queen may have been genuinely deceived but, in view of her preternaturally sensitive antennae for matters of this kind, it is not very likely. More credibly, she may well have come to the conclusion by this time that her own plan was not going to work out – she told the Spanish ambassador that it failed because Robert had not consented – and she may even have decided that she could not, after all, bear to part with him. At the same time, she obviously could not expect to prevent Mary from marrying altogether. Darnley was technically her subject, having been born and brought up in England, and encouraged by Robert she may have seen him as a possible alternative. Mary had not so far shown any signs of interest in her young relative – Darnley was three years her junior and, apart from his breeding and rather girlish good looks, was of no particular account – but if she were now to take a fancy to him, then perhaps a marriage might be arranged. On suitable terms, of course. It would, at least, be preferable to another foreign connection.

But, if Elizabeth was reasoning along these lines, she failed to reckon with Mary's obstinacy when it came to getting her own way or with the strength of her biological urges. The Queen of Scots suffered from none of her English cousin's mysterious hang-ups on the subject of marriage. At twenty-one she was a warm-blooded, very normal young woman, impatient for love. Her first reaction to Darnley was favourable – he was 'the lustiest and best proportioned long man' she had seen – and before many weeks had gone by the Queen and her cousin were inseparable.

Mary did not guess that beneath the surface of this tall handsome princeling, with his pretty manners and courtly accomplishments, lay a spoilt, loutish, unstable youth with all the makings of a vindictive bully. Since her return home the young Queen of Scotland had often been lonely. She missed the brilliance and the civilised gaiety of the French court, and she had had to put up with a good deal of John Knox's conversation. Darnley crossed her path at a time of mounting disappointment and frustration and it is not in the least surprising that she should have seen him as an answer to prayer. But it was extremely unfortunate that she should have allowed her infatuation to blind her to all considerations of statecraft, of caution or even of plain common sense. Opposition to the match, of which there was plenty, only hardened her resolve and she quarrelled disastrously with her powerful kinsman, the Earl of Moray, who had so far guarded and guided her through the bloodstained jungle of Scottish politics. Nor, it seemed, did she any longer care if she offended Queen Elizabeth.

Queen Elizabeth was – or, at least, professed to be – deeply offended and promptly clapped the intriguing Lady Lennox into the Tower; but a suspicion persisted that she, or some other 'great person', had deliberately sent Darnley to Scotland in the hope of trapping Mary into an unhappy and demeaning marriage. William Cecil regarded the projected union of these two strong contenders for the English succession with deep misgiving – believing that it would inevitably comfort and encourage 'all such as be affected to the Queen of Scots, either for herself or for the opinion of her pretence to this crown or for the desire to have a change of the form of religion in this realm'.[22]

Thomas Randolph in Edinburgh believed that Mary had been bewitched and frankly despaired of her future, finding her 'so altered with affection towards Lord Darnley that she hath brought her honour in question, her estate in hazard, her country to be torn in pieces! I see also', he went on, 'the amity between the countries like to be dissolved, and great mischiefs like to ensue. To whom this may chiefly be imputed, what crafty subtlety or devilish device hath brought this to pass, I know not, but woe worth the time! (and so shall both England and Scotland say) that ever the Lord Darnley did set foot in this country.' Darnley's overweening arrogance was already making him intolerable to all honest men, but Mary, transported by love, would heed no warning, listen to no advice. Randolph could only speculate gloomily on what would become of her or what her life with such a husband would be and was moved to genuine pity for 'the lamentable estate of this poor Queen'.[23] She was so changed, he wrote, that she hardly seemed the same woman. 'Her majesty is laid aside – her wits not what they were – her beauty another than it was; her cheer and countenance changed into I wot not what.'[24]

Few people would have predicted a happy outcome for the marriage solemnised in the Chapel Royal at Holyrood House on 31 July 1565; but equally no one foresaw that it would end so soon and so melodramatically, or that it would have such far-reaching long-term consequences for both England and Scotland.

CHAPTER IX

Talk Is All of the Archduke

So for better or worse, the Queen of Scots was married while the Queen of England was still a maid and, at over thirty, in danger of becoming an old maid. Surely, people asked themselves, surely she must now recognise the urgent necessity of acquiring a husband before it was too late to provide the country with an heir no one could dispute? And in 1565 it did look rather as though Mary Stuart's marriage was forcing Elizabeth to reconsider her position. But in fact she had been reconsidering her position, or at least seeking to reopen certain avenues of approach, for nearly two years. Sooner or later she would have to face Parliament again and, if she was to avert a major confrontation with that increasingly vociferous body, would have to show that some attempt was being made to redeem the promise given to both Houses at Easter 1563.

In the autumn of 1563, therefore, William Cecil had been given the go-ahead to start the first cautious moves towards a possible resumption of negotiations with the Habsburg family. It all had to be done with exquisite tact. On no account must Elizabeth appear too eager and thus lose her initial advantage in the ritual dance of diplomatic courtship. On the contrary, elaborate precautions must be taken to conceal her interest in the affair. So Cecil wrote to Strasbourg to Dr Christopher Mundt, for many years the English government's agent and general go-between in German affairs. Mundt contacted the Duke of Württemberg, a close friend of the Imperial family, mentioning that, for various reasons, he personally believed this might be a propitious moment for raising the English marriage project again; and the Duke wrote to the Emperor, mentioning that he had recently received a visit from his old acquaintance Dr Mundt who, amongst other things, had discussed with him how 'the action of a marriage between Your Imperial Majesty's son, the Archduke Charles and the Queen of England, might best be resumed'.[1]

Although he was too much of a gentleman to say so, the Emperor probably had little difficulty in making an accurate guess as to the real origin of this new initiative. His reaction was guarded but sufficiently favourable to encourage the Duke of Württemberg to send an envoy to London in January 1564 – ostensibly to take the Queen a present of Lutheran books but actually to explore the situation on the spot and report accordingly. This individual, a Frisian who rejoiced in the name of Ahasverus Allinga, found the court at Windsor and on the day after his arrival had a very private interview with Elizabeth at which only Cecil and two maids of honour were present.

After listening patiently to a long harangue on the manifold advantages of marriage in general and marriage to the Archduke in particular, the Queen remarked that it was unnecessary to advance so many reasons at present, 'for she would never be induced by any appeals to reason but only by stern necessity, as she had already inwardly resolved that if she ever married it would be as Queen and not as Elizabeth'. There followed a somewhat inconclusive argument about whose fault it was that negotiations had been broken off last time. Elizabeth blamed the Emperor who, as she said, was behaving like an old woman and complained that he had treated her very badly over the matter of his son's visit to England. What did emerge with absolute clarity was that the Queen remained as determined as ever to have a good look at Charles before she committed herself to anything, and that the first move towards reopening negotiations would have to come from the Emperor. Elizabeth could not begin again 'without covering herself with ignominy' and was certainly not going to fall into the trap of declaring that she wanted to marry the Archduke. If she were to follow her own inclinations, she would far rather be a beggarwoman and single than a queen and married. Only necessity, she repeated, would ever induce her to marry.[2]

After this, Ahasverus Allinga was, not surprisingly, so discouraged that he told Cecil he could see no point in pursuing discussions any further. Not at all, replied the Secretary. The Queen had told him how much she had enjoyed the conversation and he believed she was by no means disinclined to the marriage. Allinga went home to Württemberg, no doubt to ponder on the peculiar mating habits of the English, and there for the moment the matter rested. Then, in July, the Emperor Ferdinand died – an event which might provide the opportunity for making a fresh start.

That autumn the talk in London was all of the Archduke, of how an important embassy would soon be going to offer condolences and congratulations to the new Emperor (he was Maximilian, eldest of

Ferdinand's three sons), and at the same time to reanimate the Austrian marriage. But somehow argument and confusion over who should be sent to Vienna prolonged themselves into October, and in early November Christopher Mundt was writing again to Württemberg to tell the Duke that the Queen of England had been expecting Maximilian to return his father's insignia of the Garter, as was customary. It seemed that the neglect of this courtesy had caused Elizabeth to delay sending her own emissaries, and Mundt warned that these unfortunate hesitations and misunderstandings might prove fatal to the happy outcome of a connection so honourable to Christendom and greatly desired by the English nobility.[3]

The Queen gave her nobility another nasty fright in December by falling 'perilously sick' with an attack of enteritis. She recovered quickly but, as William Cecil told his crony Sir Thomas Smith, ambassador in Paris, 'for the time she made us sore afraid'. Cecil had always been in the forefront of those urging matrimony on the reluctant Elizabeth, praying that God would direct her heart to procure a father for her children. Now he prayed that the Almighty would take an even closer interest in the matter and 'lead by the hand some meet person to come and lay hand on her to her contentation'. If that were to happen, he told Smith, he could wish himself more health to enjoy the benefits he trusted would follow. 'Otherwise, I assure you, as now things hang in desperation, I have no comfort to live.'[4]

Cecil seems to have believed, although the wish may have been father to the thought, that the Queen was now thinking seriously about a foreign alliance, and during the early part of 1565 another project came under discussion. This time the suggested bridegroom was Charles IX of France but, apart from the other obvious difficulties, the fact that the King of France was fifteen years old to Elizabeth's thirty-one did not really make it seem a very likely proposition. Elizabeth herself remarked drily that people would say she was marrying her grandson. However, the Queen was never averse to being courted and, in view of the current trend of affairs in Scotland, even the most improbable-sounding Anglo-French connection could be turned to use. So there was much solemn confidential talk about young Charles' remarkable precocity, about an exchange of portraits, perhaps a secret exchange of visits. But, although these conversations were carried on with every outward appearance of serious intent, and were spun out over the best part of six months, the Austrian Archduke remained unchallenged in his apparently permanent position as the Queen of England's chief suitor.

In May 1565 another Imperial envoy arrived in London. The outward purpose of Adam Zwetkovich's visit was to take advantage of the proffered opening and return the late Emperor's Garter insignia. In reality, as everyone knew, he had come to make one more attempt to revive the marriage negotiations. Always provided, so his instructions ran, that he was satisfied with regard to the Queen's unspotted virtue – the Habsburgs still had misgivings about the real nature of her relationship with Robert Dudley.

Robert, of course, was the joker in the pack. If Elizabeth married the Archduke (or anyone else, for that matter), his unique position as her 'brother and best friend' would be gone, and even the fact that he now had his earldom and a seat on the Council would not compensate for its loss. Let him once be ousted from his place at the Queen's side and his enemies would close in for the kill. He could therefore be expected to fight the Austrian marriage tooth and nail. On the other hand, the Queen might yet decide to marry him after all, and there were those who believed that his chances were as good now in the spring of 1565 as they had ever been.

Robert himself alternated between hope and despair. He told the Spanish ambassador that the Queen would never marry him 'as she has made up her mind to wed some great Prince, or at all events no subject of her own'. Then, suddenly changing direction, he said he thought the Queen of Scots' marriage would mean that his business might be more easily arranged, as the reason Elizabeth had refused him before was because of her fear that Mary meant to marry some powerful foreign prince.[5]

There was a new Spanish ambassador in London by this time. Bishop de Quadra had died in the plague summer of 1563 and his replacement, Don Diego Guzman de Silva, was proving to be a perceptive and sympathetic character with a nice sense of humour who, alone of King Philip's envoys to Elizabeth's court, made a genuine effort to promote the cause of Anglo-Spanish understanding. The Queen and William Cecil both liked and trusted him; and Robert, of course, had wasted no time in getting on terms with him. Unlike his predecessor, de Silva was being careful to avoid too close an involvement in the tangled web of the Austrian marriage and had already resisted an attempt on the part of the English government to use him as an intermediary, wisely refusing to enter into any negotiations 'without some firm assurance that the affair would be carried through'. This assurance had not been forthcoming and de Silva strongly suspected that there was no serious intent behind the recent resurgence of interest in the Archduke – that it was, in fact, simply a diversion. From his various conversations with the Queen, with Robert and from hints reaching him from other sources, the ambassador had come to believe that 'Lord Robert's affair is not off', while he had many reasons for being doubtful about the Archduke. He therefore made up his mind to adopt a strictly neutral attitude – doing what he could to advise and assist the Emperor's ambassador, while at the same time keeping Robert in play, 'helping him in such a way that if ever his marriage to the Queen should come off, he will be bound to continue friendly'.[6]

To the outward eye Robert's relations with the Queen seemed as intimate as ever. There was a well-publicised incident in March 1565 when he and the Duke of Norfolk were playing tennis, Elizabeth looking on, and Robert took the Queen's napkin out of her hand to wipe his sweaty face. Norfolk, outraged by the sight of this casual familiarity, had to be restrained from hitting his opponent over the head with his racquet, but Elizabeth was apparently unperturbed and her wrath lighted on the Duke.[7] There were, however, liberties which Robert was not allowed to take – witness that other, equally famous occasion when one of his henchmen attempted to take a high hand with a member of the royal household. This led to a furious telling-off. 'God's death, my lord, I have wished you well, but my favour is not so locked up for you that others shall not participate thereof... and if you think to rule here, I will take a course to see you forthcoming. I will have here but one mistress and no master.'[8] Robert took the warning. He knew Elizabeth too well to make that sort of mistake twice and, according to one commentator, 'his feigned humility was long after one of his best virtues'.

Robert might be good at managing the Queen, and was probably as close to her as any other human being, but not even he could read her mind. Early in June, de Silva heard that the Earl of Leicester had again become more hopeful about his marriage and was moving in the matter. 'It looks as if the Queen favoured it also,' he went on, 'and the French ambassador has been pointing out to her the objections to the Archduke's match, saying that he is very poor and other things of the same sort to lead her away from the project.'[9] The Emperor's ambassador was getting a similar message and told the Earl of Sussex that he believed the Queen was determined never to marry or that, if she did, she would take no one but the Earl of

Leicester. Sussex who, like Norfolk and William Cecil, strongly supported the Austrian marriage, pooh-poohed the idea – the Queen had promised the kingdom she would marry, and if she refused the Archduke there was no one else. All the same, round about this time Cecil was facing up to the fact that it looked very much as if Elizabeth still meant to have Robert Dudley in the end. The objections to such a match were the same as they had always been. Nothing would be gained for the country 'either in riches, estimation or power'. On the contrary, Robert was heavily in debt and would think of nothing but enriching himself and his friends, which would inevitably lead to bitter dissension and faction. He was 'infamed' by the death of his wife and, if he and the Queen were to marry now, not only would all the old scandals be revived but it would be thought that 'the slanderous speeches of the Queen and the Earl have been true'. Added to this, Cecil believed Robert was likely to prove an unkind and jealous husband.[10]

Then, in July, the weather suddenly changed and the court realised with fascinated interest that Elizabeth was treating her old friend with marked coolness. More than that, for the first time since the eclipse of William Pickering, she was bestowing smiles and favours on another Englishman, Thomas Heneage, one of the gentlemen-in-waiting and 'a young man of pleasant wit and bearing and a good courtier'. Robert did not conceal his annoyance, and angry words passed between the two men. De Silva thought at first that it was 'all make believe and simply devised to avoid jealousy', especially as Heneage was 'a great intimate' of Robert's, but he heard later that the trouble had started with Robert paying court to the pretty young Viscountess of Hereford, born Lettice Knollys and a cousin of the Queen's, apparently in an attempt to test the strength of the Queen's affection for him. Elizabeth had retaliated by taking up Thomas Heneage, and Robert had asked leave to go away to his own place to stay 'as other noblemen do'. The result was a violent quarrel between the Queen and her best friend. 'The Queen was in a great temper,' reported de Silva, 'and upbraided him with what had taken place with Heneage and his flirting with the Viscountess in very bitter words.' Heneage was sent away and Robert sulked in his lodgings for several days. Finally, the Earl of Sussex and Cecil smoothed things over, although, as de Silva remarked, 'they are no friends of Lord Robert in their hearts'. Robert was sent for, and he and Elizabeth shed tears and made it up.[11]

It all sounded trivial enough, but the episode rankled and during the Twelfth Night festivities in January 1566 there was another furious altercation between Heneage and the Earl of Leicester. According to the gossip retailed at the French court, the Queen was once more very angry with Lord Robert, saying 'that if by her favour he had become insolent he should soon reform, and that she would lower him just as she had at first raised him'. But, the same correspondent added, it was also being said that she would shortly proclaim him a duke and marry him![12] A few weeks later Elizabeth herself told de Silva that, if only Robert were a king's son, she would marry him tomorrow. 'She is so nimble in her dealings,' remarked the Spaniard, 'and threads in and out of this business in such a way that her most intimate favourites fail to understand her, and her intentions are therefore variously interpreted.' Nevertheless, de Silva saw no reason to change his own view that, although the Queen loved the business of being courted and having all the world running after her, she would end by marrying Robert or no one – an opinion which was coming to be shared by other European observers.[13]

Meanwhile, negotiations over the terms of a marriage contract with the Archduke were continuing. In general both sides accepted the precedents for the marriage of an English queen regnant established by Mary Tudor – the laws of England and the rights of Englishmen to remain sacrosanct, and neither the Queen nor any children of the marriage to be taken out of the realm without the consent of the realm – but there was still plenty of scope for argument over other matters. For example, who was going to pay for the Archduke's keep? The Emperor maintained that his brother's household expenses should be charged to the English exchequer but the English, remembering those rumours so assiduously spread by the French ambassador that Charles had no money of his own, were making it a condition that the Queen's husband must not become a burden on the taxpayer. Then there was the question of status. The Habsburgs were demanding that the Archduke should at once be crowned king and rule jointly with Elizabeth, also that he should retain his footing in England in the event of her death – terms which found little favour on the English side.[14]

These, though, were bargaining-points capable of being resolved by negotiation. More serious was the great religious divide. The English insisted that Charles must conform to the rites and observances of the Anglican Church, while the Emperor was equally definite that his brother must be allowed the full, free and open practice of Roman Catholicism. Elizabeth herself was now saying flatly that she could not possibly marry anyone who did not share her religious persuasion, for two persons of different faiths could never live peaceably in one house. When it was pointed out to her that she had always known Charles was a Catholic, she answered that on the contrary she had always been led to believe he was not set in his ways and would be willing to change his opinions.[15] The Queen was apparently ready to use the religious difficulty as an excuse for rejecting the whole plan, but others felt that even this obstacle might be overcome. The Earl of Sussex told Adam Zwetkovich he thought the matter could be arranged if the Archduke would agree to accompany the Queen to church in public and hear mass privately in his own apartments.[16]

On the other outstanding issue – that old bone of contention, the Archduke's visit to England – neither side had shifted from its previously entrenched position. Elizabeth told Zwetkovich that she would take no man she had not seen. She had already said this a thousand times, she remarked irritably, and was still and ever would be of the same mind. She wanted Charles to come incognito, hinting that if they took a fancy to each other everything else would be plain-sailing. If they did not – and she would never give the Archduke cause to curse portrait-painters and envoys as Philip had done when he first set eyes on Queen Mary – then it could be given out that it had not been possible to agree on the articles of the marriage contract and no one need be any the wiser.[17]

Elizabeth considered this perfectly reasonable, but the Emperor could not approve a plan which he clearly regarded as thoroughly feminine and frivolous and 'entirely novel and unprecedented' among kings and queens. He also feared a trap – that the English would wait until the Archduke had arrived and then put forward a pre-posterous set of conditions which he would not be able to accept. In any case, there could be no question of secret visits or suchlike romantic nonsense – the union of realms and princes was a serious matter. When the Archduke went to England it would be 'with all befitting ceremony' and not until negotiations over the terms of the contract had been satisfactorily completed.[18] In other words, the Habsburgs were still determined to bind the Queen in advance, while she was equally determined not to be bound to anything – not until she had seen Charles with her own eyes would she start taking an interest in the small print. She would not even consider a suggestion by Adam Zwetkovich that she should send some distinguished personage to have a look at the Archduke and report back to her. Surely she would take the word of such an old and trusted friend as the Earl of Leicester, for instance? This ingenuous plan was rejected, but Zwetkovich still took the precaution of warning Vienna that Charles should henceforward be careful to wear his best clothes on all occasions and only be seen riding 'fiery steeds' – especially important this, as a reputation for dashing horsemanship would do him more good with the English than the possession of millions in gold.[19]

Elizabeth continued to nag about the visit, asking de Silva at frequent intervals if he thought the Archduke would come. One day in early August, when she was walking in the park at Windsor with both the Spanish and Imperial ambassadors, the subject came up again and de Silva could not resist the opportunity to do a little teasing. Had the Queen, he asked solemnly, noticed anyone she had not seen before among the gentlemen who accompanied the Emperor's ambassador and himself, as perhaps she was entertaining more than she knew? Elizabeth was momentarily taken in. She looked quickly at the faces round her, went quite white and became so agitated that de Silva could not keep a straight face and gave the game away by laughing. The Queen recovered her composure and remarked that it would not be at all a bad way for the Archduke to come, if his dignity would allow it. 'I promise you plenty of princes have come to see me in that manner,' she added airily.[20] In fact, probably nothing would have been more embarrassing for the Queen than if Charles had taken her at her word and come courting in person.

On 14 August, Adam Zwetkovich was dismissed with 'an honourable answer' and a personal letter from Elizabeth to the Emperor. Zwetkovich himself apparently felt satisfied that progress had been made, and William Cecil believed 'the Queen's Majesty, thanked be God, is well disposed towards marriage'. He told Thomas Smith that 'common opinion is that the Archduke Charles will come, which if he do and will accord with us in religion and shall be allowable for his person to her Majesty, then ... we shall see some success'.[21] Guzman de Silva remained sceptical. He was being careful to stay friendly with the Earl of Leicester and still thought that 'if any marriage at all is to result from all this it will be his'.

In the spring of 1566 attention was temporarily diverted from the Queen of England's matrimonial prospects to the startling events beginning to unfold themselves in Scotland. Mary Stuart's marriage was already going badly. As early as the previous October, Thomas Randolph had been reporting 'jars' between the Queen of Scots and her husband, and by the New Year the rift gaped for all to see.

Darnley, furiously disappointed at being refused the crown matrimonial, was drinking heavily and neglecting his wife for the whores
of Edinburgh, while Mary, who was now carrying his child, treated
him with cold contempt. On 13 February, Randolph wrote: 'I know
now for certain that this Queen repenteth her marriage – that she
hateth Darnley and all his kin.'

The Queen of Scots' domestic problems were rendered even more
explosive by the favours Mary was lavishing on her private secretary
and constant companion, the Piedmontese musician David Riccio.
John Knox and the elders of the Calvinist kirk saw him as a papist
snake-in-the-grass; the nobility furiously resented the low-born
foreign interloper and Darnley believed, or was easily persuaded to
believe, that 'that villain Davy' had done him 'the most dishonour
that can be to any man'. In fact, despite the scurrilous rumours going
about that he was the real father of her child, there is no more reason
to suppose that David Riccio was ever Mary Stuart's lover than there
is to suppose that Robert Dudley was ever Elizabeth Tudor's, but her
obvious preference for his cheerful and uncritical society, though
understandable, was in the circumstances extremely unwise. Six years
earlier Caspar von Breuner had wondered why no Englishman could
be found to stab milord Robert with a poniard. In Scotland, as its
queen should surely have guessed, men did not suffer from such
inhibitions and no one was particularly surprised when, at about
eight o'clock in the evening of Saturday, 9 March, a gang of thugs,
admitted by Darnley, burst into Mary's private apartments at Holyrood Palace, interrupting a decorous little supper party. Riccio was
dragged screaming into an adjoining room and savagely stabbed to
death, while the Queen, who had been forcibly restrained from going
to his aid, was, so she afterwards alleged, threatened with a loaded
pistol.

Scottish national pride had been salved by the slaughter of the
wretched Italian, but the murder was only an incidental part of a
plan to imprison the Queen in Stirling Castle and set up Darnley as
the puppet king of a new régime untainted by popery. It was a plan
which might well have succeeded had not the conspirators seriously
underestimated the Queen's recuperative powers. She herself believed
they had hoped she would miscarry and die, but for a delicately
nurtured young woman six months pregnant who had just been
subjected to an experience of nightmarish horror and fear, Mary
displayed astonishing qualities of resilience, courage and self-com-
mand. Concealing her revulsion, she worked on Darnley all the

following day to persuade him that he, as much as she, was in deadly danger. By the Monday evening she had contrived a means of escape and by dawn on Tuesday, 12 March, after a wild ride through the night, she and her husband were safe at Dunbar. With Darnley's desertion and the Queen once more a free agent, the *coup d'état* collapsed and Mary survived to bear her child, Prince James Charles, at Edinburgh Castle on 19 June.

In England the shocking events of that March weekend were regarded with disapproval and, early in April, Queen Elizabeth received Guzman de Silva wearing a portrait of the Queen of Scots hanging from a gold chain at her waist. Had she been in Mary's place, she told him energetically, she would have seized her treacherous husband's dagger and stabbed him with it, but added hastily that the Emperor must not think she would ever treat the Archduke in such a way![22]

Elizabeth had been given yet another object lesson in the perils and pitfalls of royal marriage but she could not avoid the issue for long. That autumn the much postponed confrontation with Parliament was due to take place with the succession still unsettled, the Queen still unmarried and in the embarrassing position of having to ask for money in time of peace. The problem of the succession had not grown any easier over the last three years. On the contrary, it was if anything even more highly charged than before and there were now signs of an organised campaign of agitation to have the matter 'proceed in Parliament' whether the Queen liked it or not.

In spite of her continued disgrace and imprisonment, Catherine Grey's claim to be recognised as heir presumptive still commanded strong support among the increasingly influential and militant left-wing Protestants – a faction powerfully represented in the House of Commons. On the other hand, the Queen of Scots' position had been greatly strengthened by the birth of her son – already being hailed in some quarters as the future King of England – and she was not likely to stand aside while another successor was nominated; indeed she demanded the right to send commissioners to London to represent her if the matter were to be raised in Parliament. Add to this Queen Elizabeth's well-known determination not to name any successor at all, and there seemed every prospect of a first-class political row in the offing.

Both Houses assembled at Westminster on 30 September but the government, uncomfortably aware of the gathering storm, hesitated to precipitate it. Instead, at a council meeting on 12 October, they made a somewhat forlorn attempt to soften up the Queen. The Duke of Norfolk, acting as spokesman for the nobility, reminded her as tactfully as he could of the petitions presented by the Lords and Commons in 1563. So far no action had been taken because they still awaited her final answer, but now all those who had the welfare of the country at heart most humbly begged that she would allow Parliament to discuss both the succession and her marriage. Elizabeth was not impressed. The succession was her business, she retorted, and she wanted no one's advice on how to handle it. She had no intention of being buried alive like her sister. She remembered only too well how people had flocked to her at Hatfield in the last months of Mary's reign and wanted no such journeyings during her lifetime. In any case, they knew quite well that her marriage was not far off. As for Parliament, she bade the members do their duty and with that she brought the proceedings to a close.[23]

It did not sound hopeful and when, a week later, the subsidy bill had finally to be presented to the Commons the storm broke. The Lower House, or at any rate a well-organised and belligerent pressure group within the Lower House, was no longer prepared to be put off with promises and in the subsidy bill had seen a weapon which could be used to coerce the Crown. There would be no supplies until those far more urgent and important issues, the succession and the Queen's marriage, had been disposed of. Government efforts to cool the situation met with no success and the reply to one councillor who urged a little more patience was uncompromising : 'We have express charge to grant nothing before the Queen gives a firm answer to our demands. Go to the Queen and let her know our intention, which we have in command from all the towns and people of this Kingdom, whose deputies we are.'[24] After a bad-tempered debate which lasted two days and during which, according to the Spanish ambassador, the members even came to blows, it was then decided to make another approach to the Lords with a view to renewing joint pressure on the Queen. 'These heretics', commented Guzman de Silva, 'neither fear God nor obey their betters.'[25]

Elizabeth was very angry and possibly a little taken aback over this open insubordination. She told de Silva that the Commons had offered to vote her £250,000, if she would allow the nomination of Catherine Grey as her successor to be discussed, but she had refused. Apart from the fact that she had no intention of allowing Parliament to meddle in the matter at all, she was not going to make bargains. The money she was asking for was for the common good, to strengthen the Navy and to suppress trouble in Ireland, and it should be given freely and graciously. De Silva sympathised with her predicament but pointed out that if she married the Archduke all this trouble would automatically come to an end. She was aware of that, replied the Queen, and meant to send a message to the Emperor within a week 'signifying that her intention was to accept the marriage'. De Silva's information was that negotiations with Vienna were virtually at a standstill, but he kept his scepticism to himself.[26]

On Monday, 21 October, a committee of the Commons formally requested the Lords to join them in another petition to the Queen. Their lordships were just as worried about the general situation but, as befitted a more conservative and responsible body, they shrank from a head-on collision with their sovereign lady. Before answering the Commons, therefore, an imposing deputation headed by the Lord Treasurer, the old Marquis of Winchester now over eighty years old, waited on the Queen in her Privy Chamber. One by one they reminded her yet again of the need to provide for the future in good time. Parliament was being reduced to expensive futility by the present stalemate and one by one the peers begged the Queen to declare her will in the matter of the succession – either that or dissolve Parliament and let everyone go home before things got any worse. Elizabeth's answer gave no hint of concession. The Commons, she declared, were no better than rebels and would never have dared to treat her father in such a way. As for the Lords, they could do as they pleased and so would she. The succession was far too serious to be left to such a light-witted assembly and she was thinking of taking advice from the best legal brains in the country.[27]

Three days later the House of Lords agreed to combine with the Commons in their suit to the Queen. Elizabeth felt herself cornered and reacted accordingly. De Silva heard that she had called the Duke of Norfolk a traitor or something very like it and that, when the Earl of Pembroke tried to remonstrate, she told him he talked like a swaggering soldier. As for the Marquis of Northampton, who was also present, the Queen remarked that he had better remember the arguments which got him married again while he had a wife living, instead of mincing words with her. Nor was the Earl of Leicester immune. Elizabeth said she had thought that, if all the world abandoned her, he would not, and, when Robert hastily protested his readiness to die at her feet, she retorted crossly that that had nothing to do with the matter. Then, having ordered them all to get out of her sight and stay out of it, she flounced off to pour her grievances into the receptive ear of the Spanish ambassador who, in her present state of almost total isolation, seemed the only friend she had. The Queen, reported de Silva, was especially incensed against the Earl of Leicester and asked what de Silva thought of such ingratitude from one to whom she had shown so much kindness and favour that even her honour had suffered. However, she was glad now to have such a good opportunity for sending him away and the Archduke would be able to come without any suspicion.[28]

Meanwhile the Commons were staging what amounted to a sit-down strike – after nearly a month virtually no government business had been transacted. Several behind-the-scenes attempts to reach a settlement had failed – according to de Silva, the Queen appeared to think it would be 'an affront to her dignity to adopt any compromise' – and tension was mounting. By 4 November the joint committees of the Lords and Commons were ready to make a new approach to the Palace and William Cecil optimistically assured the Spanish ambassador that he was sure everything would soon be favourably settled. De Silva himself thought the Queen 'will give them fair words with regard to the marriage and will defer the succession for a future time and the whole matter will thus be quieted for the present'.[29] They both underrated the Queen. There were to be no more fair words. Elizabeth was about to take the offensive.

On the morning of 5 November she commanded a delegation of thirty members from each House to appear before her that afternoon. The Speaker was expressly excluded. On this occasion the Queen intended to do all the speaking herself. After some stinging remarks about unbridled persons in the Commons whose mouths had never been snaffled by a rider and certain members of the Lords who might have been expected to know better, she burst out: 'Was I not born in the realm? Were my parents born in any foreign country? Is not my kingdom here? Whom have I oppressed? Whom have I enriched to other's harm? What turmoil have I made in this Commonwealth that I should be suspected to have no regard to the same? How have I governed since my reign?'

After this Elizabeth turned to the matter in hand. She had already said she would marry and would never break the word of a prince, spoken in a public place, for her honour's sake. She could only say again that she would marry as soon as she conveniently could, adding 'and I hope to have children, otherwise I would never marry'. As for the succession, she made another reference to her experiences during Mary's reign when she had 'tasted of the practices' against her sister and had herself been 'sought for divers ways'. There were individuals now sitting in the Commons, she observed, who knew exactly what she was talking about. But none of them had had personal experience of what it was like to be 'a second person', or any notion of what it would mean for her as Queen to have an impatient heir presumptive breathing down her neck. It was not convenient to settle the succession, 'nor never shall be without some peril unto you and certain danger unto me'. However, if she ever did see a suitable opportunity to name an heir, then she would 'deal therein for your safety, and offer it unto you as your Prince and head, without request; for it is monstrous that the feet should direct the head'.

One thing Elizabeth made abundantly clear. 'Though I be a woman, yet I have as good a courage, answerable to my place, as ever my father had. I am your anointed Queen. I will never be by violence constrained to do anything.' And she went on, 'I thank God I am endued with such qualities that if I were turned out of the realm in my petticoat, I were able to live in any place in Christendom.'[30]

When an expurgated version of this remarkable piece of Elizabethan rhetoric was passed on to the full House of Commons, it was received in stony silence. Two days later someone suggested that the House should proceed with its controversial suit for the limitation of the succession regardless of the Queen's attitude. The Queen retaliated by forbidding any further discussion of the matter, ordering the members to 'satisfy themselves with her Highness's promise of marriage'. This led to another revolt – Paul Wentworth, a leader of the militants, going so far as to raise the question of whether the Crown had any authority to prevent the Commons from debating a matter of urgent public concern.

By the middle of November the main issue at stake was no longer the succession or the Queen's marriage but royal violation of Parliament's 'accustomed lawful liberties', and it was beginning to look as if a serious constitutional crisis might be impending. The Queen had allowed temper and something very like panic to ride her and in consequence had got herself into an untenable position. Only two courses of action were now open to her. Either she must dissolve Parliament forthwith, which would not only mean doing without her much-needed cash but would also be a damaging admission of defeat for a sovereign who took justifiable pride in her warm relationship with her subjects – either that or she must surrender. Elizabeth surrendered and on 25 November she lifted her embargo. This sensible action, which was 'most joyfully taken of all the House', took the heat out of the situation, but it was not quite enough by itself and two days later the Queen sent another message to the Commons offering to sacrifice one-third of the subsidy payment. This time the bait was irresistible. The succession debate was dropped and the subsidy bill got its reading.

The battle was over – apart from one final skirmish. Subsidy bills normally carried preambles and a group of irreconcilables among the radicals conceived what seemed to them the brilliant idea of recording the Queen's promises to marry and to settle the succession as soon as a suitable opportunity arose in the preamble of the present bill. They would thus, they hoped, compel their artful mistress to honour her verbal assurances by incorporating them in the solemn and public apparatus of an Act of Parliament. It was an ingenious ploy but it failed. When Elizabeth saw the draft text she scribbled a furious comment in the margin. 'I know no reason why any my private answers to the realm should serve for prologue to a subsidies book. Neither yet do I understand why such audacity should be used to make without my licence an act of my words.' The draft was scrapped and in its final form contained only a pious hope that the succession would be settled at some future time.[31]

The Queen might be said to have won on points. The succession remained a contest open to all comers but at least the decision remained in her hands and, in spite of all her promises, the prospect of a royal wedding seemed as remote as ever. Elizabeth did, though, make one more move in the direction of the Habsburgs by sending the Earl of Sussex to Vienna during the summer of 1567.

After making the Archduke's acquaintance, Sussex was able to assure the Queen that she need have absolutely no qualms about his personal appearance. He was of a good height, his hair and beard a light auburn colour, 'his face well-proportioned, amiable, and of a very good complexion, without show of redness or over paleness; his countenance and speech cheerful, very courteous and not without some state; his body well-shaped, without deformity or blemish; his hands very good and fair; his legs clean, well-proportioned, and of sufficient bigness for his stature; his foot as good as may be'. Altogether, upon his duty to her Majesty, honest Sussex could say that he had not found 'any thing to be noted worthy misliking in his whole person'. So much for all those stories that the Archduke had an oversized head! He spoke fluent Spanish and Italian as well as Latin and, of course, his native German. He seemed popular with his own people; was reported to be wise and liberal and had proved his courage in the recent war with the Turks. He delighted in hunting, riding, hawking and all the manly exercises. Sussex had seen him run at the ring and was able to commend his horsemanship unreservedly. He was fond of music and took an interest in such intellectual matters as astronomy and cosmography.

The Earl was also able to nail the slander that Charles was a poor man. On the contrary, he was a great prince with wide territories in south-eastern Austria and Croatia, where he could ride for nearly three hundred miles without leaving the boundaries of his own estates. He drew large revenues from gold, silver and lead mines, as well as from the customs duties on grain and wine, and lived in 'great honour and state'.[32]

But unhappily all this splendour and excellence was not for sale, since Charles was quite definitely not prepared to change his religion. He would, he told Sussex, do anything else to please Queen Elizabeth, but no consideration in the world would induce him to abandon the Catholic faith of his ancestors. He would promise not to admit any Englishman to his chapel; he would be careful never to say or do anything to prejudice the Church of England; he would even, if necessary, be present with the Queen at an occasional Anglican service; but in return he insisted that he must be given proper facilities in a decent public place of worship where he and his household could attend mass freely and openly, for he did not intend to be reduced to practising his religion in secret. Until this had been clearly conceded he could not come to England, and that was his final and unalterable decision.[33]

These convenient scruples of conscience on Charles's part gave Elizabeth an unexceptionable excuse for bringing the long farce of their courtship to a close. She could not, she explained, allow the laws of her country to be broken, not even – or perhaps especially not – by her own husband. She too had a conscience, and in any case she prized the continuance of a peaceable reign more highly than all the favours which the princes of the world and all kingdoms could confer on her. Charles could have a room in the palace fitted up as a chapel where he and his personal attendants could have a private mass, but in no circumstances would she allow him the use of a public church with its music, choristers 'and all the other solemnities usual in the chapels of princes, such as the Archduke would wish to have'.[34]

It would never have done, of course. An arrangement which might have been reluctantly tolerated in 1559 or 1560 would have provoked an insupportable alienation of feeling in the atmosphere of the late sixties, which were seeing a steady hardening of attitudes on both sides of the ideological divide. A Catholic consort, however tactful, however discreet he might honestly try to be, would inevitably become a focal point for lobbying and intrigue by all those English Catholics and crypto-Catholics who were still hoping for better times. A nest of papists openly practising their idolatrous abominations under the protection of the Queen herself would cause instant and furious offence to all law-abiding Protestants, while the radicals would not hesitate to make their displeasure felt in the crudest terms. Elizabeth was perfectly well aware that all those 'Protestant gentlemen' in the Commons who had been so impudently urging her to hurry up and get married would be the first to take exception to her Catholic husband.

So, in a civil exchange of letters early in 1568, the Austrian marriage project finally died. Two years later, when she was once more under severe political pressure, Elizabeth had the gall to try to revive it yet again; but the joke was now definitely over as far as the Habsburgs were concerned, and good patient Charles, released from his ten-year bondage, was courting the Duke of Bavaria's daughter. He lived on till 1590 and became, ironically enough, something of a persecutor of Protestants.

CHAPTER X

To Marry with France

THE 1560s drew to a close in an atmosphere heavy with the sense of impending crisis. In Scotland young Darnley was dead – murdered in the house at Kirk o' Field with, there is really very little reason to doubt, the prior knowledge and consent of his wife. Few people privately would have blamed the Queen of Scots for choosing this drastic solution to her marital difficulties – Darnley had proved himself impossible as a husband and was becoming an increasingly dangerous nuisance all round – but even in sixteenth-century Scotland appearances had to be kept up. When Mary showed not the slightest interest in bringing the killers to justice but instead was regularly seen in the company of the Earl of Bothwell who, there is no reason at all to doubt, had personally supervised the assassination, her days of queenship were numbered and her spectacular rampage of self-destruction during the spring of 1567 brought its inevitable nemesis. By the summer Bothwell had been driven into exile and Mary had been deposed by her outraged subjects; her infant son had been proclaimed as King James VI and she herself imprisoned in Loch-leven Castle.

That the nobility would have taken an even shorter way with her had it not been for the furious reaction of the Queen of England is something else which cannot reasonably be doubted. Elizabeth, in common with every other western European head of state, had been horribly shocked by Mary's recent conduct; but an anointed queen was still an anointed queen and not to be insulted, threatened and put in fear of her life by subjects, no matter what the provocation. This she made clear beyond any possibility of misunderstanding to the new Scottish government. Her own councillors openly deplored their mistress's unfortunate determination to protect her cousin from the natural consequences of her misdeeds. They deplored it even more when, a year later, Mary escaped from her island prison and presently landed up on the coast of Cumberland, a refugee with nothing but the clothes she stood up in. 'I fear that our good Queen hath the wolf by the ears,' lamented the Archbishop of Canterbury, and how right he was. The presence of the *de facto* Catholic heiress on English soil (and the recent death of Catherine Grey had left her with no serious competitor) was to prove a violent and eventually an intolerable irritant to the Protestant body politic. It also presented the Protestant Queen with a socially embarrassing, personally dangerous and politically insoluble problem.

It was no coincidence that less than eighteen months after Mary's arrival the first and, as it turned out, the only serious domestic rebellion of Elizabeth's reign broke out. The rising in the predominantly Catholic north country was due as much to social and economic as to political and religious grievances, but its best-remembered incident remains the descent of the rebels on Durham Cathedral, where they defiantly celebrated mass and 'rent and trampled underfoot the English bibles and books of Common Prayer'. The dissidents made no further headway towards their declared objective of restoring the true and Catholic religion, and never got within miles of releasing the Queen of Scots from the Midlands mansion where she was currently residing as the involuntary houseguest of the Earl and Countess of Shrewsbury. In fact, the movement soon collapsed, being suppressed without difficulty and with a good deal of savagery. Just the same, the Earl of Sussex, as Lord President of the North, had lived through some anxious days while waiting for reinforcements to reach him from the south, for he dared not rely on the loyalty of his local levies, and the rising served as a warning to the central government not to take national unity for granted – especially now that the Catholic population had so seductive a figurehead and potential leader in their very midst.

Mary Stuart's legendary beauty and charm, together with the romantic story of her escape from Lochleven and natural human sympathy for her present predicament, were by this time rapidly effacing the memory of the antics which had brought that predicament about, and by the end of the sixties the rehabilitation of the Queen of Scots was virtually complete. In January 1569, Don Guerau de Spes, who had taken over from de Silva as Spanish ambassador in London, described Mary as 'a lady of great spirit' and told King Philip that she was gaining so many friends in England that 'with little help she would be able to get this kingdom into her hands'.[1]

If the situation at home looked unsettled, abroad it was definitely menacing. Relations with Spain had been deteriorating rapidly during the past two years of the decade and not only for ideological reasons. Spain's determination to claim a monopoly of the vast wealth and trading potential of her American empire was becoming the cause of considerable ill-feeling; and the nasty episode at San Juan de Ulloa in September 1568, when an English fleet seeking shelter in the harbour was treacherously set upon by order of the local Spanish viceroy, sowed the seeds of an implacable hatred and distrust of all things Spanish in the hearts of the English mercantile and seafaring community.

A more immediate cause for concern existed much nearer home – just across the North Sea, in fact, where the Netherlanders, England's traditional allies and trading partners, had risen in revolt against Spanish rule. The Dutch and Flemish nobility resented the loss of many of their ancient liberties under Philip's heavy-handed régime, the merchants and burghers resented his taxation, but armed conflict had been touched off by the spread of a militant form of Calvinism in the north and east and in Antwerp, commercial capital of northern Europe. Philip might be forced to tolerate heresy in other countries for reasons of political expediency, but in no circumstances would he tolerate it within his own dominions, and in 1567 he had despatched the notorious Duke of Alva with an army of ten thousand 'black-beards' to pursue a policy of blood and iron in the disaffected provinces. Dutch resistance, under the dour leadership of William of Orange, proved unexpectedly tenacious, but no one could be in much doubt as to the eventual outcome and England faced the all too likely prospect of seeing a victorious and unemployed Spanish army camped within a day's sail of her all too vulnerable south-eastern coastline.

It was not a comforting thought – especially not in February 1570 when the Pope, apparently acting on inaccurate and out-of-date reports inspired by the Northern Rising, finally came down off the fence and issued his long-threatened bull of excommunication against the heretical and bastard Queen of England, depriving her of her 'pretended title' and absolving her Catholic subjects from their allegiance. Although this papal thunderbolt might be dismissed in London as 'a vain crack of words that made a noise only', its implications were deeply disturbing and the perennial Protestant dread that 'some monster was a-breeding' – that a league of Catholic powers dedicated to the extirpation of the gospel was in the making – inevitably grew sharper.

In the midst of all these perils the Queen of England stood as though in a spotlight, the target of enemies from both within and without the realm. In her late thirties Elizabeth Tudor had matured into an elegant, vigorous, self-confident woman who had won the respect, if not always the approval, of her fellow-sovereigns. But she was still single and unprotected by family ties with any other royal house; still childless when she would soon be past the normal child-bearing age. To the society in which she lived, the Queen's freely expressed aversion to the holy state of matrimony, her stubborn re-fusal to accept her proper role as wife and mother, remained totally incomprehensible and more than a little shocking. As she herself once remarked to Guzman de Silva: 'There is a strong idea in the world that a woman cannot live unless she is married, or at all events that if she refrains from marriage she does so for some bad reason'.[2]

That Elizabeth's innermost reason for refraining from marriage had to do with childhood traumas seems at least a plausible theory. After all, had not her father killed her mother and her mother's cousin for crimes perhaps only dimly understood, but yet demon-strably connected with sexual guilt? It would scarcely be surprising if, by the time she was eight years old, a conviction that for the women of her family there existed an inescapable correlation between sexual intercourse and violent death had taken root in her subconscious mind – a conviction which could only have been strengthened by her own adolescent experience at the hands of Thomas Seymour. On a less speculative level, the adult Elizabeth had watched the shame and misery of unrequited physical passion ravage her sister, another reigning queen. Of one thing she could be certain – that to surrender to passion, to surrender her body to a man, any man, would diminish if not destroy her power, both as a woman and as a queen; and, if it is possible to be certain of any one thing about Elizabeth Tudor, it is that she lived and throve on the exercise of power over men.

The row with Robert Dudley which had blown up during the 1566 Parliament rumbled on into the following spring. In May 1567, Robert was having a good moan about royal ingratitude and general unreasonableness, and seeing no future for himself but a cave in a corner of oblivion. This time it was Nicholas Throckmorton (who had once been so afraid that Robert would run off with the Queen but was now one of his closest friends) who acted as peacemaker, and Elizabeth rather grudgingly agreed to make it up. By the summer they were back on their old cosy footing, but the hectic courtship, the blazing rows and tearful reconciliations of the sixties seemed to be over, giving place to a steadier, altogether more businesslike partner-ship. Robert, although never a popular figure, was becoming accepted

as a permanent feature of the Elizabethan landscape – a sort of unofficial grand vizier through whose hands an enormous amount of
patronage flowed and with whom it was wise to keep on good terms.
Apart from his personal influence, the Earl of Leicester was now an
important member of that charmed inner circle of the Queen's
intimates who governed the country under her supervision and were
honoured with pet names. As William Cecil was her Spirit, so
Robert was her Eyes.

His public duties and responsibilities increased with the years
(as well as everything else, he was still Master of the Horse), but
Robert Dudley never forgot or neglected the very special relationship
on which his career was founded. In July 1575, he entertained the
Queen at Kenilworth, the Warwickshire estate she had bestowed on
him twelve years earlier. The royal visit lasted for three exhausting
ostentatious weeks – three weeks of plays, masques, pageants, feasts,
revels, hunts, bear-baiting and firework displays, presented against a
backdrop of idyllic countryside through a succession of hot, still
summer days. The Princely Pleasures of Kenilworth cost Robert a
small fortune but they established him beyond question as a great
man who knew how a queen should be treated. Elizabeth accepted
the tribute and the hospitality graciously enough, but she almost
certainly preferred the small informal house-parties arranged for her
at country houses like Rycote in Oxfordshire, home of the Norris
family, where she could relax quietly with Robert and a few close
friends. She was apparently quite content with the peculiar compromise she had evolved – a compromise which kept him constantly
at her side, her consort in all but name, her lover in all but physical
fact.

If, by the early seventies, Elizabeth had organised her private life
to her own satisfaction, that did not mean she had abandoned the
public game of political courtship – far from it. She had so far always
avoided aligning herself too closely with either of the two great
European power-blocs, preferring to follow the classic pattern of
English foreign policy of playing one off against the other. Now,
however, with the shadow cast by Spain growing ever longer and
darker, some form of Anglo-French *rapprochement* seemed inevitable.

The idea that this might be achieved by a marriage between the
Queen of England and the French king's younger brother Henry,
Duke of Anjou, had been in the wind since 1568 but was first openly
suggested in the autumn of 1570. In December the French am-

F

bassador, de la Mothe Fénélon, had a long conversation on the sub-ject with the Earl of Leicester and found him apparently all in favour. Fénélon then saw the Queen, who received him dressed in her best and in her most sprightly mood. She told him that if she ever did decide to marry it would only be to a prince of some important royal house, and when the ambassador mentioned Anjou's name her re-action was sufficiently encouraging for him to write to the French Queen-Mother, Catherine de Medici, saying that he thought it was time for an official proposal to be made.[3]

Meanwhile, Elizabeth had brought the matter up with her own council. Someone said doubtfully that the Duke was rather young and added that 'it would be well to consider deeply before they broke entirely with the House of Burgundy'. The other members, according to the Spanish ambassador, 'were silent, surprised to see her so set upon this marriage which they had always thought was merely a fiction'.[4] Considering that Anjou was nineteen years old to Elizabeth's thirty-seven and had the reputation of being an adherent of the ultra-Catholic party in France, their surprise was understand-able. But 'I perceive her Majesty more bent to marry than heretofore she hath been', wrote Leicester to Francis Walsingham, the new English ambassador in Paris, on 14 February and at this stage of the game the eagerness seemed to be rather on the English side than the French.

Relations between the two countries were traditionally cool, when not actively hostile, and were now further complicated by the prob-lem of the Queen of Scots. The King of France was in honour bound to protest at the restraint of his former sister-in-law and had been lending at least token support to her party in Scotland; while Eliza-beth, on her side, was known to be lending moral and some financial support to the embattled French Protestants. If any sort of *entente* was to be arrived at, it would be based purely on mutual self-interest and not on any warmth of mutual trust or friendship. The Queen of England needed a counter weight to balance the threat from Spain and the Papacy. The French royal family, as represented by the young Valois King Charles IX and his strong-minded Italian mother, needed a counterweight to balance the threat to their freedom of action from the encroaching Guise family and their party of pro-Spanish Catholic ultras.

The most recent religious civil war in France had just ended more or less in a draw and the Queen-Mother was anxious to keep things that way – peace based on a measure of toleration for the Huguenots

appearing to offer the best chance of keeping herself and her son on
the top of the pile of warring factions. But, to achieve this desirable
state of affairs, Catherine urgently needed to find a 'harbourage' for
her second son. Anjou, ambitious, unstable and, since the end of the
civil war, unemployed, would be easy prey for the Guises. Left to
hang about at home, he would be at best a nuisance, at worst a
serious menace to Valois domestic tranquillity. In the circumstances,
therefore, the English marriage seemed to offer a solution to many of
the Queen-Mother's problems – not only would France acquire a
strong ally against Spain, but the House of Valois would also be
buttressed against the House of Guise and her son (and Anjou was
her favourite) would be handsomely provided for and kept out of
mischief. The trouble was that Catherine could not be certain that
Elizabeth was in earnest and she hesitated to commit herself to a
formal proposal, knowing that as soon as the matter became official
the advantage of being the one sought would pass to the Queen of
England – and all Europe knew just how ruthlessly the Queen of
England could exploit that advantage.

At last, in March 1571, Catherine took the plunge, setting out four
major conditions as a basis for negotiation – Anjou and his household were to have full freedom to exercise their religion; on the day
after the wedding he was to be crowned and rule jointly with Elizabeth; he was to be paid an annual allowance of £60,000 out of the
English exchequer; and, if Elizabeth died first without leaving heirs,
he was to enjoy both his title and his allowance for the rest of his life.
Elizabeth was prepared to agree that her husband should rule with
her as Philip had done with Mary and also that he should be called
king, but she would not admit his right to be crowned. She agreed to
provide him with a suitable allowance but not a life pension. Again,
though, these were bargaining-points and, as before, it was the
religious question which soon isolated itself as the main obstacle.
Elizabeth offered to excuse the Duke from attendance at the Anglican
service but was firm in refusing to allow him the exercise of his own
religion, even in private.

This did not sound encouraging, and any prospects of reaching a
compromise were not improved by Anjou's own lukewarm attitude
towards the marriage. His Catholic friends were naturally doing all
they could to stiffen his resistance, telling him that, apart from being
a heretic, the Queen of England was old and probably barren. Gossip
at the French court that Anjou had better marry Queen Elizabeth,
who was an old woman with a sore leg, and then give her a 'potion'

so that he would be free to wed the younger and prettier Queen of Scots and rule over both kingdoms soon reached Elizabeth's ears and annoyed her very much. It was true that she had been suffering from an ulcer on her leg which had been slow to heal but, she told the French ambassador crossly, it was a pity he had not been present at the Marquis of Northampton's ball where he could have seen her dance and would have been able to assure the Duke that he was in no danger of marrying a cripple.[5]

Negotiations continued throughout the summer, but everything really turned on whether either side would make concessions over the religious issue. Both sides, however, seem to have been imbued with the idea that, if they stood firm, the other would eventually give way. Certainly Elizabeth was sticking rigidly to her refusal even to allow Anjou a private mass. She remarked, characteristically enough, that she failed to see why he could not worship according to the Church of England rite without damage to his conscience – after all, the service was not so very different from the Roman one – and offered to have the Book of Common Prayer translated into Latin for him if that would help.[6] On the French side, Catherine de Medici told Francis Walsingham that, while she could understand Elizabeth's problems in marrying a Catholic, hinting that in due course her son might be willing to be converted, they could not in any circumstances agree to an unconditional surrender. She and the King, though, were obviously eager that the marriage should go through, if only to get Anjou out of the country and away from the Guises, and Walsingham was of the opinion that Monsieur was nowhere near so convinced a Catholic as he liked to make out. Walsingham also believed that the French probably *would* give way rather than lose Elizabeth altogether, but the English ambassador, himself something of a Protestant zealot, may have been over-influenced by the optimistic assurances of his Huguenot friends who were naturally working hard to promote the English alliance.

Opinion in England was generally in favour of the marriage, in spite of the religious difficulty. William Cecil, now Lord Burghley, certainly favoured it and so did the Earl of Sussex – both of them believing that a husband and a major European alliance were the only sure means of protecting the Queen from the dangers threatening her on every side. Nicholas Bacon, the Lord Keeper, had contributed a long memorandum on the subject, carefully balancing the pros and cons and pointing out that, by marrying Anjou, Elizabeth would be 'delivered of the continual fear of the practices with the Queen of that Bacon said nothing about the 'matter of religion' which, as he admitted, was the weightiest consideration of all.[7]

The Earl of Leicester maintained his outwardly favourable stance, but Lord Burghley felt certain that it was Leicester who was behind the Queen's unwontedly hard Protestant line; that it was Leicester Scots'; that the King of Spain would be made 'more conformable'; that the Pope's malice would 'vanish like smoke'; and the Emperor would have the Queen in more estimation. It was noticeable, though, who had been whispering to the French to stand fast over Monsieur's mass and the Queen would compromise in the end. As for Elizabeth, no one, not even Burghley or Leicester, could say for certain whether she was serious or not. With the benefit of hindsight it is not difficult to guess that she was hoping to use the French marriage just as she had used the Austrian marriage – as a delaying tactic, a diplomatic ploy to create uncertainty and keep the Catholic powers off balance. Count, now the Duke, de Feria was most probably right when he wrote in May 1571 that the Queen was simply teasing Spain 'with inventions and fears that she will marry in France'. 'She will no more marry Anjou than she will marry me,' declared Elizabeth's old adversary bluntly.[8] All the same, in June, Alvise Contarini, the Venetian ambassador in Paris, was reporting to the Signory that 'the negotiation for the marriage between the Queen of England and Monsieur d'Anjou still continues. The Court is at Gaillon and the English ambassador has been granted a long and most gracious audience by the Queen-Mother who, for the great love which she bears her son, is doing her best to bring the affair to a conclusion; and although there are many reasons to the contrary, and amongst others the disparity of age and the difference of religion, it is nevertheless the opinion of many that the negotiation will be successful.'[9]

But, by July, Walsingham had pretty well come to the conclusion that the marriage was off. Anjou had turned obstinate and neither his mother nor his elder brother had been able to persuade him to agree to go to England without a public assurance that 'he might enjoy his religion there'. Catherine was very much annoyed but had not yet given up hope of changing her son's mind – or Elizabeth's. With this end in view a special envoy, Paul de Foix, a former French ambassador at the Court of St James's, went over to London in August; but, although he was warmly received, he failed to shift the Queen on the religious issue. When he returned to France in September, the Venetian ambassador heard that the marriage scheme was now

definitely off but that a 'good understanding' had been established
between the two countries.[10]

The marriage, though, was not yet quite dead. Events that autumn
were to revive interest in it, at any rate on the English side. De Foix
was still having talks in London as details of the Ridolfi Plot – so
called after Roberto Ridolfi, Italian banker-cum-conspirator and
builder of castles in the air – began to come to light. The aims of the
plot were fourfold : to seize Elizabeth alive or dead, release the Queen
of Scots, set her on the English throne with the Duke of Norfolk as
her consort and, of course, restore the Catholic religion. These interesting feats – at least according to the blueprint Ridolfi had been
offering for Philip of Spain's approval – were to be accomplished by
the English Catholics led by Norfolk, in conjunction with an army
provided by the Duke of Alva from the Netherlands.

The Mary–Norfolk marriage plan was not a new one. It had first
been suggested early in 1569 and may, in its original form, have been
an honest, if naïve, attempt to find a solution to the problem of the
Queen of Scots by subjecting her to a suitably high-ranking and
trustworthy English husband. Just the same, it was noticeable that
none of its promoters, least of all the bridegroom-elect, could quite
bring himself to mention it to Elizabeth. But Elizabeth had soon got
to hear about it and had squashed it flat – she was under no illusions
as to who would be the dominant member of such a partnership or
what would be the consequences for herself. In spite of his categorical
denials that he had ever sought to marry 'so wicked a woman, such a
notorious adulteress and murderer', the Queen sensed a shiftiness in
Norfolk which roused her suspicions and when, just before the outbreak of the northern rebellion, he suddenly bolted for his East
Anglian estates, she ordered him back to London and incarcerated
him in the Tower.

But the Duke was an important public figure, popular and
respected. His integrity had always been taken for granted, and the
idea that he could have been dabbling in treason seemed unthinkable.
In the summer of 1570 he made a solemn submission to Elizabeth,
binding himself on his allegiance never to have anything to do with
the Queen of Scots again, and in August he was allowed to go home.
But his promises were not worth the paper they were written on. In
September 1571 he was caught in the act of sending money to Mary's
partisans in Scotland, ciphers were found hidden under the roof tiles
in his London house and it soon became only too clear that he had
been in regular correspondence with Mary herself, lending her

money, exchanging presents with her, even advising her on how to conduct the current round of negotiations with Elizabeth for her possible release and restoration.

The alarming revelations of the Ridolfi Plot made a deep impression on the public mind and served as a grim reminder of England's dangerous isolation. They strengthened the case of those who were urging the necessity of an alliance with France at almost any price and, for a time at least, it looked as if Elizabeth would be driven in this direction. Certainly she was now prepared to make a major concession in an effort to resuscitate the Anjou marriage by indicating that she would, after all, be willing to allow the Duke to practise his religion in private. Francis Walsingham, as the man on the spot, thought this was a mistake. His information was that the marriage project was beyond revival, 'the Duke of Anjou utterly refusing the match, all being granted that he desires'. Walsingham could find no one willing to deal any further in the matter and he was afraid that the Queen would be laying herself open to a damaging rebuff if she persisted.[11]

There remained the possibility of a defensive league without a marriage and, in December, Elizabeth sent Sir Thomas Smith, an old hand at dealing with the French, to see if, Walsingham regardless, the marriage could be revived and, failing that, to open negotiations for a simple treaty of friendship. The unhappy Smith had a very bad crossing and was so sick 'that life and death were to him but one' but on reaching Calais he was gently entertained and soon felt better. He was received at court by King Charles on 4 January and two days later saw the Queen-Mother. Catherine repeated that the only obstacle to the Anjou marriage was the religious one but went on to say that her son had grown so devout that he was becoming quite 'lean and evil-coloured' from fastings and vigils. When Smith asked if the Duke would be content with a private mass in his own apartments, Catherine had to admit that he would not; he was now demanding public high mass with full ceremonial and would accept nothing less. 'Why, madame,' exclaimed Smith in disgust, 'then he may require also the four orders of friars, monks, canons, pilgrimages, pardons, oils and creams, relics and all such trumperies. That in no wise can be agreed.'[12]

This conversation marked the effective end of the Anjou courtship but not the end of the French marriage project. Catherine de Medici had yet another son and now she asked Smith if he thought the Queen of England might fancy him instead. Unfortunately, the

Duke of Alençon was younger still, only seventeen, and while Anjou
had been a tall, reasonably good-looking youth Alençon was under-
sized and disfigured by smallpox. But Catherine, who took a severely
practical view of matrimony, remarked that if Elizabeth was disposed
to marry at all 'she saw not where she might marry so well, and
pointed out that without a marriage she could not see any league or
amity being so strong or so lasting'. Smith quite agreed with her. It
was an axiom of the times that 'the knot of blood and marriage was a
stronger seal than that which was printed in wax, and lasted longer,
if God gave good success'.[13]

Thomas Smith had always been in the forefront of those urging
marriage on Elizabeth and apparently he could see nothing out of the
way in a more than twenty-year disparity of age. He wrote home
eagerly recommending the new proposal; Alençon might be young,
dwarfish and pock-marked but he was less papistical and less pig-
headed than his brother. He was also, it seemed, likely to be 'more
apt for the getting of children' – perhaps Smith had been hearing
about Anjou's homosexual tendencies. At any rate, the ambassador
clearly hoped that here at last might be the solution to an intractable
problem and was even ready to face more Channel crossings in such
a good cause, though he were never so sick for it.[14]

But Elizabeth was not enthusiastic. She considered she had been
shabbily treated over the Anjou affair and was disposed to take
offence. The French need not think she was going to marry any old
prince they happened to have handy. Burghley explained tactfully to
Fénélon that, the Queen's natural repugnance to the idea of marriage
having been overcome by Anjou's remarkable qualities, it would
need a lot of persuasion to bring her to the point of accepting a
substitute, and Fénélon warned Catherine that she might be wiser
to conclude a treaty with England first and talk about marriage later.

The Queen-Mother took the hint, but some time in March she and
Thomas Smith had another talk on the subject. After discussing
Elizabeth's danger from the Queen of Scots (it had not escaped
French notice that Mary was turning to Spain for help), Catherine
exclaimed impatiently: 'Jesu, doth not your mistress, Queen Elizabeth, see plainly that she will always be in such danger till she marry?
If she marry into some good house, who shall dare attempt aught
against her?' Again, Smith was in complete agreement. Treaty or no
treaty, he remained totally convinced that Elizabeth's only true
safeguards would be marriage and children. If she had even one
child, 'then all these bold and troublesome titles of the Scotch Queen

or others, that make such gaping for her death, would be clean choked up'. But why stop at one child, cried Catherine, why not five or six? 'Would to God,' answered Smith, 'she had one.' 'No,' the Queen-Mother persisted, 'two boys, lest the one should die, and three or four daughters to make alliance with us again and other princes, to strengthen the realm.' 'Why then,' said Smith, 'you think that Monsieur le Duc shall speed?' With that Catherine laughed and said 'she desired it infinitely and trusted to see three or four at the least of her race, which would make her indeed not to spare sea and land to see her Majesty and them'. After all, if Elizabeth had been able to fancy Anjou, why not Alençon who was 'of the same house, father and mother, and as vigorous and lusty or rather more' – especially now that his beard had begun to sprout.[15]

While the Italian matriarch was making these optimistic plans, negotiations for an Anglo-French treaty of perpetual friendship were proceeding and on 19 April 1572 the draft protocol was signed at Blois. It was primarily a defensive alliance and not, as Francis Walsingham and his radical friends would have liked, an offensive league against Spain. It did not bar the way to a possible future renewal of the Burgundian connection, nor did it in any way commit England to involvement with French intervention in the Nether-lands – something which Charles IX, persuaded by the great Huguenot leader Admiral Coligny, was now beginning seriously to contemplate. Even more usefully, France had now to all intents and purposes recognised the *de facto* government of little King James of Scotland under the pro-English Regent the Earl of Mar – thus virtually abandoning Mary Stuart to her fate.

Having got pretty well everything she wanted, Elizabeth showed even less interest in the Alençon match, but the French were not giving up. In June a high-powered embassy, headed by the Duke de Montmorenci came over to London to ratify the Treaty of Blois and to make the Queen a formal offer of marriage on behalf of the young Duke. Elizabeth received them graciously, entertained them lavishly and invested Montmorenci with the Garter, but she was lukewarm about the proposal. Alençon was too young, too short and really she did not feel she could stomach those pockmarks. However, as usual, she did not close the door. The embassy was dismissed with thanks and a promise that she would think the matter over and send her answer within a month. Lord Burghley was instructed to ask Francis Walsingham for a full report about Alençon, 'of his age in certainty, of his stature, of his condition, his inclination to religion' and so on.[16]

Walsingham, who was as much in favour of the marriage as
Thomas Smith, did his best. Alençon was seventeen years old; he was
wise and stalwart, of a tractable disposition, commendably free from
French light-mindedness and in religion 'easily to be reduced to the
knowledge of the truth'. Walsingham, however, could not conceal
the fact that the young man was nothing to look at. Those wretched
pockmarks were not a very serious disfigurement, since they were
'rather thick than great and deep' and that sprouting beard would
help to cover them. But they were still definitely visible, and Walsingham feared that to the well-known 'delicacy of her Majesty's eye'
they would prove an insurmountable obstacle.[17] So did Lord
Burghley, in spite of Fénélon's assurances that he knew of a doctor
who could remove this defect by a sure and simple remedy.

In July, Catherine de Medici sent one of her son's friends, M. la
Mole, to England to plead his cause. La Mole was an attractive young
man whose charm and gallantry were much to Elizabeth's taste. She
entertained him at Warwick Castle, had him to supper, played the
spinet to please him and invited him to watch a firework dislay, but
she was not committing herself to anything. She told Fénélon that she
had discussed the matter with her council but was still very much per-
plexed. The disparity of age and the difference in religion presented
serious problems and, in any case, she could not possibly decide until
she had seen Alençon for herself. Fénélon replied that the King and
the Queen-Mother would be delighted to arrange this, if only they
could be assured that her Majesty was really in the mind to marry. To
date her attitude had been so doubtful that they hesitated to go
further. But Elizabeth was firm. She must see the Duke and be
certain that they could love each other before making any sort of
commitment. It was Charles of Austria all over again.

La Mole went home in August without, apparently, having
achieved anything very much; but he had made an excellent impression in official circles, and Lord Burghley, ever optimistic, told
Walsingham that 'as it seemeth, the Queen's Majesty is come nearer
to the matter than I hoped for'. But the Queen's Majesty had her
suspicions that all these French attentions were designed to trap her,
through marriage, into an anti-Spanish crusade in the Netherlands
which would ultimately benefit only the King of France. She distrusted Catherine de Medici as strongly as Catherine distrusted her
and had very little faith in the stability of Charles IX's government.

Elizabeth's doubts were soon to be tragically justified, for before
any further progress could be made in the marriage negotiations the

violent forces of sectarian hatred simmering just below the surface of sixteenth-century French society had erupted in a particularly horrible manner. The spark which ignited the explosion of St Bartholomew's Day is generally held to have been the Queen-Mother's jealousy of Admiral Coligny and his growing influence over the weak impressionable king; but what began as an effort to curb the undesirable ascendancy of the Huguenot Party by murdering its leader ended in a bloodbath. In Paris the Catholic mob is estimated to have slaughtered between three and four thousand Huguenots. The killing spread to the provinces and altogether something like ten thousand men, women and children were butchered during the last week of August 1572.

News of the massacre roused Protestants all over Europe to a deep and bitter anger more than tinged with fear. In England especially, where a stream of terrified refugees poured across the Channel into the south-coast ports, public opinion was profoundly shocked. A great wave of anti-Catholic, anti-French feeling surged through the country and any notion of a French marriage for the Queen had become unthinkable. Even the future of the French alliance looked distinctly precarious as preachers thundered for revenge from their pulpits, indignation meetings were held on street corners calling for the repudiation of the Treaty of Blois and the expulsion of the French ambassador, and anyone who did not join in the general outcry was in danger of rough handling from his neighbours. 'It is incredible', wrote Fénélon, sadly contemplating the ruin of his work, 'how the confused rumours . . . of the events in Paris have stirred the hearts of the English who, having heretofore shown a great affection for France, have suddenly turned to extreme indignation and a marvellous hatred against the French . . .'[18]

Events in Paris had put Queen Elizabeth in an awkward position. For the past two years her foreign policy had been based on the French connection and in the present international situation she could not risk an open break with her new friends. On the other hand, she certainly could not give any appearance of condoning the massacre of her co-religionists. She therefore received Fénélon, after keeping him in suspense for three days, and listened in chilly silence while he presented his government's version of the 'accident' of St Bartholomew's Day. It seemed that an assassination plot had been discovered among the Huguenot leaders gathered in Paris for the wedding of the King's sister to the Huguenot Prince Henry of Navarre – a plot already so far advanced that the lives of the royal

family were in imminent danger and this emergency forced the King
into sanctioning a counter-attack which had, no doubt, led to some
very regrettable occurrences. But there was no question of any change
of policy towards the Huguenots in general and no intention of
revoking their edicts of toleration. King Charles sincerely hoped that
the Anglo-French *entente* would not be affected and he, for his part,
intended to stand by the alliance.

Elizabeth heard Fénélon out and then remarked that this was a
different story from the one she had been told by her own ambassador.
She was bound to accept Charles's explanation as that of a monarch
and a gentleman but she hoped he would now do all in his power to
make amends for so much blood so horribly shed, if only for the sake
of his own honour, now so blemished in the eyes of the world.[19] 'I
can assure you, madame,' Fénélon told Catherine de Medici, 'that the
late accident has wounded the Queen and her subjects so deeply that
only a very skilful surgeon and a very sovereign balm can affect a
remedy.'

Catherine was only too anxious that such a balm should be applied
without delay. The monster she had so unwisely let loose on St
Bartholomew's Day had seriously upset the delicate balance of power
in France and the Duke of Guise was now to be seen striding about
the streets of Paris wreathed in smiles. The Queen-Mother therefore,
in spite of all that had happened, began to push the Alençon marriage
again. It was true that Alençon, unlike either of his brothers, had
played no part in the massacre and had indeed spoken out against it,
but in the circumstances Catherine cannot surely have expected much
of a response. She certainly did not get it. The recent slaughter of
Protestants had filled Elizabeth's mind with doubts and she could
come to no decision until she saw how the King of France meant to
treat his Huguenot subjects in future. In any case, as she wrote
reasonably enough to Walsingham, 'if that religion of itself be so
odious to him that he thinks he must root out all the possessors of it,
how should we think his brother a fit husband for us? Or how should
he think that the love may grow, continue and increase betwixt his
brother and us, which ought to be betwixt the husband and the
wife?'[20] But Catherine still persisted, although her ingenuous suggestion that a meeting between Elizabeth and Alençon might be
arranged on some neutral ground – say, the island of Jersey – was
coldly rejected.

By the summer of 1573 the renewal of the civil war, precipitated
by St Bartholomew's, had died down again and a truce was once

more arranged. This peace, said the Queen-Mother, had been made largely to please Elizabeth and Alençon had been one of its prime movers. She and the King were now prepared to let the Duke come to England to be inspected with no strings attached. They were even ready to yield over the religious question – the Queen of England might rule in this matter at her pleasure.

But, if Catherine expected, by these blanket concessions, to drive Elizabeth into her son's arms, she underestimated that lady's inventive powers. The Queen was now rather averse to a meeting. She was afraid she would not like the Duke when she saw him – he would have to give her an undertaking not to be offended if she rejected him.

Matters continued in this way for several months – the French importuning Elizabeth for an answer, Elizabeth always retreating yet always contriving to leave just a little room for hope – until the early spring of 1574 when France at last began to lose interest. The political situation was changing again and Charles IX was dying – the judgement of God said the Protestants, though his early death was more likely due to the effects of congenital syphilis which riddled the Valois family. By that summer it seemed as if yet another Elizabethan courtship had faded into the mist.

CHAPTER XI

A Frog He Would a-Wooing Go

WHAT is conveniently known as the second Alençon courtship opened in 1578 and continued intermittently into the early 1580s. Like all Elizabeth's foreign flirtations with matrimony, it was initiated and prolonged for purely political reasons. What marks it out from its predecessors is the undoubted fact that, for a period of several months during the summer of 1579, Elizabeth managed to convince almost everyone – including perhaps herself – that this time she really was in earnest; that after all those years of obstinate and apparently contented spinsterhood she really did genuinely want to marry an ugly little Frenchman more than twenty years her junior.

Except that they had become considerably more complex and more menacing, the problems facing the Queen in the late seventies were basically much the same as those of the late sixties. On the home front, Mary Queen of Scots, that perennial threat to the government's peace of mind, was still a state prisoner, still intriguing incessantly with her friends abroad, still hoping against hope that her Guise relations, or the Pope, or Philip of Spain, or all three together would one day succeed in getting her out of the Earl of Shrewsbury's custody and on to Elizabeth's throne. Since Elizabeth flatly refused to consider the solution to the problem of Mary favoured by the House of Commons after the discovery of the Ridolfi Plot – to cut off her head and make no more ado about her – and since the prospect of finding a formula by which she could safely be returned to Scotland looked as remote as ever, there seemed nothing for it but to continue to keep her under restraint in England and hope to frustrate her more flamboyant schemes.

A new complication at home was the apparent revival of English Catholicism under the leadership of missionary priests, trained in seminaries in Douai and Rome, who had begun to infiltrate the country by the middle of the decade. In spite of the somewhat hysterical publicity they attracted, the missionaries came too late and too few to do much more than blow on the embers of a dying fire and coax the spark of faith into a tiny flame. By themselves they could never have caused much more than a minor irritation to the Protestant state. But taken in conjunction with the papal bull of excommunication, with the lack of a Protestant heir and the presence of a vigorous Catholic claimant on English soil, they represented a potentially serious danger which could not be ignored, and as a result many brave and sincere men suffered the unpleasant form of death normally reserved for more obvious traitors.

Abroad, European politics were still dominated by the growing might of Philip's empire. In the years immediately following the holocaust of St Bartholomew, when it seemed as if the French alliance would have to be written off, Elizabeth had succeeded, at least temporarily, in mending her fences with Spain. In 1578, Elizabeth and Philip were still just about on speaking terms, but few informed observers of the international scene believed that a confrontation could be postponed indefinitely. Harassed by the depradations of English privateers on his American trade, and increasingly convinced that he would never suppress his Dutch rebels while they continued to receive handouts from Elizabeth, even the slow-moving Philip would sooner or later use the Pope's interdict as an excuse for dealing with the heretical Queen as she deserved.

It was the war in the Netherlands which led more or less directly to the resumption of the Alençon courtship. Elizabeth, to the sorrow of her more radical Protestant advisers, did not like the Dutch. She lent them enough money to keep the rebel forces in being, but regarded them as greedy, quarrelsome, unreliable and Calvinist. In present circumstances, William of Orange and his brother Count Louis were performing a useful service by tying Philip down in a costly and unprofitable war of attrition, but Elizabeth was determined that her own involvement should be kept to a minimum. In the long term she was interested in a negotiated settlement, for in the long term England's national security and economic prosperity depended heavily on a peaceful and prosperous Netherlands. She was therefore alarmed and irritated when the French King's brother began to take an interest in Dutch affairs. Least of all did she want to see another round of the perennial Habsburg–Valois quarrel fought out on her own doorstep; besides which it had always been a cardinal point of English foreign policy to keep the French out of the Low Countries.

But when, in the spring of 1578, it became apparent that Alençon was playing a lone hand Elizabeth's attitude changed. If the Duke could be lured by the bait of marriage she ought, with any luck, to be able to control his future activities and use him to serve her purposes by making trouble for Philip without involving her too closely. It would certainly be considerably cheaper than the alternative course of paying the Dutch to send him away. It would also be safer, for if Philip should turn nasty the threat of approaching Anglo-French nuptials would serve to put the frighteners on.

Alençon himself was nothing loath, and indeed the first approaches seem to have come from him. Charles IX having died childless, the French throne was now occupied by Henry of Anjou, Elizabeth's former reluctant suitor, and the Valois family pattern was repeating itself. Alençon, restless, ambitious and dissatisfied with his lot, was on bad terms with his brother and rapidly becoming as much of a domestic nuisance as ever Anjou had been. His attempts to carve a career and a patrimony for himself in the Netherlands had not so far met with any noticeable success and he knew he could expect no help from home. The Queen of England was still, as Francis Walsingham put it, 'the best marriage in her parish' and even to become her official suitor would give him useful additional status. If she could be cajoled into financing his plans for his own self-aggrandisement, so much the better, and the Duke began to write winning letters assuring the Queen of his entire devotion and willingness to be guided by her in all his doings.[1]

By late summer the courtship was once more a live issue, although at this stage no one seriously supposed that it would lead to anything more than another prolonged bout of negotiations. The character of the affair began to change early in 1579 when Alençon sent his best friend, Jean Simier, to England with full powers to negotiate and conclude the marriage contract and also, it would appear, instructions to do his best to sweep Elizabeth off her feet, for Simier, who proved to be the epitome of every Englishman's idea of a gallant Frenchman – 'a most choice courtier, exquisitely skilled in love toys, pleasant conceits and court dalliances' – at once embarked on an ardent proxy wooing. Presumably he and his master reckoned that such an approach would be irresistible to a middle-aged spinster and it looked, for a time at least, as if they might have guessed right.

Elizabeth was charmed with Simier. He was rapidly admitted to the ranks of those privileged few known by royal nicknames, becoming the Queen's Monkey in a punning reference to his own surname. He was allowed to capture 'trophies' in the shape of gloves and handkerchiefs – even to mount a daring raid on the royal bedchamber and carry off one of the royal nightcaps. But, although Elizabeth blossomed under the life-giving rain of Simier's admiration (the French ambassador told Catherine de Medici that the Queen seemed quite rejuvenated and more beautiful than she had been fifteen years before), and appeared in some danger of losing her heart, she showed absolutely no signs of losing her head. Not all her new friend's skill in love toys or pleasant conceits could induce her to make any commitment. She told the current Spanish ambassador, Bernardino de Mendoza, that it was a fine thing for an old woman like her to be thinking of marriage and more than hinted that she was only encouraging Alençon to get him out of the Netherlands. In any case, she said, nothing could be settled until he had been over to see her.[2]

But by this time most people thought he would come and that he would not come in vain. Elizabeth herself had promised him that his honour would not suffer and Catherine de Medici was urging her son to take the plunge. 'I am sure', she wrote on 29 March, 'she [Elizabeth] will not be so ill advised as to let you return discontented, for she knows the wrong she would do in abusing the brother of so great a king.'[3] Gilbert Talbot told his father, the Earl of Shrewsbury, in a letter written from the court on 4 April that for the past five days the Privy Council had been continuously in session from eight o'clock in the morning until dinner time, 'and presently after dinner and an hour's conference with her Majesty, to council again and so till supper time. And all this,' he went on, 'as far as I can learn, is about the matter of Monsieur's coming hither, his entertainment here and what demands are to be made unto him in the treaty of marriage ... and I can assure your lordship it is verily thought this marriage will come to pass of a great sort of wise men.'[4]

A committee of the Council had now begun to negotiate with Simier on the basis of the proposals put forward by the French when the Anjou marriage had been under consideration eight years previously, but it was clear that no real progress would be made unless and until Alençon himself came to England. In any case, the councillors were deeply divided over the advisability of the whole project. The Earl of Leicester and Francis Walsingham (now back at home as Principal Secretary of State) were both strongly opposed, while Lord Burghley and the Earl of Sussex were in favour. The arguments in favour of the Queen's marriage were basically the same as they had always been – the obvious advantages of an alliance with a major foreign power sealed by family ties and the hope of an undisputed heir to the throne. The old arguments against – that the only possible husband for the Queen was a foreigner and a Catholic – were now reinforced both by the deepening of the ideological divide and by fears that Elizabeth's life would be endangered if she were to become pregnant – she would be forty-six on her next birthday.

Leicester's objections were probably mainly personal but, as was shortly to become apparent, he was hardly in a position to complain. Walsingham's opinion, set out in a closely reasoned memorandum, was coloured by his deep distrust of all the Catholic powers. While not minimising the dangers facing the Queen at home and abroad, he believed that her best policy would be to trust in the Protestant God and keep clear of any entanglement with the representatives of anti-Christ. Alençon might not be a bigoted Catholic, but he was still a Catholic and as heir presumptive to the French throne would hardly be willing to jeopardise his inheritance by abjuring his religion. However compelling the political case for the marriage, Walsingham, after St Bartholomew, was convinced that every right-thinking Englishman would far rather Elizabeth stayed single than see her ally herself to a nasty unhealthy set of foreigners like the Valois and perhaps risk her life in childbirth.[5]

Against this, Sussex and Lord Burghley clung to the old-fashioned belief that any husband would be better than none and Burghley pooh-poohed the idea that the Queen was too old to have a child. The proportions of her body were excellent and she suffered from no physical impediment such as smallness of stature or largeness of body, 'nor no sickness, nor lack of natural functions in those things that properly belong to the procreation of children' he wrote in one of his careful *aides-mémoire* to himself. In the judgement of her doctors and those women who knew her estate in such matters and were most intimately acquainted with her body, there was no reason at all why she should not safely bear children for some time to come. Indeed there was every reason to believe that her Majesty was 'very apt for the procreation of children'. Burghley even thought that the therapeutic effects of sexual intercourse might cure Elizabeth's neuralgic pains and improve her health and spirits generally, for she would be spared 'the dolours and infirmities as all physicians do usually impute to womankind for lack of marriage, and specially to such women as naturally have their bodies apt to conceive and procreate children'.[6]

But Burghley seems to have been pretty much alone in his optimistic assessment of Elizabeth's childbearing prospects, and the

Queen's closest advisers remained divided and hesitant in the face of the Queen's unexpected enthusiasm. According to Mendoza, writing early in May, she was now expressing 'such a strong desire to marry that not a councillor, whatever his opinion may be, dares to say a word against it'.[7] Nevertheless, at a full council meeting held a few days later, opinion was almost universally hostile. Again according to Mendoza, the new Lord Chancellor, Thomas Bromley, pointed out 'how bad this talk of marriage was, both for the Queen and the nation, since no succession could be hoped from it, and great confusion might be caused by the coming hither of Catholics, and above all Frenchmen, who were their ancient enemies'. Simier was then summoned and told that several of Alençon's demands – including coronation immediately after the marriage, a life pension of £60,000 and the garrisoning of a port by French soldiers for his own protection – were totally inadmissible.

At this the normally suave Simier lost his temper and, slamming his way out of the room, went straight to the Queen. She listened to him 'with much graciousness and many expressions of sorrow that her councillors disapproved of her marriage which she desired so much', and proceeded to assume a settled air of lovelorn melancholy. Mendoza heard that she had 'twice said when she was retired in her chamber "they need not think that it is going to end in this way; I must get married" '.[8]

There was much coming and going of envoys from France over the next few weeks, with the result that Alençon abated most of his preconditions – though he was still insisting on the private exercise of his religion. The negotiations were on again and Simier was ordered 'to use every possible means to attract and satisfy the lords and gentry of the kingdom', for which purpose money would be available. 'Simier has begun to do this already,' commented Mendoza on 14 May, 'and has given two grand banquets this week to the Council.'[9]

But in spite of the free food, and in spite of a lavish scattering of bribes and expensive presents, the opposition was not appeased. There were two rather amateurish attempts to assassinate Simier during the summer, both of which were blamed on the Earl of Leicester's party. It was after the second of these that a justifiably irritated Simier, who had been keeping his ear to the ground since his arrival in England, decided that the time was ripe to strike back at his most dangerous adversary and chose a propitious moment to pass on to the Queen an interesting piece of information about her precious Robert Dudley.

He had, it seemed, been secretly married for nearly a year to Lettice, the widowed Countess of Essex – the same Lettice who, as Viscountess Hereford, had been the cause of so much ill-feeling back in the sixties.

If the Frenchman had hoped to provoke an explosion of wrath against the opponents of the marriage and smooth the way for Alençon's visit, he certainly succeeded brilliantly. The Queen, according to William Camden's account of the matter, 'grew into such a chafe that she commanded Leicester not to stir out of the Palace of Greenwich and intended to have committed him to the Tower of London, which his enemies much desired. But the Earl of Sussex, though his greatest and deadliest adversary, dissuaded her. For he was of opinion that no man was to be troubled for lawful marriage, which estate amongst all men hath ever been held in honour and esteem.'[10]

Good faithful old Sussex managed to calm Elizabeth down and prevent her from making a fool of herself in public, but her rage against Robert was still terrible. Not only had he deceived and betrayed her, but he'd also had the unspeakable gall to oppose her own marriage when all the time he was married himself! As for Robert, after a brief period of house arrest at Court, he retreated to his house at Wanstead and wrote mournfully to Lord Burghley of his grief at the Queen's bitter unkindness after twenty years' faithful service. 'And,' he went on, 'as I carried myself almost more than a bondman many a year together, so long as one drop of comfort was left of any hope, as you yourself, my Lord, doth well know, so being acquitted and delivered of that hope, and, by both open and private protestations and declarations discharged, methinks it is more than hard to take such an occasion to bear so great displeasure for.'[11]

It might seem hard that, having refused him herself, Elizabeth should now be creating such an uproar over Robert's marriage. But, as Robert very well knew, this was not an area ruled by logic. He had always occupied a unique position – the Queen's own creation and her special property. It was a position which had always carried its drawbacks as well as many solid material advantages, and while he could still dream of one day founding a royal Dudley dynasty he had been prepared to put up with any number of drawbacks. Now that old dream was finally dead and buried and it was time, more than time, to think of the future. Robert still loved Elizabeth in his own way, a relationship such as theirs could not have survived as it did without a solid basis of mutual affection and respect, but, as he

stoutly told Lord Burghley, he was not prepared to be her slave. He
wanted a wife and he wanted a son to carry on his name. This, of
course, was a perfectly legitimate aspiration and one which Robert
had evidently reasoned he should now be in a strong enough place
to achieve without losing the Queen altogether. But, knowing the
Queen's autocratic and naturally possessive temperament, he can
hardly have expected to achieve it without an almighty row – hence
his reluctance to make the matter public and face the inevitable
consequences.

Meanwhile Elizabeth was showing a determinedly sprightly face to
the world as she got ready to welcome her latest suitor – for Alençon
was at last on the point of leaving for England to try his luck in
person. 'She is burning with impatience for his coming,' commented
Mendoza rather sourly, 'although her councillors have laid before her
the difficulties which might arise . . . She is largely influenced by the
idea that it should be known that her talents and beauty are so great,
that they have sufficed to cause him to come and visit her without
any assurance that he will be her husband.'[12]

The Duke reached Greenwich in the early hours of 17 August and
later that day Elizabeth dined with him privately in Simier's rooms.
His presence in the Palace was supposed to be a secret, which put
councillors and royal servants in the embarrassing position of having
to pretend to be deaf and blind, but one thing was clear from the out-
set – from a personal point of view the visit was proving a triumphant
success. Alençon might be a funny little man with a pock-marked
complexion and a bulbous nose, but he was also charming, intelligent
and witty. He became the Queen's Frog and the French ambassador
hastened to inform Catherine de Medici that 'the lady has with
difficulty been able to entertain the Duke, being captivated, overcome with love. She told me she had never found a man whose nature
and actions suited her better.'[13] Mendoza, too, was obliged to admit
to Philip that 'the Queen is delighted with Alençon and he with her,
as she has let out to some of her courtiers, saying that she was pleased
to have known him, was much taken with his good parts and
admired him more than any man. She said that, for her part, she will
not prevent his being her husband.'[14]

A grand ball was held at Greenwich on Sunday the twenty-third at
which Elizabeth danced much more than usual, constantly waving
and smiling at the Duke, who watched the proceedings not very
adequately hidden behind a curtain. But for all this showing off, and
for all the billing and cooing going on at the Palace, there had so far

been, as Mendoza did not fail to point out, no sign 'that any resolution has been arrived at' and King Philip remained highly sceptical,
convinced that the whole thing was mere pretence. Nevertheless, the
party which opposed the marriage had taken grave alarm. 'Leicester,'
reported Mendoza on 25 August, 'is in great grief.' Robert had
recently had an interview with the Queen, after which his emotion
was remarked, and that same evening a meeting of the opposition
took place at the Earl of Pembroke's house, the Sidneys and various
other friends and relatives of the Dudley clan being present. According to Mendoza, 'some of them afterwards remarked that Parliament
would have something to say as to whether the Queen married or not.
The people in general', he added hopefully, 'seem to threaten a
revolution about it.'[15]

Alençon went home on the twenty-ninth and, although he and the
Queen immediately began a hectic exchange of love letters, it seemed
that no promises had yet been given. Meanwhile popular expressions
of hostility to the marriage were growing. As far back as April,
Gilbert Talbot had noted that the preachers were busy 'to apply their
sermons to tend covertly against this marriage, many of them in-
veighing greatly thereat'; and during August, probably while
Alençon was still at Greenwich, the Puritan writer John Stubbs
published his famous pamphlet *The Discovery of a Gaping Gulf
whereunto England is like to be swallowed by another French
Marriage*.

Stubbs did not mince his words. The Queen was too old now to
think of marriage and it was all a devilish French trick to push the
matter so eagerly just at a time when childbearing was likely to be
most dangerous for her. If only she would honestly consult her most
faithful and wise physicians, they would tell her how fearful was the
expectation of death. As for Alençon, he was rotten with debauchery
– 'the old serpent himself in the form of a man come a second time
to seduce the English Eve and to ruin the English Paradise'. If his
mass was once allowed into the country it would be 'as wildfire that
all the seas could not quench' and would seriously imperil the true
Protestant faith.[16]

John Stubbs was not the only man to commit his objections to
paper. Philip Sidney, Robert Dudley's beloved and brilliant nephew,
also wrote earnestly to the Queen, begging her not to alienate the
affection of her loyal Protestant subjects – 'your chief, if not your
sole, strength' – by marrying a Frenchman and a papist, one whom

even the common people knew to be the son of 'a Jezebel of our age'.[17]

Sidney had at least had the tact to address himself to the Queen's private ear and he escaped with an angry scolding. But Stubbs' provocative diatribe, which was attracting wide publicity, roused Elizabeth to real fury. She issued a fierce proclamation against the dissemination of all such lewd and seditious libels and ordered the arrest of Stubbs and his printer. They were prosecuted, ironically enough, under a statute originally framed to protect Philip of Spain when he was Mary's consort and sentenced to lose their right hands. The execution was carried out in the presence of a silently sympathetic crowd but it did not stifle the growing radical agitation which was beginning ominously to resemble that which had preceded Mary's marriage.

However, it seemed that Elizabeth meant to go ahead with her plans. Early in October she summoned the Council to discuss the matter and give her its considered advice, but after a series of meetings, one of which lasted without a break from eight in the morning till seven o'clock at night, it was clear that a majority of the members were still very unhappy about the whole thing. Their objections were summed up in a minute in Lord Burghley's hand, dated 6 October and headed 'Causes of Misliking of the Marriage'. These included the fact that Alençon was a Frenchman, 'the people of this realm naturally hating that nation', and the fact that he would in all probability shortly succeed his ailing and childless brother as King of France, with the obvious complications that would entail. Then there was 'the doubt that her Majesty either shall not have children, or that she may be endangered in child-birth'. Much as everyone wanted an heir to the throne, no one wanted to see the Queen risk her precious life. Her constitution was, after all, so good that, without courting the perils of marriage, she seemed 'like to live long'. Also, as someone pointed out, there was no guarantee that Monsieur would prove a kind and considerate husband. On the contrary, the huge discrepancy in their ages and their difference in religion hardly augured for 'a hearty love of her Majesty'. The difference in religion, of course, remained 'the greatest inconvenience' to those council members who foresaw that Alençon's Catholicism 'shall be a comfort to all obstinate Papists in England and a discomfort to all the subjects of good religion'.[18]

In spite of the weight of opinion against him, Lord Burghley still favoured the French marriage – at least, he painted a gloomy picture of the dangers to the realm from the unsettled succession (especially as Elizabeth grew older), from the pretensions of Mary Stuart and from foreign aggression if the Queen did not marry. Probably, though, the argument which influenced him most strongly was that Elizabeth herself appeared to want the marriage so much. Eventually it was decided that this was a matter on which the Council as a body could not advise – each individual member would state his position if required and each would do his best to carry out her wishes – but the Queen would have to make up her own mind first.

When this message was conveyed to the Queen on the morning of 7 October by a four-man committee headed by Lord Burghley, it got a stormy reception. Elizabeth burst into tears and reproached her faithful councillors bitterly for doubting that there could be any better safeguard for the realm than 'to have her marry and have a child of her own body to inherit and so to continue the line of King Henry VIII'. Since this was precisely what her faithful councillors had been urging her to do throughout all the years when it might have been physically practicable – advice which she had consistently refused to accept – such reproaches must have seemed unreasonable to put it mildly, though none of those present ventured to say so. The Queen went on to curse herself for her 'simplicity' in allowing the matter to be debated at all, but she had expected, so she said, to have had 'a universal request made to her to proceed in this marriage'. Then, being too upset to continue, she dismissed the committee until the afternoon.

When they returned, the conversation was resumed along much the same lines, the Queen showing 'her great misliking' of anyone who opposed her marriage. As for the religious difficulty, 'she did marvel that any person would think so slenderly of her, as that she would not for God's cause, for herself, her surety and her people, have so straight regard thereto as none ought to make that such a doubt, as for it to forbear marriage and to have the Crown settled in her child'.[19]

After this remarkable display, there was nothing for the committee to do but report back to the full Council her Majesty's 'earnest disposition for this her marriage'. 'And thereupon,' recorded Lord Burghley, 'after long consultations had, all the Council accorded upon a new offer to be made to her Majesty of all our assents to offer our service in furtherance of this marriage, if so it shall please her.'[20]

The offer was duly made next day 'by the mouth of the Lord

Chancellor', but was not received in any very gracious spirit. 'Her Majesty's answers were very sharp in reprehending of all such as she thought would make arguments against her marriage . . . and though she thought not meet to declare to us whether she would marry Monsieur or no, yet she looked at our hands that we did so much desire her marriage and to have children of her body, as we should have with one accord have made special suit to her for the same.'[21]

In spite of having apparently got what she wanted, Elizabeth remained in an exceedingly bad temper. She was still not speaking to the Earl of Leicester and had quarrelled furiously with Francis Walsingham, whom she suspected of being behind much of the popular agitation against the marriage. According to Bernardino de Mendoza, she was 'so cross and melancholy that it was noticed by everyone who approached her'.

Meanwhile, Simier, who had now been hanging about for nearly a year, was getting impatient and badgering the Queen for a decision. On 9 November they were closeted together for several hours and on the following day she summoned the principal councillors to her chamber 'and told them that she had determined to marry and that they need say nothing more to her about it, but should at once discuss what was necessary for carrying it out'.[22] This sounded like hard news at last but, as Mendoza told Philip a fortnight later, 'these people change so constantly in whatever they take in hand, that it is difficult to send your Majesty any definite information'.[23] Elizabeth had apparently changed her mind overnight and a messenger on his way to Alençon was stopped at Dover and recalled.

The Queen was now talking about getting every councillor to give his opinion of the marriage in writing. When Simier heard of this and protested at what looked like a deliberate delaying tactic, she complained that the Council leaked like a sieve. Her next move was an attempt to persuade that much-tried body to write a collective letter to Alençon urging him to come back to England as soon as possible, 'whereupon they replied that it was not for them but for her to do that'. They also, according to Mendoza, told her that someone of greater standing than Simier should be sent to complete the negotiations. The result was more trouble with Simier's wounded feelings and eventually, towards the end of November, a small committee, from which both Leicester and Walsingham were excluded, was set up to finalise the draft of the marriage contract. This was completed within a few days and conceded to Alençon and all his household the right to hear mass in their private chapel.[24]

G

But even now Elizabeth had been careful to leave herself an escape-route. She could not marry without her subjects' consent and must therefore be granted a two months' breathing-space during which she would do her very best to win them over to the idea. If she failed, then the engagement was to be regarded as broken off.[25]

Simier left for France on 24 November, laden with expensive presents and handsomely escorted. In December, Elizabeth talked to Mendoza on the subject of her marriage and 'referred to it so tenderly as to make it clear how ardently she desired it'. In January she had become perceptibly less enthusiastic. Leicester and Walsingham were both back at court by this time, and significantly the Queen was now herself raising the religious barrier. She wrote sorrowfully to her Frog telling him that in spite of all her efforts it seemed the English would never accept his mass, so, if he could not give it up, perhaps they had better forget about marriage and remain just good friends.

Had she ever been really serious? A number of learned historians have believed that she was, at least for a time, and have seen her as an ageing lonely woman snatching desperately at an eleventh-hour chance of marriage and motherhood. Well, maybe, and yet it is some-how very difficult to visualise Elizabeth Tudor, that supremely successful career woman, surrendering herself to a man fully young enough to be her own son; being willing, as Philip Sidney put it, to deliver him the keys of her kingdom and live at his discretion. At the same time, there has to be some explanation of her uncharacteristic behaviour during the summer and autumn of 1579. She was, of course, approaching if she had not already begun the menopause and this, combined with the emotional shock of Leicester's marriage, may well have thrown her temporarily off balance. There are other possible explanations. For more than twenty years Elizabeth had been using the courtship ploy at every opportunity, likely and un-likely, in her relations with foreign countries and, apart from the obvious advantages it gave her in the diplomatic poker game, there can be little doubt that she also derived more complicated satisfac-tions from the elaborate teasing of her prospective bridegrooms – satisfactions to do with the exercise of sexual power and the gratifica-tion of sexual vanity. As little as any other woman did the Queen enjoy being reminded of the passing years, but at forty-six she knew well enough that the time for playing her favourite game was coming to an end and, like any great actress making perhaps her last appear-ance in a role which has made her famous, she would naturally want the occasion to be a memorable one. It was ironical, too, that in this her final courtship Elizabeth should for the first time have found a supporting cast worthy of her talents. Unlike the comically boorish Scandinavians, the stodgy Germanic Charles von Habsburg and sulky Anjou, young Alençon had been only too willing to enter into the spirit of the thing. He and Simier were both finished products of a society which regarded the making of courtly love as an art form and, bearing in mind the value of the prize they were after, neither grudged the expenditure of his best efforts. It was all a new and intoxicating experience for Elizabeth and perhaps it is hardly surprising that she should have allowed herself to be carried away. The illusion of renewed youth and beauty died on the morning of 7 October as she looked into the worried faces of some of her oldest friends and the awakening, it seemed, was bitter.

Illusion might be dead, but the Alençon courtship was still very much alive. The Queen was back at her old tricks of blowing hot and cold and driving sober statesmen like Francis Walsingham to distraction. 'I would to God,' he moaned, 'her Highness would resolve one way or the other touching the matter of her marriage.' Walsingham liked the idea no more than he had ever done, but he was terrified that Elizabeth would play fast and loose once too often and end up by offending the French past repair. 'If her Majesty be not already resolved touching her marriage,' he wrote to the Earl of Sussex, 'it will behove her to grow to some speedy resolution therein, for the entertaining of it doth breed her greater dishonour than I dare commit to paper, besides the danger she daily incurreth for not settling of her estate which dependeth altogether on the marriage.'[26]

Walsingham's alarm was understandable, for as the year 1580 unfolded the international scene could hardly have looked much bleaker from England's point of view. Spain's annexation of Portugal that summer gave Philip control of the entire Iberian peninsula. It gave him the use of the fine Portuguese navy and the revenues of Portugal's colonial empire in the east to add to those of his own empire in the west, making him – on paper at least – the richest and most powerful monarch the world had ever seen. Across the North Sea, Alexander of Parma, the new Spanish commander in the Netherlands, was having a considerable run of success against the Dutch rebels, and now trouble threatened even nearer home, across the Scottish Border, where Mary Stuart's son was growing up. Unfortunately, young James's adolescent revolt against the restraints of his strictly Calvinist upbringing was taking the form of an ominous desire to hobnob with his mother's Guise relations – and that connection boded no good to Protestant England. In Protestant England itself, 1580 saw the arrival of the first Jesuit missionary priests, Fathers Campion and Parsons, and their startling, if short-lived, success among the Catholic minority caused acute alarm in government circles.

It was certainly no time for the Queen to make a single unnecessary enemy and, if ever she had needed friends, surely she needed them now. But Elizabeth refused to be deflected – she would go her own way just as she had always done. She was angling now for a new league with France without marriage, just as she had done ten years earlier, but this time the King of France and the Queen-Mother stood firm. They were determined to pin down the elusive virgin, to saddle her with responsibility for the volatile Alençon and ensure that she paid her full share of the price of war with Spain. As for Alençon himself, he was in the classic position of all adventurers in pursuit of an heiress and could not afford to take offence. He grumbled over the Queen's inconstancy but he had not lost hope, and the Queen took care that he should not. In April 1581, when one of her garters fell off during the famous visit to Sir Francis Drake on board the *Golden Hind* at Deptford, she allowed the French ambassador to 'capture' it as a trophy for the lovelorn Frog.[27]

Failing marriage, Alençon's plan was to coax or blackmail Elizabeth into giving him money. He was already deep in debt, having borrowed lavishly on his expectations, and had now just about reached the end of his resources. If he could not get more backing from somewhere soon, he would have to abandon his ambitions in the Netherlands and return empty-handed to his brother's unfriendly court. In the summer of 1581 the Queen finally opened her purse to the extent of lending her impecunious suitor £30,000, which was better than nothing but still nothing like enough, and Frog came to the conclusion that his best chance of getting more would be to go a-wooing again. He landed at Rye on 31 October and received a warm welcome. All the old routine of dalliance was resumed, Elizabeth making an enormous fuss of her prince frog, her little Moor, her little Italian and, according to gossip relayed by the Venetians, visiting him every morning while he was still in bed to take him a cup of broth; while Frog himself yearned eloquently to be allowed into her bed to show what a good companion he could be.

Mendoza reported that the French ambassadors and the Duke's own companions 'look upon the marriage as an accomplished fact, but the English in general scoff at it, saying that he is only after money ... It is certain', went on Mendoza in a letter to Philip dated 11 November, 'that the Queen will do her best to avoid offending him, and to pledge him in the affairs of the Netherlands, in order to drive his brother into a rupture with your Majesty, which is her great object, whilst she keeps her hands free and can stand by looking on at the war.'[28]

What is certain is that Elizabeth was doing her utmost to inveigle the King of France into agreeing to share the cost of supporting Alençon and a good deal of hard bargaining was going on behind the screen of slightly farcical love-making. But Henri III refused to commit himself to anything until he was sure of the Queen and, although Mendoza heard from a reliable source that 'when the Queen and Alençon were alone together she pledges herself to him to his heart's content, and as much as any woman could to a man', she would not allow anything to be said publicly.

Matters came to a head on the morning of 22 November, when Elizabeth and her Frog were walking together in the gallery at Whitehall, Leicester and Walsingham being also present. Again according to Mendoza's account: 'the French ambassador entered and said that he wished to write to his master, from whom he had received orders to hear from the Queen's own lips her intention with regard to marrying his brother. She replied, "You may write this to the King: that the Duke of Alençon shall be my husband", and at the same moment she turned to Alençon and kissed him on the mouth, drawing a ring from her own hand and giving it to him as a pledge. Alençon gave her a ring of his in return, and shortly afterwards the Queen summoned the ladies and gentlemen from the presence chamber in the gallery, repeating to them in a loud voice in Alençon's presence what she had previously said.'[29]

The Queen could scarcely have gone further in her efforts to convince the French of her good faith. 'The standers-by', says William Camden, 'took it that the marriage was now contracted by promise' (a promise to marry made before witnesses constituted a legally binding contract), and the episode naturally created a considerable stir. When William of Orange heard about it he had the bells rung in Antwerp, while at home 'the courtiers' minds were diversely affected; some leaped for joy, some were seized with admiration, and others were dejected with sorrow'.[30] Camden goes on to say that the Queen quickly regretted her rash words and spent a sleepless night in 'doubts and cares' among the lamentations of her gentlewomen, but despite all appearances the Queen had, in fact, committed herself to very little. If the French took her up on her promise she had only to protest that she'd been misunderstood and raise her terms to even higher levels. (She was already demanding conditions which the King was expected to refuse.) Alternatively, she could call Parliament in the confident expectation of a Commons' veto on her marriage to a Catholic. In either case she would be able to cast the blame for failure on other shoulders. It's in the highest degree unlikely that she made her declaration unadvisedly – carried away 'by the force of modest love in the midst of amorous discourse'. The Indian summer madness of 1579 had long since faded and now, at least so she told the Earl of Sussex in December, Elizabeth hated the idea of marriage more every day for reasons which she would not divulge to a twin soul.

That Alençon had taken her seriously, even for a moment, is almost equally unlikely. The Duke was nobody's fool and had probably known for some time that the marriage was a non-starter. However, the Queen had now given him a useful card which he proceeded to play by sitting tight and indicating quite plainly that she would have to make it worth his while to go away quietly. And it's difficult to blame him. Elizabeth had made shameless use of him and she owed him something. The poor Frog may also have been growing tired of his rootless, precarious gambler's existence. It was pleasant to live comfortably and free at the English court, and the prospect of going back into the cold clearly became less and less inviting. Of all Elizabeth's suitors it is possible to feel more than a little sorry for François, Duke of Alençon.

After some indecision and a good deal of haggling, Elizabeth finally offered him a 'loan' of £60,000 – half to be paid fifteen days after he had left the country and the other half fifty days after that. Still he would not go and showed signs of turning awkward, pointing out reasonably enough that the Queen had openly pledged herself to him and, if she turned him out now, he would become the laughing-stock of the world. The Queen advanced him £10,000 and still he lingered, hoping to extort better terms. At last, just as the situation threatened to become embarrassing, he had to accept the fact that the holidays were over and, after some last-minute delays, he left London on 1 February 1582. The Queen went with him as far as Canterbury and a rather sardonic Leicester was deputed to see him safely off the premises. The farewells were affectionate, Elizabeth protesting tearfully that she would give a million to have her dear Frog swimming in the Thames again and telling all and sundry that he would be back in six weeks to marry her – if only the King of France would keep his side of the bargain. In private she is said to have danced for joy in her bedchamber.

The Queen had reason to feel relief and some satisfaction. She had succeeded in extricating herself comparatively cheaply from a potentially dangerous predicament. There had been no rupture with France; Alençon might yet cause Philip some trouble in the Netherlands and Elizabeth had gained nearly three years' valuable time. As it turned out, Alençon accomplished very little in the Netherlands – indeed, he was to prove more of a nuisance to the hard-pressed Dutch than to anyone else – and when he died of fever in June 1584 he had long outlived his usefulness to the Queen of England. Nevertheless, Elizabeth apparently mourned him deeply, shedding tears for three weeks on end and unblushingly informing the French ambassador that she regarded herself as a forlorn widow. Perhaps she did feel a mild pang. Beneath all the nonsense and the play-acting she had liked Alençon. He had been her last fling and at least he had amused her for a season.

Envoi

THERE were no more foreign suitors after the Duke of Alençon and most people were thankful for it. The English had long since resigned themselves to the extinction of the line of King Henry VIII and had become accustomed to the phenomenon of their Virgin Queen. To a nation growing increasingly prosperous and increasingly confident of its ability to survive no matter what, with the assured assistance of the Protestant God, an uncertain future seemed a small enough price to pay for freedom from foreign interference and foreign entanglements. Unmarried, the Queen belonged to every Englishman, and very few Englishmen would now have had it any other way. Indeed, it's difficult to see how it could ever have been any other way. In the absence of an acceptable native-born or foreign Protestant consort, it would have been impossible for Elizabeth to have married without splitting the country in half.

Once she had recovered from the emotional *crise* of 1579, Elizabeth herself showed no real signs of regret that her courting days were over – perhaps she too was rather thankful than otherwise. She had come to terms with the fact of the Earl of Leicester's marriage by simply ignoring it, and the new Countess was kept carefully out of her sight. Since the Queen continued to make regular use of Leicester's house at Wanstead for council meetings and conferences, this must have led to a good deal of inconvenience. But, in spite of the domestic problems caused by Elizabeth's refusal to recognise the existence of Lady Leicester, and although the longed-for son and heir, born at the end of 1579, lived only four years, Robert and Lettice seem to have been happy together and Robert proved a surprisingly uxorious husband, 'doting extremely upon marriage'.

He was not to have much leisure to enjoy it. The second half of the 1580s was a stormy period for everyone in English public life, but especially for Robert Dudley. After the assassination of William of Orange, Elizabeth had been reluctantly obliged to take a more active part in the Dutch struggle for survival, and in the autumn of 1585 Robert was appointed commander-in-chief of an expeditionary force of about five thousand men being sent to the Netherlands.

Trouble began when, after giving him a royal welcome, the Dutch Estates offered the Earl of Leicester the Supreme Governorship of the United Provinces. Trouble increased dramatically when he accepted – it was an offer of power and prestige calculated to turn stronger heads than his. It was equally calculated to enrage the Queen, who had already refused an offer of Dutch sovereignty herself and who was, in any case, still determined to keep her involvement to an absolute minimum. When the news reached her she was angrier with her old friend than perhaps she had ever been before. 'We could never have imagined,' she wrote, 'had we not seen it fall out, that a man raised up by ourself and extraordinarily favoured by us above any other subject of this land, would have in so contemptible a sort broken our commandment in a cause that so greatly touched our honour.' An extra edge was added to Elizabeth's fury by gossip that Lady Leicester was planning to join her husband, taking with her 'such a train of ladies and gentlemen, and such rich coaches, litters and side saddles as her Majesty had none such and that there should be such a court of ladies as should far surpass her Majesty's court here'. This tale, so Robert was informed, had roused her Majesty 'to extreme choler and dislike of all your doings there, saying with great oaths she would have no more courts under her obeisance but her own, and would revoke you from thence with all speed'.

Robert, as usual, was in despair over the Queen's attitude and her refusal even to listen to his explanations. 'At the least,' he complained, 'I think she would never have so condemned any other man before she heard him.' But the Council, alarmed at the possible effect on the conduct of the campaign if Elizabeth carried out her threat to recall its general in disgrace, combined to smooth things over. Gradually the Queen calmed down and was finally prepared to admit that perhaps Robert had not really meant to disobey her, that he'd believed he was acting for the best, though mistakenly. She would not allow him to keep his governorship, but there was no more talk of recalling him and by the following summer he had once more been forgiven. 'Now will I end,' she wrote in a private letter dated July 1586, 'that do imagine I talk still with you and therefore loathly say farewell to my two Eyes, though ever I pray God bless you from all harm and save you from all foes, with my million and legion of thanks for all your pains and care.'

Robert, absent in the Netherlands, missed the fearful explosion of royal temperament which followed the execution of the Queen of Scots that winter and was considered fortunate by his colleagues, riding the storm in London; but he was home again before the end of 1587, ready to take up the onerous post of Lieutenant and General of the Queen's Armies and Companies being hastily mustered to defend the country against invasion. King Philip's long-threatened Enterprise against England had at last become an imminent reality and during the crisis summer of 1588, with a Spanish fleet expected hourly in the Channel, Elizabeth was showing an alarming disposition to go down to the south coast to meet the enemy in the front line. It was to divert her mind from such an unsuitable exploit that Robert suggested she should instead spend a few days visiting his headquarters at Tilbury, to see the camp and the forts and hold a review of the citizen army which had been concentrated to the east of London to meet an attack from Parma across the North Sea. The Queen took up the idea with enthusiasm and, during her famous visit to the army at Tilbury, Robert walked bare-headed at her bridle-hand. It was to be the last time he escorted her in public and it was fitting that it should have been the greatest occasion of them all. He had grown stout, red-faced and rather bald; she had taken to wearing a crimped orange wig and over-painting her face, and they were both middle-aged. But none of that mattered. The old strong bond of a lifetime's shared experience, which reached its peak on that glorious emotional day at Tilbury, would be broken now only by death.

In the middle of August, while the Armada was being beaten up the coast towards Scotland, Robert broke camp and returned to London. He wasn't at all well – the last few months had been an appalling strain – and had promised himself a short holiday. He spent a few quiet days with the Queen, dining with her every day, and then left for the country, intending to take the waters at Buxton. On the way he sent Elizabeth a note from Rycote, the Oxfordshire manor-house where they had often stayed together in the past. He wanted to know how his gracious lady was – she had been suffering a few twinges lately – 'it being the chiefest thing in this world I do pray for, that she should have good health and long life. For my own poor case,' he went on, 'I continue still your medicine and find it amends much better than with any other thing that hath been given me. Thus hoping to find a perfect cure at the bath, I humbly kiss your foot. From your old lodging at Rycott this Thursday morning, ready to take my journey ...'

He got as far as Cornbury, a few miles from Oxford, and there, on 4 September, he died – possibly from cancer of the stomach. In the general rejoicing which followed the defeat of the Armada, the disappearance of this great landmark of the Elizabethan scene passed almost unnoticed and generally unmourned. At a time when her people expected to see her bathed in the radiance of victory, the Queen could not afford the luxury of private grief but she took that brief note scribbled at Rycote and put it by her. Fifteen years later it was found in the little coffer she kept at her bedside. Across it she had written: 'His last letter.'

The Queen continued obstinately to ignore the existence of the widowed Countess of Leicester – apart, that is, from hounding her for repayment of Robert's considerable debts to the Crown – but she could not, even if she had wanted to, ignore the widow's son. Robert Devereux, Earl of Essex, has often been described as the darling of Elizabeth's old age but it would probably be more accurate to describe him as one of its greatest headaches. Essex, still in his early twenties, was extremely good-looking and, when he chose to be, charming company. He was also spoilt, ambitious and headstrong. Unlike his stepfather, he never learnt the art of putting his passions in his pocket. Unlike Leicester, he had not grown up with Elizabeth and he made the fatal mistake of underestimating her. In his youthful arrogance and impatience he came to see her as a tiresome old woman who, if she could not be cajoled, would have to be bullied – a miscalculation which led inexorably to tragedy.

The war with Spain still dragged on, and in 1596 the Earl of Essex distinguished himself in a brilliantly successful raid on the port of Cadiz. He returned to a hero's welcome – his youth, his striking good looks, his open-handedness and his martial enthusiasm all combined to make him a favourite with the London crowds – but he was by no means universally popular. At Court two distinct and increasingly hostile factions were emerging : on the one side Essex and most of the younger element, eager for military profit and glory, who looked to him as their natural leader; on the other, what might be described as the peace party, headed by old Lord Burghley and his sober son, Robert. Elizabeth did her best to keep a balance. She was undoubtedly very fond of Essex – rather in the manner of an indulgent aunt with a wild but irresistibly attractive young nephew – but it was soon noticed that while the Earl seemed able to get anything for himself, including plenty of expensive presents, the Queen would give nothing to his friends. She had no intention of allowing him to build up too large a following, no matter how he coaxed. Essex was not used to being refused, and when he failed to get what he wanted by cajolery he would sulk and storm. These tactics led to rows, with Elizabeth swearing angrily that she would break him of his will and pull down his great heart.

One of the Earl's more sensible friends, the long-headed young lawyer Francis Bacon, tried to warn him of the risks he was running. 'A man of a nature not to be ruled,' wrote Bacon; 'of an estate not grounded to his greatness; of a popular reputation; of a military dependence: I demand whether there can be a more dangerous image than this represented to any monarch living, much more to a lady and of her Majesty's apprehension?' There would be no surer way to frighten and offend the Queen than by appearing to be too powerful or too popular, and Bacon urged his patron to break with his military followers, or at least to seem to do so, and seek advancement by peaceful means. This was excellent advice, but unhappily Essex was incapable of taking it. His unquiet spirit could find no fulfilment in the sort of career his stepfather had settled for and although the Queen, who found it difficult to be angry with him for long, continued patiently to try to tame him into becoming a useful servant of the Crown, the task was hopeless.

The last act of the Essex tragedy was played out during the winter of 1600, the year after his disastrous failure in Ireland. By this time a sick and despairing figure and probably more than a little mad, he was making wild plans to seize the court and the Queen, force Elizabeth to restore him to favour and, above all, to get rid of his arch-enemy Robert Cecil. The Queen and Robert Cecil watched and waited. Then, on Saturday, 7 February 1601, some of the more foolish members of the Essex faction bribed William Shakespeare's company of actors to put on a special performance of *Richard II*, the play in which a king is deposed and killed. That night Essex was summoned to appear before the Council. He refused to go, and next morning he and about two hundred of the rabble of 'men of broken fortunes' who had attached themselves to him attempted to raise the City, running armed through the Sunday streets crying that a plot was laid for his life and England sold to the Spaniard. But the citizens stayed indoors and by evening it was all over.

The Earl of Essex was brought to trial, convicted of high treason and executed before the end of the month; but, although the Queen sorrowed for the death of a once brilliant and beautiful young man, she never hesitated over its necessity. Her sweet Robin, whom she had tried to love and tried perhaps to mould into a substitute for that other Robin now more than ten years in his grave, had committed two unforgiveable sins. He had set out to turn her own Londoners against her, and he would have touched her sceptre. When the young Elizabeth had told William Maitland of Lethington, 'as long as I live I shall be Queen of England', she had meant just precisely what she said.

The Queen had two more years to live – busy, active years with no respite from the burden of public care which she had borne for nearly half a century. To the very end she remained in full control of her situation, allowing no man to rule her, and, by her own special brand of magic, keeping the goodwill of all her husbands – the people of England.

A Note on Sources

REFERENCES to the various marriage projects discussed for the child Elizabeth are to be found scattered through the later volumes of the compendious *Letters and Papers, Foreign and Domestic, of the Reign of Henry VIII* (1862–1910); also in the despatches of Eustace Chapuys printed in the *Calendar of State Papers*, Spanish (1862–1954), vols v and vi.

The fullest source for the Seymour episode is *A Collection of State Papers, 1542–70, from Letters and Memorials Left by William Cecil, Lord Burghley, at Hatfield*, ed. Samuel Haynes (1740). Further references can be found in P. F. Tytler, *England under the Reign of Edward VI and Mary* (1839), and *The Literary Remains of King Edward VI*, ed. J. G. Nichols (Roxburghe Club, 1857), while many of the original documents are in the *State Papers*, Domestic, Edward VI, vol. vi, at the Public Record Office. For the remainder of Edward's reign, see the *Calendar of State Papers*, Spanish, vols ix, x and xi, and the *Calendar of State Papers*, Foreign, Edward VI and Mary (1861).

For Mary's reign, the best and most detailed account is given by Simon Renard in the *Calendar of State Papers*, Spanish, vols xi, xii and xiii, but see also the *Calendar of State Papers*, Venetian, vol. vi. Other contemporary sources include *The Chronicle of Queen Jane and Two Years of Queen Mary*, ed. J. G. Nichols (Camden Society, 1850); *Chronicle of the Greyfriars*, ed. J. G. Nichols (Camden Society, 1852); *The Diary of Henry Machyn*, ed. J. G. Nichols (Camden Society, 1848); Charles Wriothesley, *A Chronicle of England during the Reigns of the Tudors*, ed. William D. Hamilton (Camden Society, 1875); and John Foxe, *Acts and Monuments*, ed. S. R. Cattley and G. Townsend (1839), which contains a highly coloured description of Elizabeth's troubles in 1554. Many of the documents relating to this period are printed in F. A. Mumby, *The Girlhood of Queen Elizabeth* (1909); and two other extremely useful modern works are H. F. M. Prescott, *Mary Tudor* (1952), and E. H. Harbison, *Rival*

Ambassadors at the Court of Queen Mary (Princeton, 1940).

The marriage projects, likely and unlikely, of Elizabeth as Queen run through all the histories of the first twenty-five years of her reign, but again the most detailed contemporary source is provided by the despatches of King Philip's ambassadors in the *Calendar of State Papers, Spanish, Elizabeth,* vols I, II and III. There was no Venetian representative in England after 1559, but the *Calendar of State Papers, Venetian,* vol. VII, contains quite a few references to the Queen's courtships relayed by the Venetian agents in Paris. The *Calendar of State Papers, Foreign, Elizabeth,* in numerous volumes, contains many of the letters and reports of her own ambassadors overseas; while, for the reports of the Emperor's special envoys during the interminable negotiations over the Austrian marriage, see *Queen Elizabeth and Some Foreigners,* ed. Victor von Klarwill, trans. T. H. Nash (1928).

The best general account of the Amy Robsart affair is George Adlard, *Amye Robsart and the Earl of Leycester* (1870); and two modern books on the subject of Elizabeth and Robert Dudley are Milton Waldman, *Elizabeth and Leicester* (1944), and Elizabeth Jenkins, *Elizabeth and Leicester* (1961).

Most of the documents relative to Mary Queen of Scots during the 1560s are printed in F. A. Mumby, *Elizabeth and Mary Stuart* (Boston, Mass., 1914), and the same author's *The Fall of Mary Stuart* (1921), but see also the *Calendar of State Papers Relating to Scotland and Mary, Queen of Scots, 1547–1603.*

For Elizabeth's encounters with Parliament, J. E. Neale's classic work *Queen Elizabeth and Her Parliament,* 2 vols (1953–7), is an invaluable guide and so, for the general political background, is Conyers Read's two-volume biography of William Cecil, *Mr Secretary Cecil and Queen Elizabeth* (1955) and *Lord Burghley and Queen Elizabeth* (1960).

For foreign policy and the French marriage projects, see Conyers Read's *Mr Secretary Walsingham,* vols I and II (1925, reprinted 1967). Many of the documents relating to the Anjou courtship are printed in *The Compleat Ambassador,* ed. Dudley Digges (1655); and, for Alençon, see *State Papers Relating to Affairs 1571–96, from Papers Left by Lord Burghley at Hatfield,* ed. W. Murdin (1759). There is also a detailed general account in M. A. S. Hume, *The Courtships of Queen Elizabeth* (1898; revised ed., 1904).

Other miscellaneous sources of contemporary material include William Camden's *Annals of the Reign of Queen Elizabeth* (best

English edition, 1688); the *Hardwicke State Papers, 1501–1726*, 2 vols (1778); *Illustrations of British History*, ed. E. Lodge, 3 vols (1838); and T. Wright, *Queen Elizabeth and Her Times*, 2 vols (1838).

Of the innumerable modern biographies of Elizabeth, J. E. Neale's *Queen Elizabeth I*, first published in 1934 and reprinted many times, remains the best. Elizabeth Jenkins, *Elizabeth the Great* (1958), and Neville Williams, *Elizabeth I, Queen of England* (1967) are both good on the personal side, and Paul Johnson's *Elizabeth I. A Study in Power and Intellect* (1974), is first-rate on Elizabeth as a political animal.

Notes

ABBREVIATIONS

Chron. Greyfriars	*Chronicle of the Greyfriars*, ed. J. G. Nichols
Chron. Queen Jane	*The Chronicle of Queen Jane and Two Years of Queen Mary*, ed. J. G. Nichols
C.S.P. Dom.	*Calendar of State Papers*, Domestic
C.S.P. Foreign	*Calendar of State Papers*, Foreign
C.S.P. Span.	*Calendar of State Papers*, Spanish
C.S.P. Ven.	*Calendar of State Papers*, Venetian
Edward VI	*The Literary Remains of King Edward VI*, ed. J. G. Nichols
Foxe	John Foxe, *Acts and Monuments*, ed. Cattley and Townsend
Hall	Edward Hall, *Chronicle*, ed. Sir Henry Ellis (1809)
Haynes	*A Collection of State Papers, 1542–70, from Letters and Memorials Left by William Cecil, Lord Burghley, at Hatfield*, ed. Samuel Haynes
L. & P.	*Letters and Papers, Foreign and Domestic, of the Reign of Henry VIII*
Machyn	*The Diary of Henry Machyn*, ed. J. G. Nichols
Scotland	*Calendar of State Papers Relating to Scotland and Mary, Queen of Scots, 1547–1603*
S.P. Dom.	State Papers, Domestic
Tytler	P. F. Tytler, *England under the Reigns of Edward VI and Mary*
Wriothesley	Charles Wriothesley, *A chronicle of England during the Reigns of the Tudors*, ed. William D. Hamilton

PROLOGUE

[1] *C.S.P. Foreign*, Mary, 537.
[2] Ibid. 542
[3] Ibid. 537.

[4] Thomas Coryat, *Coryat's Crudities* (Glasgow, 1905), vol. I.

CHAPTER I. THE KING'S LAST DAUGHTER

[1] *C.S.P. Span.*, vol. IV, pt 2, 789.
[2] Hall.
[3] *L. & P.*, vol. VI, 807.
[4] Ibid. vol. VI, 1425.
[5] Ibid. vol. VII, 366.
[6] *Statutes of the Realm*, vol. III, quoted in G. R. Elton, *The Tudor Constitution* (1960), p. 355.
[7] *L. & P.*, vol. V, 1485–6. See also Hall and *C.S.P Ven.*, vol. IV, 822–4.
[8] *L. & P.*, vol. VII, 1298.
[9] Ibid. vol. VII, 1060.
[10] Ibid. vol. VII, 1483.
[11] Ibid. vol. VIII, 174.
[12] *Statutes of the Realm*, vol. III, quoted in Elton, *Tudor Constitution*, p. 6.
[13] *L. & P.*, vol. VIII, 174.
[14] *C.S.P. Span.*, vol. V, pt 1, 112.
[15] *L. & P.*, vol. VIII, 174.
[16] Ibid. 339–43, 548, 555, 557.
[17] Ibid. 189.
[18] *C.S.P. Span.*, vol. V, pt 1, 139, p. 420.
[19] *L. & P.*, vol. VIII, 793.
[20] Ibid. 846, 909.

[21] Ibid. 910, see also 340.
[22] Ibid. 554.
[23] Ibid. 909, 1044, 1052.
[24] *C.S.P. Span.*, vol. V, pt 1, 213, p. 554.
[25] Ibid. 238, and *L. & P.*, vol. IX.
[26] *C.S.P., Span.*, vol. V, pt 1, 246.
[27] *L. & P.*, vol. X, 308.
[28] Wriothesley, vol. I.
[29] *L. & P.*, vol. XII, pt 1, 815.
[30] Ibid. vol. XIII, pt 1, 274, 338.
[31] Ibid. vol. XIII, pt 1, 241, 255, 273, 329, 338; pt 2, 484.
[32] Ibid. vol. XIII, pt 2, 622, p. 241.
[33] Ibid. vol. XVI, 885.
[34] Ibid. 1090.
[35] Ibid. 1090.
[36] *C.S.P. Span.*, vol. VI, pt 2, 20.
[37] *L. & P.*, vol. XVII, 371.
[38] Ibid, vol. XVIII, pt 1, 364.
[39] *State Papers and Letters of Sir Ralph Sadler*, ed. A. Clifford, 3 vols (1809), vol. I, p. 129.
[40] *L. & P.*, vol. XVIII, pt 1, 509.
[41] Ibid. vol. XIX, pt 2, 470.
[42] Ibid. vol. XX, pt 1, 90, 91.
[43] Ibid. pt 2, 639 (3), 764, 856, 891, 1038.

CHAPTER II. THE NOBLEST MAN UNMARRIED IN THIS LAND

[1] *L. & P.*, vol. XXI, 634.
[2] *C.S.P. Span.*, vol. IX, 7 Mar 1547.
[3] S.P. Dom., Edward VI, vol. VI.
[4] *Edward VI.*
[5] Haynes.
[6] Ibid.
[7] S.P. Dom., Edward VI, vol. VI.
[8] Haynes.
[9] Ibid.
[10] Ibid.
[11] Ibid.
[12] Tytler, vol. I.
[13] S.P. Dom., Edward VI, vol. VI.
[14] Tytler, vol. I.
[15] Haynes.
[16] Ibid.
[17] Ibid.
[18] S.P. Dom., Edward VI, vol VI.
[19] Haynes.
[20] Ibid.
[21] Ibid.
[22] *Acts of the Privy Council of England*, vol. II.
[23] *C.S.P. Span.*, vol. IX, 19 Mar 1549.
[24] Haynes.
[25] *C.S.P. Span.*, vol. IX, 19 Dec 1549.
[26] Ibid. vol. X, 4 Nov 1550, p. 186.
[27] Ibid. 1 Mar 1551, p. 230.
[28] Ibid. June 1551, p. 299.
[29] *C.S.P. Foreign*, Edward VI, 30 Aug 1551, p. 164.
[30] *C.S.P. San.*, vol. X, 6 July 1551, p. 325; 14 Sept 1551, p. 369; 16 Nov 1551, p. 394.
[31] *C.S.P. Foreign*, Edward VI, 11 Mar 1553, p. 255.
[32] Ibid. 15 Feb 1553, p. 245.
[33] *C.S.P. Span.*, vol. XI, 30 May 1553, p. 46.
[34] *Edward VI.*
[35] *C.S.P. Span.*, vol. XI, 11 July 1553, p. 81.

CHAPTER III. LE PLUS BEAU GENTILHOMME D'ANGLETERRE

[1] *Edward VI.*
[2] *Greyfriars Chron.; C.S.P. Span.*, vol. XI, 6 Aug 1553, p. 152.
[3] Ibid. 22 July 1553, p. 114.
[4] Ibid. 14 Aug 1553.
[5] Ibid. 15 Aug 1553.
[6] Ibid. 8 Sept 1553.
[7] H. F. M. Prescott, *Mary Tudor*, p. 212; E. H. Harbison, *Rival Ambassadors at the Court of Queen Mary*, p. 79.
[8] *C.S.P. Span.*, vol. XI, 14 Sept 1553, p. 236.
[9] Ibid. 20 Sept 1553, p.247.
[10] Ibid. 12 Oct 1553.
[11] Ibid. 12 Oct 1553, p. 291.
[12] Ibid. late in Aug 1553, p. 195.
[13] Ibid. 12 Oct 1553, p. 292.
[14] Ibid. 19 Oct 1553, p. 307.

[15] Ibid. 31 Oct 1553, p. 328.
[16] Ibid. 4 Nov 1553, pp. 334–5.
[17] Ibid. 28 Nov 1553.
[18] Ibid. 24 Dec 1553.
[19] Ibid. 4 Nov 1553, p. 333.
[20] Ibid. 6 Nov 1553, pp. 342–3.
[21] Ibid. 20 Nov 1553, p. 372.
[22] Ibid. 17 Nov 1553, p. 364.
[23] De Noailles to the King of France, 14 Dec 1553, in F. A. Mumby, *The Girlhood of Queen Elizabeth*, p. 97.
[24] Ibid.

[25] Harbison, *Rival Ambassadors*, pp. 121–2.
[26] Ibid. pp. 126–7.
[27] *C.S.P. Span.*, vol. xii, 24 Feb 1554, p. 125.
[28] Ibid. 8 Mar 1554, pp. 139–40.
[29] Ibid. 14 Mar 1554.
[30] Ibid. 22 Mar 1554, pp. 166–7.
[31] Ibid. 27 Mar 1554.
[32] Ibid. 22 Apr 1554.
[33] Ibid. 3 Apr 1554, p. 201.
[34] Ibid. 1 May 1554.

CHAPTER IV. NO ALLIANCE MORE ADVANTAGEOUS THAN THAT WITH THE DUKE OF SAVOY

[1] *Chron. Queen Jane*, app. x, John Elder's letter.
[2] *C.S.P. Span.*, vol. xii, 8 Mar 1554.
[3] *Chron. Queen Jane.*
[4] *C.S.P. Span.*, vol. xiii, July 1554, p. 11.
[5] Ibid. 17 Aug 1554.
[6] Ibid. 24 Aug 1554.
[7] Ibid. 17 Aug and 18 Sept 1554.
[8] Ibid. 14 Nov 1554, p. 90.
[9] Ibid. 14 Nov 1554, p. 92.
[10] Ibid. p. 104 n.
[11] Ibid. Mar/Apr 1555, p. 151.
[12] Ibid. Mar/Apr 1555, p. 152
[13] *C.S.P. Ven.*, vol. vi, pt 1, 8 Apr 1555
[14] Foxe, vol. viii.
[15] *C.S.P. Span.*, vol. xiii, 24 June 1555

[16] *C.S.P. Ven.*, vol. vi, pt 2, 13 May 1557, p. 1059.
[17] Ibid. pt 1, 21 Apr 1556.
[18] Ibid. pt 1, 28 Apr 1556, p. 423.
[19] Ibid. pt 1, 19 July 1556, p. 532.
[20] Ibid. pt 2, 13 May 1557, p. 1060.
[21] Ibid. pt 1, 9 June 1556.
[22] Ibid. pt 1, p. 571 n.
[23] *C.S.P. Span.*, vol. xiii, 20 Mar 1556.
[24] *C.S.P. Ven.*, vol. vi, pt 1, 10 Oct 1556.
[25] Ibid. pt 2, 27 Dec 1556, p. 887.
[26] Ibid. pt 2, 26 Apr 1557.
[27] Ibid. pt 3, 29 Oct 1558, p. 1538.
[28] *C.S.P. Span.*, vol. xiii, Mar (?) (?) 1558, p. 372.
[29] Mumby, *Girlhood*, pp. 236–8.
[30] *C.S.P. Ven.*, vol. xiii, 1 May 1558, pp. 379–80.

[31] *C.S.P. Ven.*, vol. vi, pt 3, 29 Oct 1558, p. 1538.

[32] *Documents from Simancas relating to the Reign of Eliza-* beth, 1558–68, trans. T. Gonzalez (1865).

[33] Machyn.

CHAPTER V. I AM ALREADY WEDDED TO AN HUSBAND

[1] Printed by J. E. Neale in *English Historical Review* (July 1950), p. 305.

[2] *C.S.P. Ven.*, vol. vi, pt 3, 10 Dec 1558.

[3] *C.S.P. Span.*, Elizabeth, vol. i, 21 Nov 1558.

[4] Ibid. 14 Dec 1558.

[5] Ibid. 14 Dec 1558.

[6] Ibid. 14 Dec 1558, p. 9.

[7] Ibid. 10 Jan 1559.

[8] Ibid. 10 Jan 1559.

[9] Ibid. 31 Jan 1559.

[10] William Camden, *Annals of the Reign of Queen Elizabeth.*

[11] Ibid.

[12] J. E. Neale, *Queen Elizabeth and Her Parliaments*, vol. i.

[13] Ibid.

[14] *C.S.P. Span.*, Elizabeth, vol. i, 20 Feb 1559.

[15] Ibid. 11 Apr 1559, p. 51.

[16] *Queen Elizabeth and Some Foreigners*, ed. Victor von Klarwill, pp. 28–9.

[17] Ibid. Report of Count von Helfenstein, pp. 31–45.

[18] Ibid. pp. 46–7.

[19] See Neale, *Queen Elizabeth and Her Parliaments*, vol. i.

[20] *C.S.P. Span.*, Elizabeth, vol i, 11 Apr 1559, p. 49.

[21] Ibid. 12 Apr 1559, p. 54.

[22] Ibid. 12 Apr 1559, p. 53.

[23] Ibid. 18 Apr 1559, p. 57.

[24] Ibid. 18 Apr 1559, p. 57.

[25] Ibid. 29 Apr 1559, p. 63.

[26] Ibid. 10 May 1559, p. 67.

[27] *C.S.P. Ven.*, vol. vii, 10 May 1559.

CHAPTER VI. IF THE EMPEROR SO DESIRES ME FOR A DAUGHTER

[1] *C.S.P. Span.*, Elizabeth, vol. i, 30 May 1559.

[2] *Queen Elizabeth and Some Foreigners.*

[3] *C.S.P. Span.*, Elizabeth, vol. i.

[4] *Queen Elizabeth and Some Foreigners.*

[5] Ibid.

[6] *C.S.P. Span.*, Elizabeth, vol. i, 1 July 1550.

[7] Forbes, *A Full View of the Reign of Queen Elizabeth*, 2 vols (1740); see also F. A. Mumby, *Elizabeth and Mary Stuart.*

[8] *C.S.P. Span.*, Elizabeth, vol. i, 1 July 1559, p. 82.

[9] Ibid. 7 Sept 1559.
[10] Ibid. 7 Sept 1559.
[11] Ibid. 2 Oct 1559.
[12] Ibid. 2 Oct 1559.
[13] Mumby, *Elizabeth and Mary Stuart*, pp. 77–9.
[14] Haynes; see also Mumby, *Elizabeth and Mary Stuart*, p. 67.

[15] *Queen Elizabeth and Some Foreigners.*
[16] Ibid.
[17] *C.S.P. Span.*, Elizabeth, vol. 1, 13 Nov 1559.
[18] Ibid.
[19] Ibid.
[20] *Queen Elizabeth and Some Foreigners.*

CHAPTER VII. LORD ROBERT WOULD BE BETTER IN PARADISE

[1] *C.S.P. Span.*, Elizabeth, vol. 1, 19 Feb 1560.
[2] Ibid. 28 Mar 1560.
[3] Ibid. 11 Sept 1560.
[4] George Adlard, *Amye Robsart and the Earl of Leycester*, p. 35.
[5] Ibid. p. 36.
[6] Ibid. p. 32.
[7] Ibid. pp. 36–7.
[8] Ibid. pp. 38–9.
[9] Haynes.
[10] Adlard, *Amye Robsart*, p. 40.
[11] Aird, 'The Death of Amy Robsart', *English Historical Review*, Jan 1956.
[12] *C.S.P. Span.*, Elizabeth, vol. 1, III, 10 Oct 1560.
[13] *C.S.P. Foreign*, Elizabeth, vol.

III, 10 Oct 1560.
[14] Printed in E. S. Beesley, *Queen Elizabeth* (1892).
[15] *C.S.P. Span.*, Elizabeth, vol. 1, 15 Oct 1560.
[16] *Hardwicke State Papers*, 1501–1726, vol. 1, p. 167.
[17] Mumby, *Elizabeth and Mary Stuart*, p. 153.
[18] *C.S.P. Foreign*, Elizabeth, vol. III, 30 Dec 1560.
[19] *C.S.P. Span.*, Elizabeth, vol. 1, 22 Jan 1561.
[20] Ibid. 23 Feb 1561.
[21] Ibid. 23 Feb 1561, pp. 181–2.
[22] Ibid. 25 Mar 1561, pp. 187–8.
[23] Ibid. 25 Mar 1561, p. 188.
[24] Ibid. 12 Apr 1561, p. 194.
[25] Ibid. 5 May 1561, pp. 200–2.

CHAPTER VIII. WITHOUT A CERTAIN HEIR, LIVING AND KNOWN

[1] *C.S.P. Span.*, Elizabeth, vol. 1, 30 June 1561.
[2] See Mumby, *Elizabeth and*

Mary Stuart, ch. v, for documents.
[3] See Hester Chapman, *Two*

Tudor Portraits (1960).

4 *C.S.P. Span.*, Elizabeth, vol. I, 27 Nov 1561.

5 Ibid. 31 June 1562, pp. 225–6.

6 Ibid. 20 June 1562, p. 248.

7 Ibid. 25 Oct 1562, p. 262

8 Ibid. 25 Oct 1562, nos 189 and 190, pp. 262–3.

9 Ibid. 25 Oct 1562, nos 189 and 190, p. 263.

10 Ibid. 30 Nov 1562.

11 Neale, *Queen Elizabeth I and Her Parliaments*, vol. I, p. 94.

12 Ibid. pp. 105–6.

13 Ibid. pp. 109–10.

14 Ibid. pp. 107–9.

15 *C.S.P. Span.*, Elizabeth, vol. I, 7 Feb 1963, p. 296.

16 Neale, *Queen Elizabeth I and Her Parliaments*, vol. I, p. 127.

17 *A Letter from Mary Queen of Scots to the Duke of Guise, January, 1562* (Scottish Historical Society, 1904).

18 *C.S.P. Span.*, Elizabeth, vol. I, 28 Mar 1563, p. 313.

19 *Scotland*, vol II, pp. 56–8. See also Mumby, *Elizabeth and Mary Stuart*, p. 307.

20 James Melville, *Memoirs of His Own Life (1549–93)*, ed. T. Thomson (Bannatyne Club, 1827).

21 Ibid.

22 Conyers Read, *Mr Secretary Cecil and Queen Elizabeth*, p. 318.

23 Mumby, *Elizabeth and Mary Stuart*, p. 378.

24 Ibid. p. 382.

CHAPTER IX. TALK IS ALL OF THE ARCHDUKE

1 *Queen Elizabeth and Some Foreigners*, pp. 173–6.

2 Ibid. pp. 180 ff.

3 Ibid. p. 201.

4 T. Wright, *Queen Elizabeth and Her Times*, vol. I, pp. 183–5.

5 *C.S.P. Span.*, Elizabeth, vol. I, 5 May 1565, p. 429.

6 Ibid. 16 June 1565, p. 437; 25 June 1565, p. 439.

7 *Scotland*, vol. II, 30 Mar 1565.

8 Sir Robert Naunton, *Fragmenta Regalia* (1824).

9 *C.S.P. Span.*, Elizabeth, vol. I, 9 June 1565, pp. 435–6.

10 Haynes, p. 444.

11 *C.S.P. Span.*, Elizabeth, vol. I, 23 July 1565, p. 454; 3 Sept 1565, p. 472.

12 *C.S.P. Ven.*, vol. VII, 19 Feb 1566, p. 374.

13 *C.S.P. Span.*, Elizabeth, vol. I, 4 Feb 1566, p. 523; 28 Jan 1566, p. 514; 20 Aug 1565; *C.S.P. Ven.*, vol. VII, 1 June 1566, p. 381.

14 *Queen Elizabeth and Some Foreigners*, pp. 240 ff; *C.S.P. Span.*, Elizabeth, vol. I, 23 July 1565, pp. 452–3.

15 *Queen Elizabeth and Some*

Foreigners, pp. 248–9.

16 *C.S.P. Span.*, Elizabeth, vol. I, 6 Aug 1565, p. 461.

17 *Queen Elizabeth and Some Foreigners*, pp. 218 and 229.

18 Ibid. pp. 239–42.

19 Ibid. p. 228.

20 *C.S.P. Span.*, Elizabeth, vol. I, 13 Aug 1565, pp. 465–6.

21 Wright, *Queen Elizabeth and Her Times*, vol. I, pp. 206–7.

22 *C.S.P. Span.*, Elizabeth, vol. I, 11 Apr 1566, p. 540.

23 Neale, *Queen Elizabeth and Her Parliaments*, vol. I, p. 136.

24 Ibid. vol. I, p. 140.

25 *C.S.P. Span.*, Elizabeth, vol. I, 19 Oct 1566, p. 589.

26 Ibid. 26 Oct 1566.

27 Neale, *Queen Elizabeth and Her Parliaments*, vol. I, p. 142.

28 *C.S.P. Span.*, Elizabeth, vol. I, 4 Nov 1566, pp. 591–2.

29 Ibid. p. 593.

30 Neale, *Queen Elizabeth and Her Parliaments*, vol. I, pp. 146–50.

31 Ibid. pp. 163–4.

32 *Illustrations of British History*, ed. E. Lodge, vol. I, pp. 366–7.

33 Ibid. pp. 368–73; *Queen Elizabeth and Some Foreigners*, pp. 269, 275 and 295.

34 Ibid.; *C.S.P. Ven.*, vol. VII, 22 Jan 1568, p. 410.

CHAPTER X. TO MARRY WITH FRANCE

1 *C.S.P. Span.*, Elizabeth, vol. II, 8 Jan 1569.

2 Ibid. vol. I, 24 Mar 1565, pp. 409–10.

3 François de Salignac de la Mothe Fénélon, *Correspondence*, 11 vols (1827–9), vol. III, pp. 414–20; see also Read, *Mr Secretary Walsingham*, vol I, p. 101.

4 *C.S.P. Span.*, Elizabeth, vol. II, 22 Jan 1571.

5 Ibid. p. 295 n.

6 *The Compleat Ambassador*, ed. Dudley Digges, p. 97.

7 *C.S.P. Dom.*, Elizabeth, Addenda, vol. VII, pp. 328–32.

8 *C.S.P. Span.*, Elizabeth, vol. II, 10 May 1571, p. 309.

9 *C.S.P. Ven.*, vol. VII, 7 June 1571, p. 468.

10 Ibid. 28 Sept 1571, p. 476.

11 *C.S.P. Foreign*, Elizabeth, vol. IX, 8 Oct 1571, pp. 544–5.

12 Ibid. vol. X, Jan 1572.

13 John Strype, *The Life of Sir Thomas Smith* (Oxford, 1820), p. 11.

14 *C.S.P. Foreign*, Elizabeth, vol. X, and Strype, *Smith*, p. 112.

15 Ibid. pp. 112–13.

16 *Compleat Ambassador*, p. 218.

17 Ibid. pp. 219–21. See also Read, *Walsingham*, vol. I, pp. 206–7.

18 Fénélon, *Correspondence*, vol. V, p. 121.

19 Ibid. vol. V, pp. 120–33, and *Compleat Ambassador*, p. 246.

See also Read, *Lord Burghley and Queen Elizabeth*, pp. 89–90.

[20] *Compleat Ambassador*, p. 259. See also Read, *Walsingham*, vol. i, p. 235.

CHAPTER XI. A FROG HE WOULD A-WOOING GO

[1] Read, *Walsingham*, vol. ii, pp. 3–4. See also Read, *Lord Burghley and Queen Elizabeth*, pp. 200–2.

[2] *C.S.P Span.*, Elizabeth, vol. ii, 26 Feb 1579.

[3] *Lettres de Catherine de Médicis*, 10 vols (1880–1909), vol. 7, 29 Mar 1579. See Read, *Walsingham*, vol ii, pp. 14–18.

[4] *Illustrations of British History*, vol. ii, *p.* 212.

[5] Read, *Walsingham*, vol. ii, pp. 14–18.

[6] Printed in Read, *Lord Burghley and Queen Elizabeth*, pp. 210–11.

[7] *C.S.P. Span.*, Elizabeth vol. ii, 3 May 1579, p. 669.

[8] Ibid. 14 May 1579.

[9] Ibid. 14 May 1579, p. 675.

[10] Camden, *Annals*.

[11] Wright, *Queen Elizabeth and Her Times*, vol. ii, pp. 103 5.

[12] *C.S.P. Span.*, Elizabeth, vol. ii, 24 June 1579.

[13] M. A. S. Hume, *The Courtships of Queen Elizabeth*, p. 212.

[14] *C.S.P. Span.*, Elizabeth, vol. ii, 25 Aug 1579, p. 693.

[15] Ibid.

[16] J. A. Froude, *History of England from the Fall of Wolsey to the Death of Elizabeth*, 12 vols (1856–70), vol. xi, p. 175.

[17] Philip Sidney, *Works*, 4 vols (1922–6), vol. iii, pp. 51–60.

[18] *State Papers . . . Left by Lord Burghley at Hatfield*, ed. W. Murdin, pp. 322–36.

[19] Ibid. pp. 336–7.

[20] Ibid. p. 337.

[21] Ibid.

[22] *C.S.P. Span.*, Elizabeth, vol. ii, 11 Nov 1579.

[23] Ibid. 28 Nov 1579.

[24] Ibid. 28 Nov 1579, p. 705.

[25] *Calendar of Salisbury Manuscripts*, vol ii, pp. 275–6.

[26] Read, *Walsingham*, vol. ii, pp. 75–6.

[27] Hume, *Courtships*, pp. 235–6.

[28] *C.S.P. Span.*, Elizabeth, vol iii, 11 Nov 1581, pp. 211–12.

[29] Ibid. 22 Nov 1581, p. 226.

[30] Camden, *Annals*.

Index